I0819088

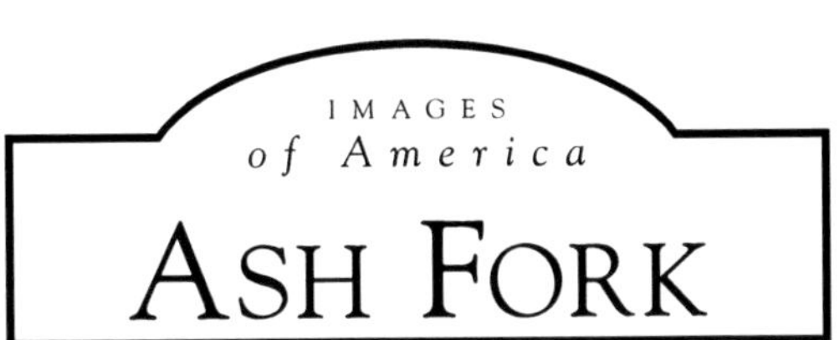
IMAGES
of America
ASH FORK

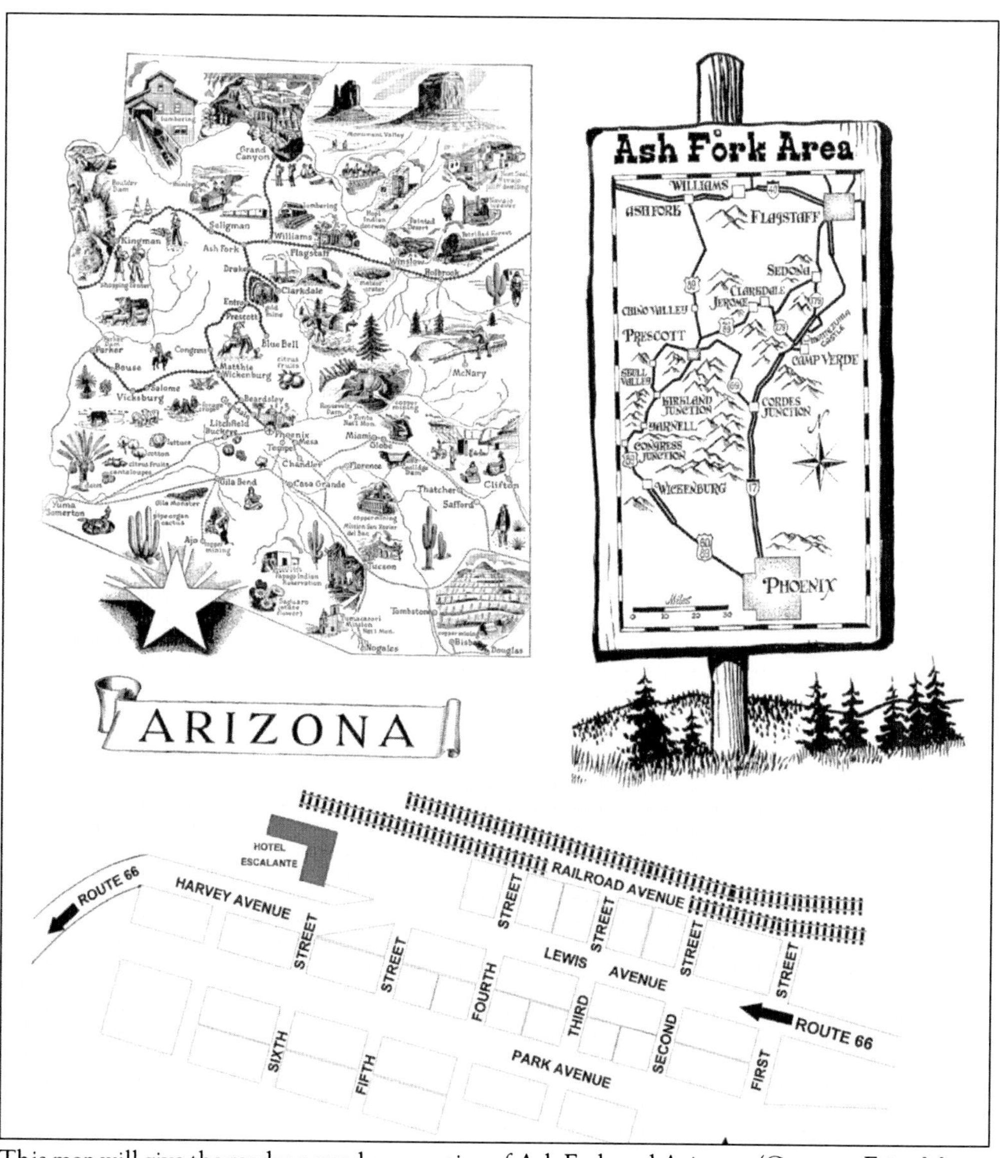

This map will give the reader a good perspective of Ash Fork and Arizona. (Courtesy Erica Moore and Kearney Egerton.)

On the Cover: Ash Fork's volunteer firemen sit on and around their brand new 1946 Dodge fire truck in the late 1940s. The fire department was founded in 1941, and a fire station was built in 1946. (Courtesy Hume collection.)

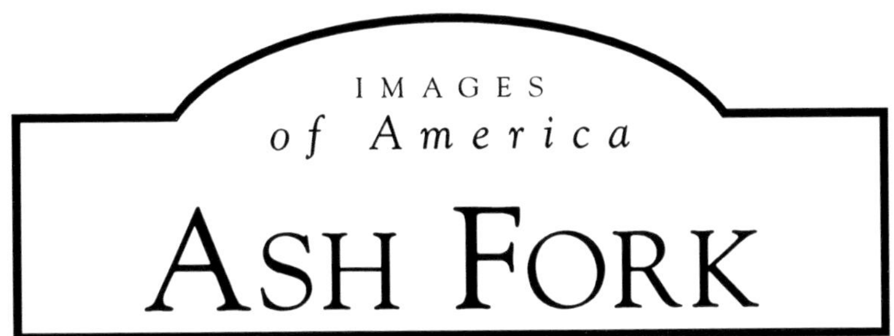

Marshall Trimble

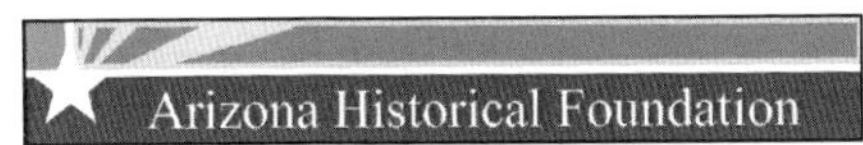

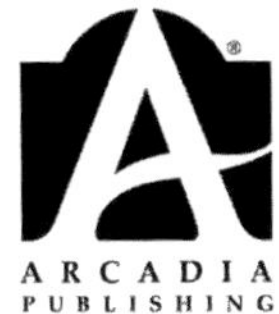

ISBN 978-0-7385-4832-6

Published by Arcadia Publishing
Charleston, South Carolina

Printed in the United States of America

Library of Congress Control Number: 2007934175

For all general information contact Arcadia Publishing at:
Telephone 843-853-2070
Fax 843-853-0044
E-mail sales@arcadiapublishing.com
For customer service and orders:
Toll-Free 1-888-313-2665

Visit us on the Internet at www.arcadiapublishing.com

To Fayrene Martin Hume

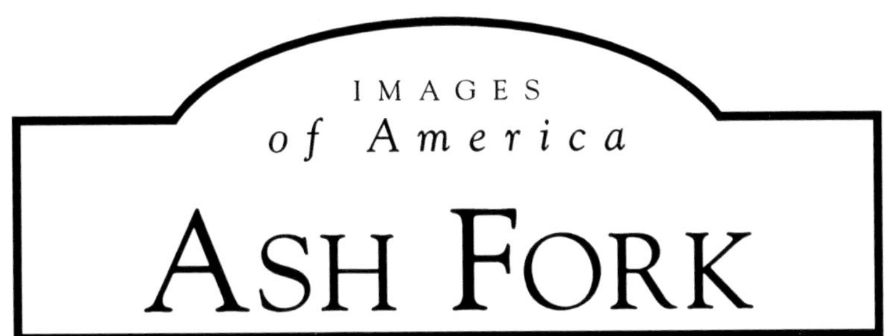

Marshall Trimble

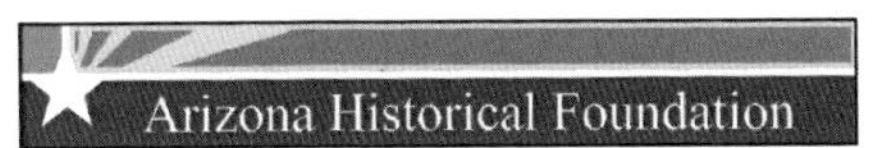

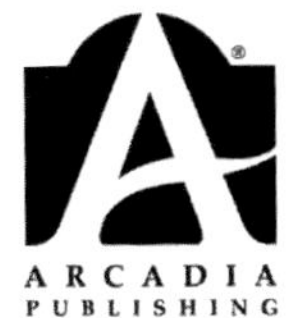

ISBN 978-0-7385-4832-6

Published by Arcadia Publishing
Charleston, South Carolina

Printed in the United States of America

Library of Congress Control Number: 2007934175

For all general information contact Arcadia Publishing at:
Telephone 843-853-2070
Fax 843-853-0044
E-mail sales@arcadiapublishing.com
For customer service and orders:
Toll-Free 1-888-313-2665

Visit us on the Internet at www.arcadiapublishing.com

To Fayrene Martin Hume

CONTENTS

ACKNOWLEDGMENTS

Writing *Ash Fork* has taken me on a special ride down memory lane. I was eight years old in 1947 when my family moved to Ash Fork and 16 when we moved away in 1955; those were my formative years, and many of the stories in this work are gathered from a youngster's personal experiences and observations.

Special thanks go to Jared Jackson, director of publications for the Arizona Historical Foundation, for his helpful assistance on the layout. Jared was always there to patiently answer questions on format and everything else necessary in bringing this work to fruition. My request for his assistance, no matter how trivial, was always answered with, "You got it."

I'm also deeply indebted to a very special lady, Vanessa Logas, who spent many hours advising, cutting, pasting, and preparing captions for more than 200 photographs.

I want to thank all those Ash Forkians, past and present, who so generously loaned me their precious photographs to copy. Copies of all these photographs will be donated to the Ash Fork Historical Museum for their collection.

The genesis of this work began back in 1982, when Ash Fork historian Fayrene Martin Hume and I worked together to compile a history of the town for the centennial celebration. Fay spent countless hours gathering photographs and stories from residents and former residents, many of whom were scattered across the nation. For almost 50 years, Fayrene not only has worked tirelessly to preserve the history of Ash Fork, but she has also been a leader in a myriad of community activities spanning entire generations. Past, present, and future residents are deeply indebted to this Arizona culture-keeper.

Our friendship goes back to the early 1950s, and it is my privilege and honor to dedicate this book to her.

Unless otherwise indicated, images appearing in this book have been drawn from the author's own collection.

—Marshall Trimble
Official Arizona State Historian

Introduction

The tiny community of Ash Fork lies slumbering on the gentle, juniper-studded hills some 15 miles west of Bill Williams Mountain. Because of the watering holes in nearby Johnson Canyon, travelers have passed through the area since prehistoric times. Evidence of primitive civilizations is scattered throughout the region. In the late 1500s, Spanish explorers found rich mineral deposits around today's Jerome, a few miles further south. When this land was a part of Mexico, traders and trappers like Ewing Young, Kit Carson, Bill Williams, Antoine Leroux, and Joe Walker passed through on their way from Santa Fe to California.

During the 1850s, the storied Army Corps of Topographical Engineers surveyed routes along the 35th parallel for a proposed railroad. The Civil War delayed the building of the transcontinental railroad for several years. When the surveyors and construction crews finally arrived in 1881, Northern Arizona changed quickly, as small towns like Holbrook, Winslow, Flagstaff, and Williams were established along the tracks.

Building further west across Arizona, the Atlantic and Pacific Railroad, later to become the Santa Fe, established a siding in October 1882. The stage station became known as Ash Fork, and on April 2, 1883, the post office was established.

By 1900, Ash Fork had a population of 140. The railroad employed about 20, and most of the others worked in saloons, restaurants, and lodging establishments.

Like many towns in the Old West, Ash Fork had a vigilance committee to deal with troublemakers. In 1884, a gang of cattle rustlers invaded the town. After a few hours of drinking and raising hell, they pulled their six-guns and began firing at random. Locals decided to put a scare into the rowdies by stuffing hay into some clothing and hanging the dummy from a tree limb with a sign that read: "Leave town or this will be your fate. Beware."

The dummy's appearance must have been convincing, because a tourist with a fertile imagination later claimed he actually heard it crying for help. Others kept a respectable distance. Whether this had any effect on the outlaws is lost to history.

The committee was active again a year later, proclaiming they'd rid the town of "murders, cutthroats, bunko men, tin horn gamblers, loafers and worthless characters."

Gunfighting was prohibited in town, as was the firing of rifles and pistols. Committee members were confident the miscreants would give Ash Fork a wide berth in the future.

In the years following the completion of the Atlantic and Pacific Railroad along the 35th parallel, cattle and sheep ranching boomed in Northern Arizona, where old-timers said the grasses grew stirrup high.

On April 25, 1885, the first of many fires in the town's history destroyed nine buildings in the small business district. With no water protection from the flames, residents had to stand by and watch their business district devoured by fire. Another disastrous fire occurred in 1893, burning the original town on the north side of the railroad tracks. In 1905, another fire destroyed most of the business district, including the original Harvey House. On November 20, 1977, the so-called "Big Fire" destroyed most of the downtown business district. By then, however, the buildings were closed for business, as the town had gone into a steep decline. On the morning of October 7, 1987, the town's last major fire destroyed most of the rest of the buildings along the two-block business district on the south side of Route 66.

Water has always been a precious commodity in Ash Fork. Old-timers used to claim there were more saloons than water fountains and whiskey was cheaper than water. Water was hauled in daily by train from Chino Valley. The railroad agreed to run the water train even during a labor strike, but in 1976, the Santa Fe notified the town it would no longer be hauling water.

Thanks to the Farmers' Home Administration and the Four Corners Commission, along with nearly $300,000 in grant monies, a well-drilling project was completed in March 1976. At a cost of nearly $550,000, the wet stuff was found at a depth of 1,700 feet, but experts were not sure if there was an adequate water supply. A few years later, a second well went down 1,400 feet. It registers 147 gallons a minute, enough to adequately supply the town and surrounding area.

Although Ash Fork had been an important east-west corridor for almost a century, it became a north-south road as well when a new railroad line running south to Prescott and Phoenix was completed in 1895. It was the only connecting point by rail between Northern and Southern Arizona. Phoenix was now linked by rail to both the northern and southern transcontinental railroads. Historians consider this the official closing of the frontier period in Arizona history.

When the horseless carriage coughed and sputtered into Arizona, the demand grew for better roads. During the 1920s, horse-drawn scrapers, gravel lories, and steamrollers cut, gouged, leveled, and packed their way across Northern Arizona to construct what would become the nation's "Mother Road," Route 66. The advent of the automobile added a new dimension to the economy of towns like Ash Fork. Motels, restaurants, curio shops, and gas stations sprang up to accommodate a restless America on the move.

During the Great Depression, thousands of displaced Midwestern families loaded their belongings in the family jalopy and headed for California. They took little more with them than hope, and Route 66 was their highway to the Promised Land. During World War II, the booming wartime economy dealt an end to the Depression. Trains carrying equipment and soldiers made regular stops in Ash Fork, adding to the town's prosperity. The postwar building boom brought a new industry to Ash Fork, as the flagstone business began to flourish. Today the town boasts that it is the "Flagstone Capital of the World."

While the fortunes of mining towns waxed and waned with the price of gold, silver, and copper, the prosperity of towns like Ash Fork was driven by transportation. During the late 1950s, to avoid the steep climb to Williams, the railroad moved its main line 15 miles north of town. The Williams-to-Crookton Bypass, completed in 1960, delivered the final blow to the railroad in Ash Fork. It cut off 16 miles of track and avoided the steep climb up Johnson Canyon. It didn't end rail traffic completely, as trains heading south from Williams to Phoenix on the old Peavine that still passed through Ash Fork, but the rail business was sharply curtailed. The population dwindled sharply as railroad families had to pack up and move.

The final coup de grâce came two years later, when the new Interstate 40 opened a half-mile south of town. Overnight the steady flow of Route 66 traffic through town stopped.

The citizens of Ash Fork who remained stubbornly refused to concede defeat. As the 20th century passed into history and a new century was born, the citizens of Ash Fork have developed a new community spirit and hopes for a brighter future.

One

Destiny Road
The Great Camel Experiment

Arizona has always been a land of anomalies, where bizarre events were accepted as normal. One of the strangest of all occurred in January 1858, when a caravan of camels looking like something out of the *Arabian Nights* plodded across Northern Arizona, carving out a wagon road and creating what would one day become the Santa Fe main line and storied Route 66.

At the time, the federal government was planning to survey a wagon road along the 35th parallel from New Mexico to California and wanted to test the feasibility of using camels as beasts of burden. The camel experiment was the pet project of Secretary of War Jefferson Davis, who believed that camels were the solution for transporting cargo across the arid lands of the American West.

The man chosen to lead the experiment was a colorful adventurer named Lt. Edward F. "Ned" Beale of the Army Corps of Topographical Engineers. Beale's camel expedition was unique in the annals of exploration in the American West. The camel's amazing ability to pack a heavy load, travel great distances without water, and thrive on natural forage along the trail made it a natural for hauling cargo across the arid Southwest.

In the summer of 1857, the U.S. Camel Corps set out from Albuquerque with 23 camels, 350 sheep, and 56 men, bound for California.

Beale and his camels managed to successfully open the wagon road along the 35th parallel. At a cost of $210,000, it was the first federally funded road in the Southwest. The road roughly followed what later became the storied Route 66 and is today Interstate 40. They passed about 15 miles north of today's Ash Fork.

This brief but romantic event in Arizona history came to an end just before the Civil War began and was overshadowed in history by the great events that took place in the east.

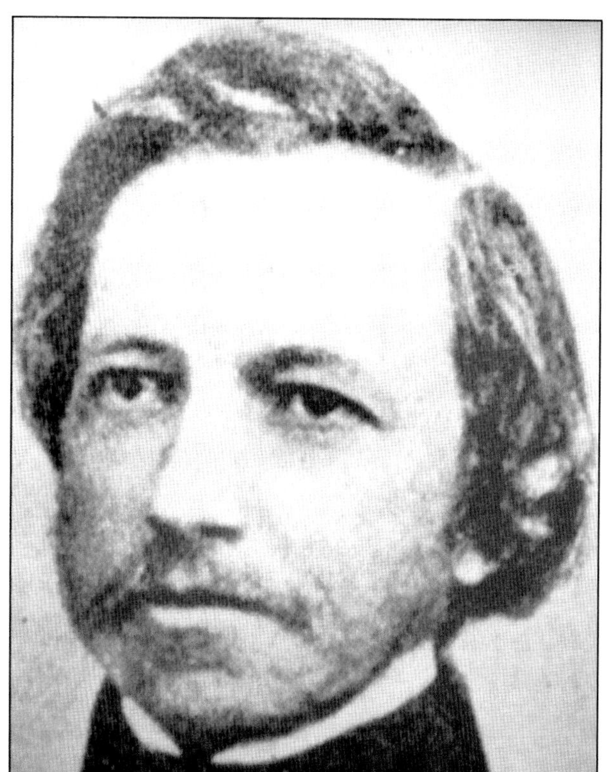

In the years immediately following the California Gold Rush, there was a loud clamor for transcontinental roads. In the winter of 1853–1854, Lt. Amiel Whipple of the Army Corps of Topographical Engineers was the second to survey a route along the 35th parallel. He also surveyed routes along the Gila River and the Mexican border. He was killed in 1863 at the Battle of Chancellorsville.

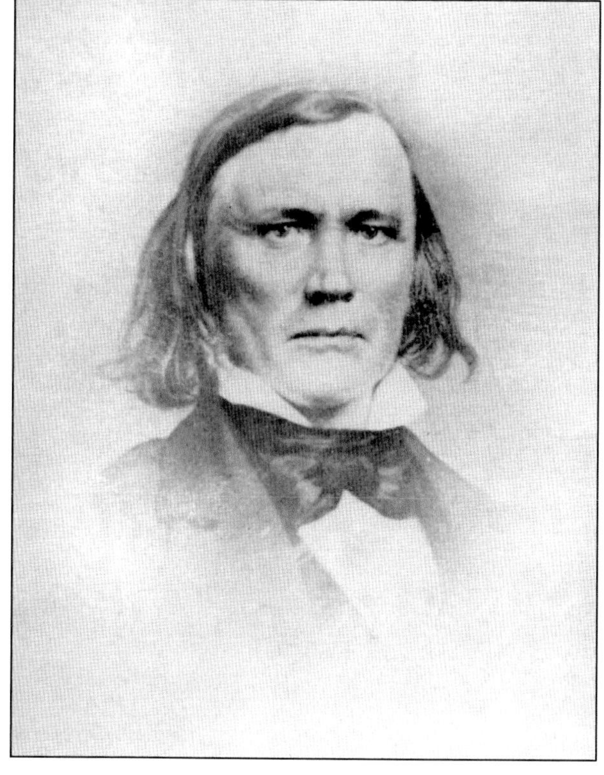

Christopher "Kit" Carson was one of the Old West's greatest legends. As a youth, he ran away from Missouri and came to Santa Fe, where he joined Ewing Young's company of mountain men. In 1827–1828, they trapped in the dangerous Apache country of Arizona then passed through where Ash Fork is today on their way to California. Carson explored much of Arizona over the next few years.

Ned Beale was one of the great unsung heroes of Western history. He and Kit Carson were heroes during the Battle of San Pasquel. He carried the first samples of California gold to Washington. When he died in 1893, an old Native American who'd served on the frontier many years with him lamented, "Beale's dead, there's no reason to go on living." He died two days later.

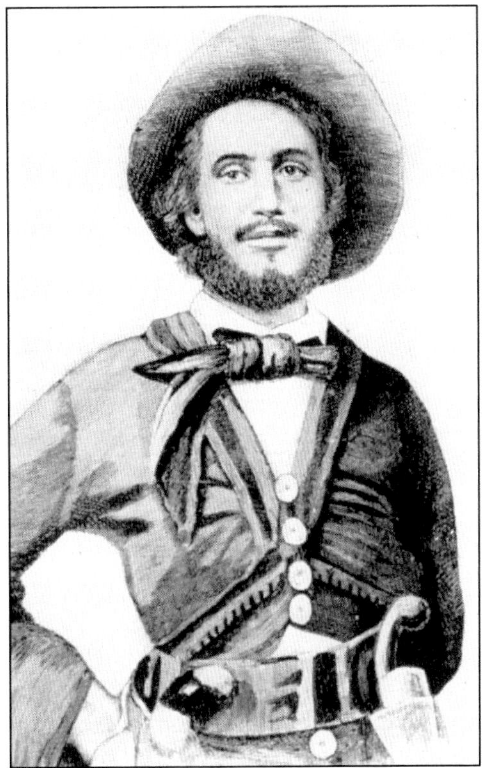

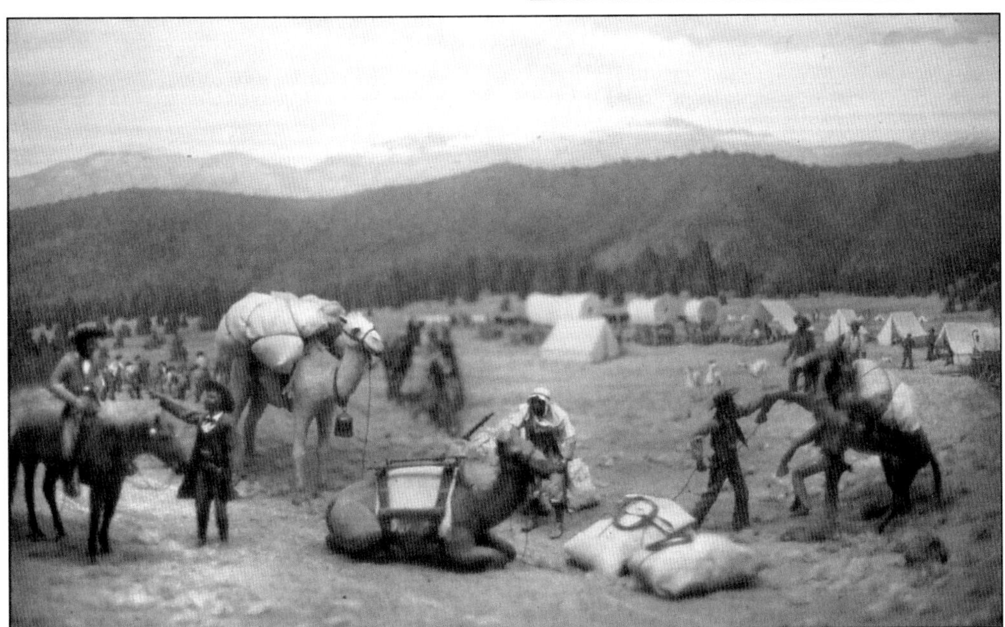

This diorama at the Arizona Historical Society in Tucson depicts the Camel Corps camp near today's Flagstaff. The splendid work mapping the West by the Army Corps of Topographical Engineers during the 1850s was overshadowed by the Civil War, but most of the transcontinental railroads and highways used today were mapped by these men. A combination of science, romance, and adventure, they were the prototypes of today's astronauts.

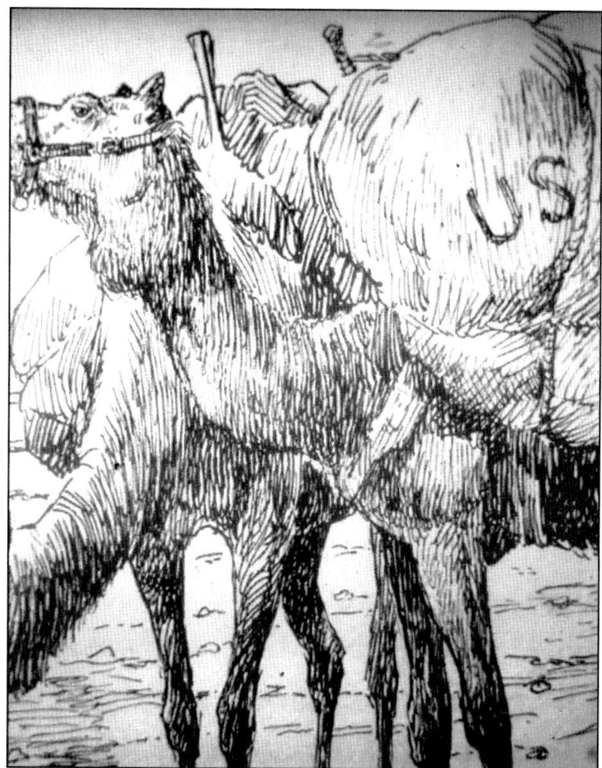

The camels passed a supreme test when Beale was challenged to pit them against the packers' mules on a 60-mile endurance trek. A 2.5-ton load was divided among six camels, and a like amount was loaded on two army wagons drawn by six mules each. The camels finished the trip in two and a half days, while the mules took four.

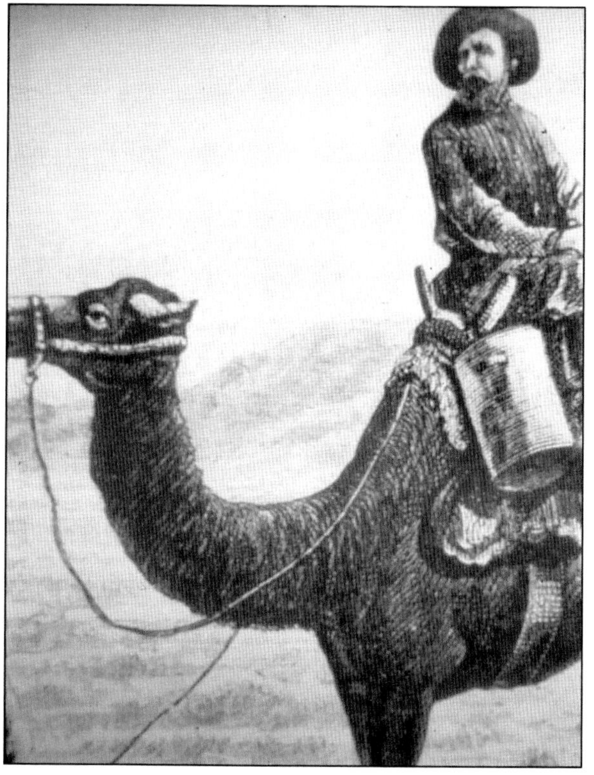

Although Beale championed his illustrious camels, referring to them as the "noblest brute alive," his mule skinners scorned them. They were especially upset when entire herds of mules stampeded at the mere site of the homely creatures. The camel's strong body odor and propensity to be extremely stubborn and spit at the mule skinners certainly didn't endear them to their American handlers.

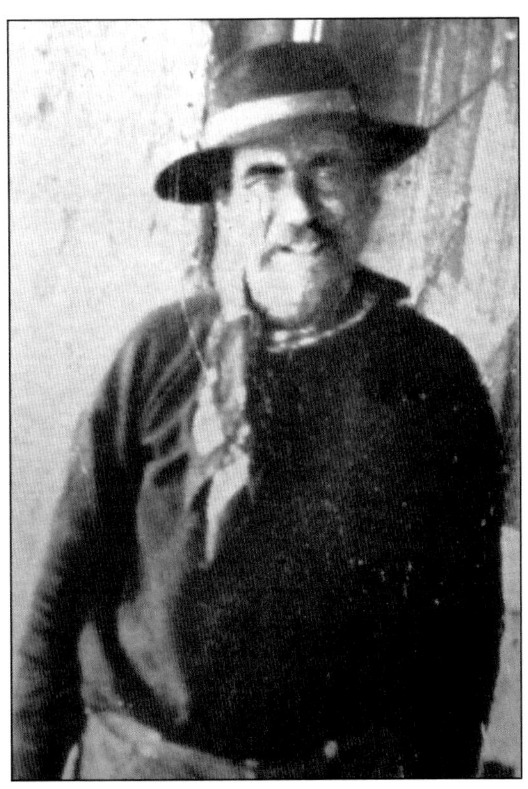

The American packers and mule skinners couldn't speak Arabic, and the stubborn camels wouldn't learn English, so camel drivers were imported from the Middle East. They were a colorful bunch with names like Long Tom, Short Tom, and Greek George. The most famous was Hadji Ali. The Americans quickly corrupted his name to "Hi Jolly." After the expedition, Hi Jolly remained in Arizona, got married, and became a prospector. He and his beloved camels are memorialized on a pyramid-shaped monument topped off with a lone camel at Quartsite, Arizona. The inscription reads: "The Last Campground of Hi Jolly." The camels were sold, auctioned off, or turned loose to roam the deserts, and the Camel Corps was almost forgotten.

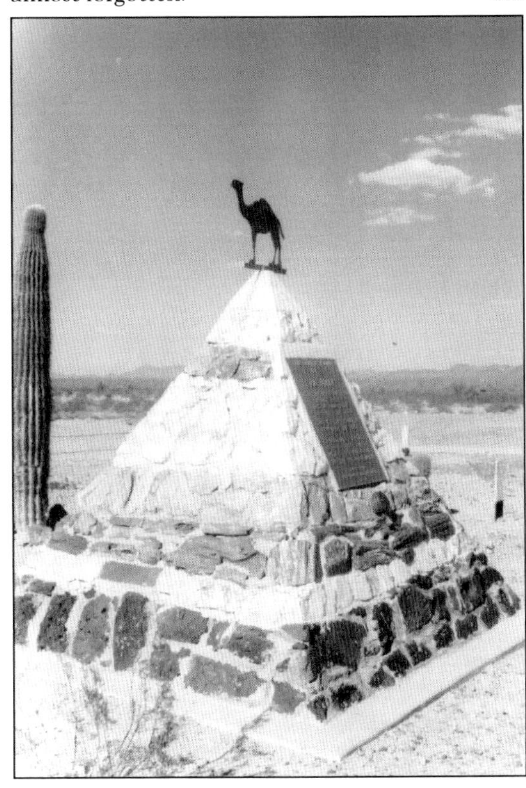

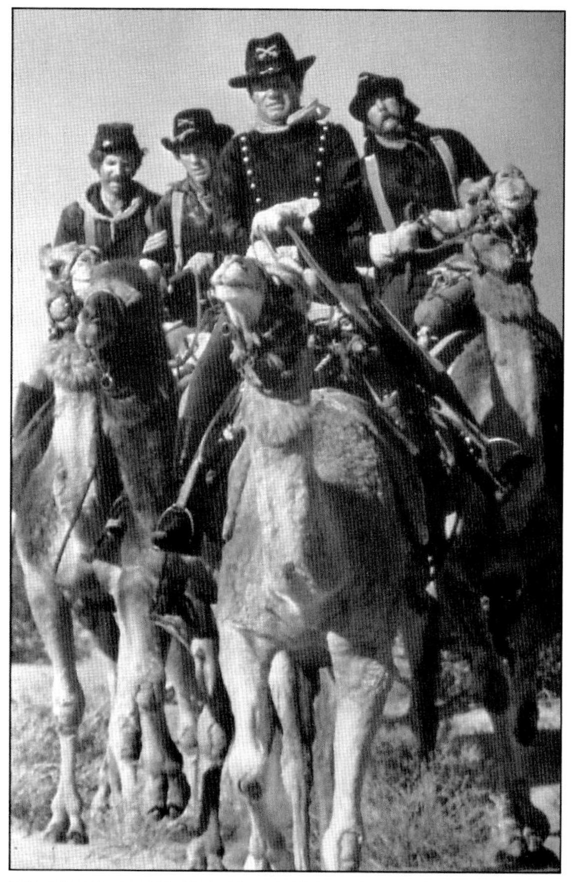

In 1976, Hollywood released a cornball comedy called *Hawmps*, which was loosely based on the U.S. Camel Corps. It was filmed at the Old Tucson movie studio. There was no love lost between the Americans and camels, but Hollywood couldn't resist providing one passionate scene. A straight version of the great camel experiment was the B Western *Southwest Passage* in 1954, starring Rod Cameron as Ned Beale. The real story of the camels was far better than anything to come out of Hollywood. In 1883, unknown people tied a dead body on the back of a stray camel. The camel was sighted many times with a skeleton tied to its back, and it became known as the "Red Ghost." It went on a rampage, tearing through mining camps, destroying property, and even killing a woman before it was shot to death.

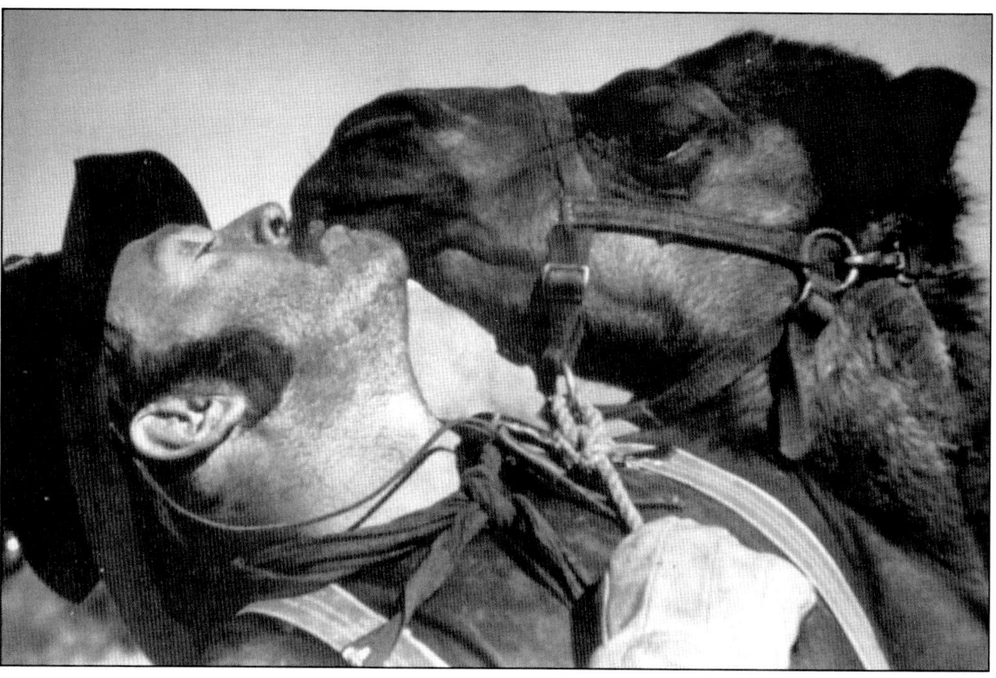

Two

Santa Fe All the Way
The Arrival of the Railroad

Although surveyors for the Army Corps of Topographical Engineers had mapped out a route across Northern Arizona along the 35th parallel in the 1850s, the Civil War delayed construction for many years. By the early 1880s, the Santa Fe had stretched its steel ribbons west from Kansas and into New Mexico. By November 1881, the tracks reached Sunset Crossing, Arizona, now called Winslow.

In 1882, when the tracks reached the site where Ash Fork is located today, freighting companies pressured the railroad for a more convenient location than the one at Williams. In October of that year, the railroad established a new siding 18 miles west of Williams. Before long, passengers and freight were being unloaded at what was now Ash Fork.

Neither Prescott nor Phoenix was linked to a railroad, and residents in both cities were clamoring for one. A king's ransom in gold and silver lay buried in the Bradshaw Mountains, and a railroad was desperately needed to haul in the equipment and haul out the rich ore.

In July 1885, Tom Bullock, a smooth-talking promoter, proposed a railroad line to link Prescott with the main line about 24 miles west of Ash Fork, calling it the Prescott and Central Railroad. The line was completed on December 31, 1886, but it was constructed over land subject to flooding. It was poorly run, and by 1893, it was out of business.

Two years earlier, railroad entrepreneur Frank Murphy began planning a new line running south from higher ground at Ash Fork. On August 17, 1892, the first spike was driven at Ash Fork as tracklayers, or gandy dancers as they were known, worked their way south. The Santa Fe, Prescott, and Phoenix Railroad was better known as the "Peavine" for its twisting, winding curves. The 57-mile line reached Prescott on April 24, 1893, and arrived in Phoenix on March 4, 1895, linking the capital city with the northern main line.

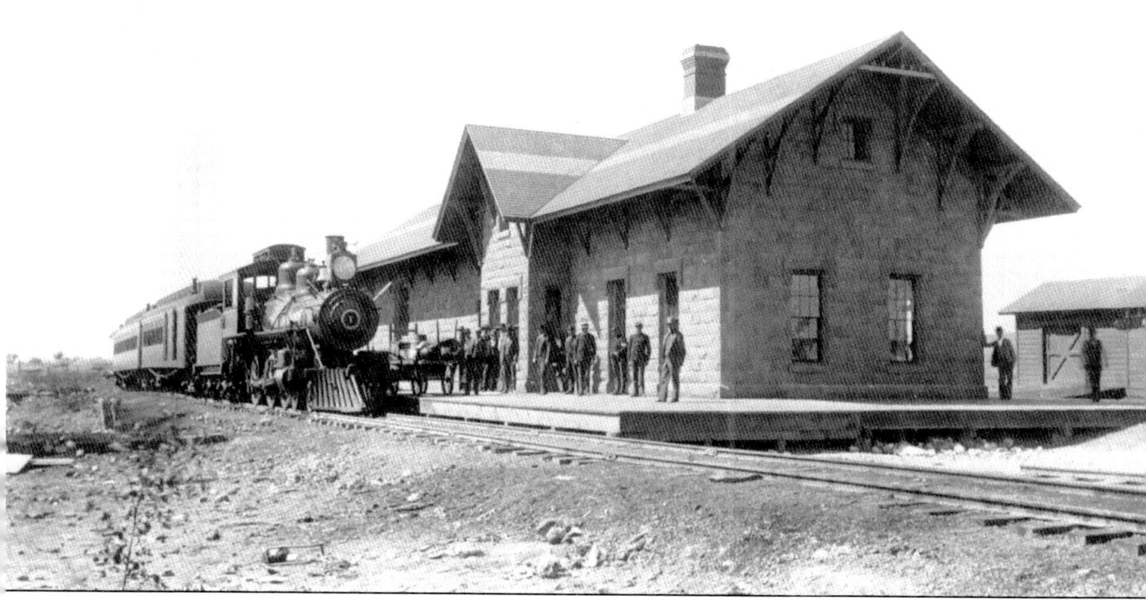

Ash Fork's original train depot was built in 1893 of red Coconino sandstone. It is quite similar to the depot still in operation at Flagstaff. The comfortable waiting room was a popular gathering place for passengers waiting to make a connection. Following the fire in 1905, a new depot, part of the famous Escalante, was built and completed by 1907. Railroads dramatically changed travel. In 1849, during the first year of the Gold Rush, it took 166 days to travel from coast to coast. By the 1860s, the trip still took about 60 days. A decade later, traveling by train, the journey took 11 days. By the 1880s, a train roaring down the track averaging 15 miles an hour could reduce the journey to a little more than a week. Folks referred to the little steam engines affectionately as "coffee pots" and "peanut roasters," and it was said a reasonably sober fat lady could outrun one of them in a downhill race, but for a young nation on the move, this was progress.

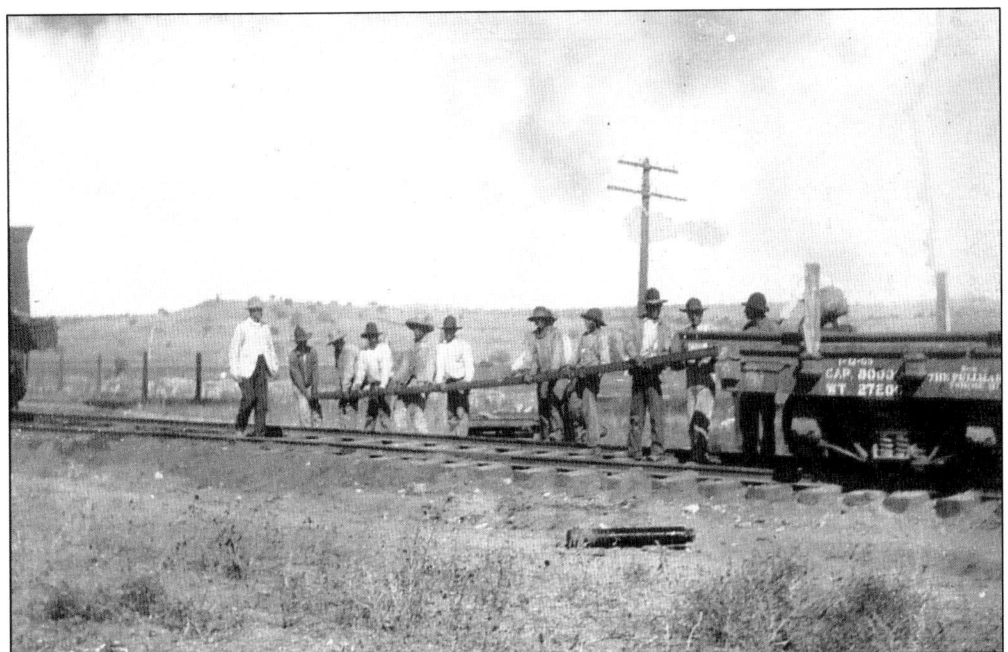

Tracklayers were called gandy dancers. The name was derived from the early section hands who used a 5-foot-long iron tamping bar made by the Gandy Manufacturing Company. The company made tools used by the railroad laborers to set the ties in the gravel track bed. A workman literally danced on the bar, called a gandy, until the tie was properly set.

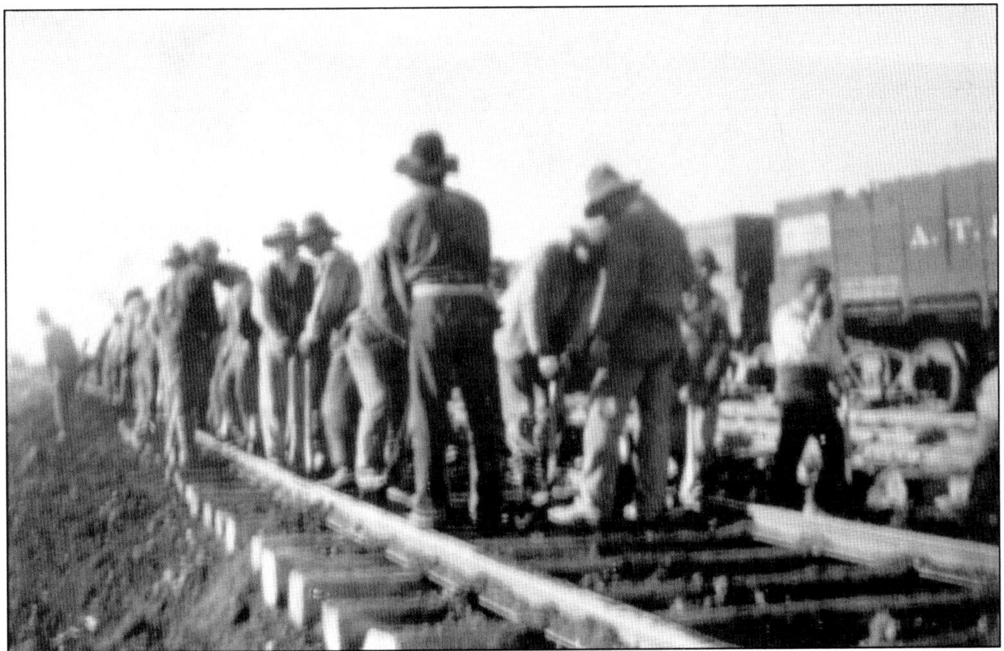

Congress granted the Atlantic and Pacific Railroad millions of acres of public lands as an incentive to build a transcontinental railroad along the 35th parallel. The land granted was 40 odd-numbered sections for each mile of track laid, which in turn could be sold to ranchers, settlers, and businesses.

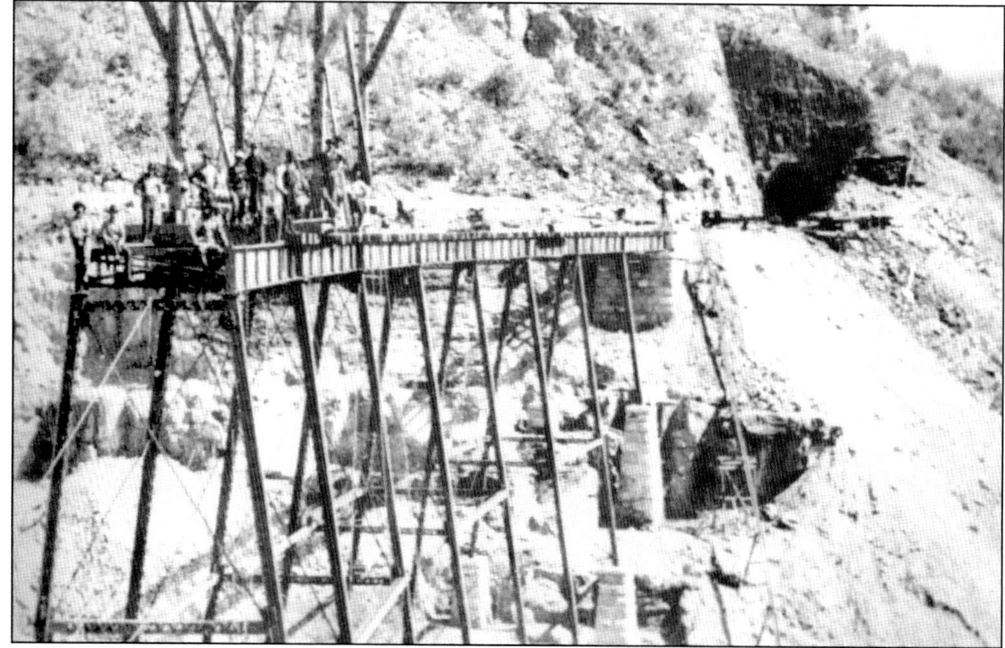

During construction of the 328-foot tunnel and trestles at Johnson Canyon, there were between 2,000 and 3,000 construction workers at the site. A city of tents, shacks, and dugouts was built and named Simms. It had at least three saloons and two general stores. Workers were paid $2.40 a day, and boardinghouses charged $5.50 per week. Accidents, murders, and sickness helped fill the tiny graveyard.

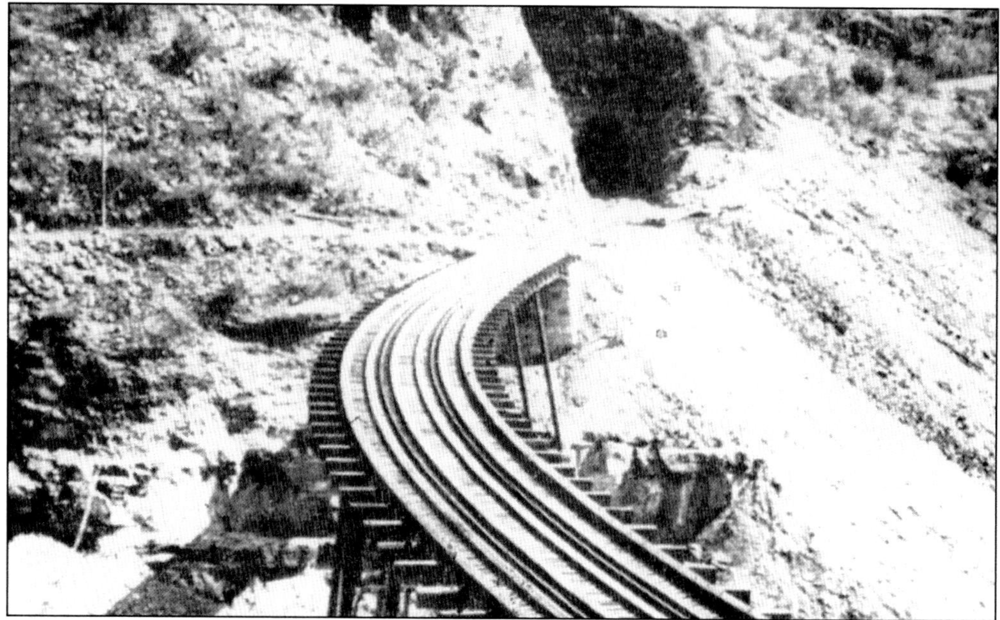

Johnson Canyon, named for a local rancher, was at the time of its construction the only tunnel on the Atlantic and Pacific Railroad between Kansas City and Los Angeles. This view looks east up Johnson Canyon towards the entrance of the tunnel. The tunnel and two trestles took almost a year to complete.

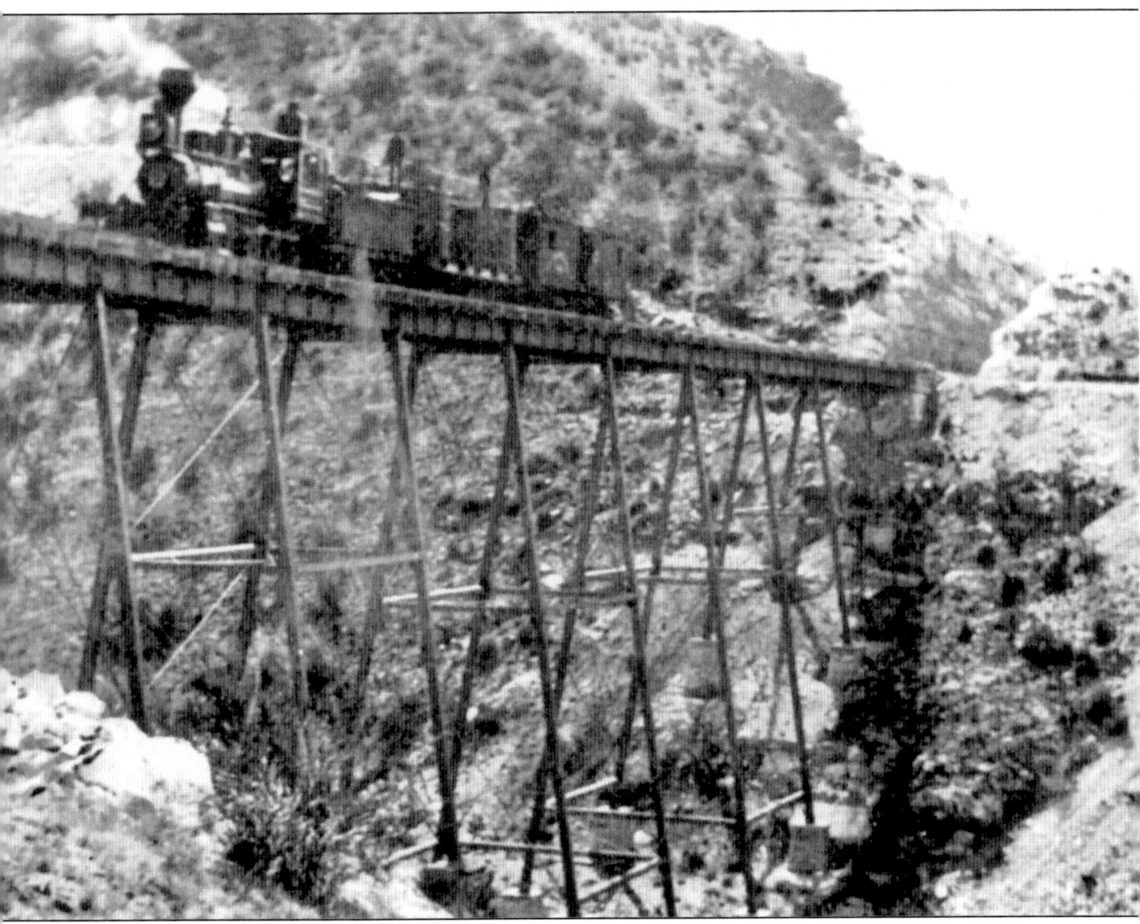

When the Atlantic and Pacific Railroad began construction across Northern Arizona in 1880, there were only two major question marks: Canyon Diablo east of Flagstaff and Johnson Canyon east of Ash Fork. Canyon Diablo was bridged by a 222-foot-high wooden trestle. Johnson Canyon would prove equally daunting with its two trestles and a tunnel. A train has just emerged from the tunnel and will cross this trestle and another while making the long run down Johnson Canyon. Steam locomotives need a lot of water to operate the huge boiler, and water from Johnson Canyon was piped down to Ash Fork.

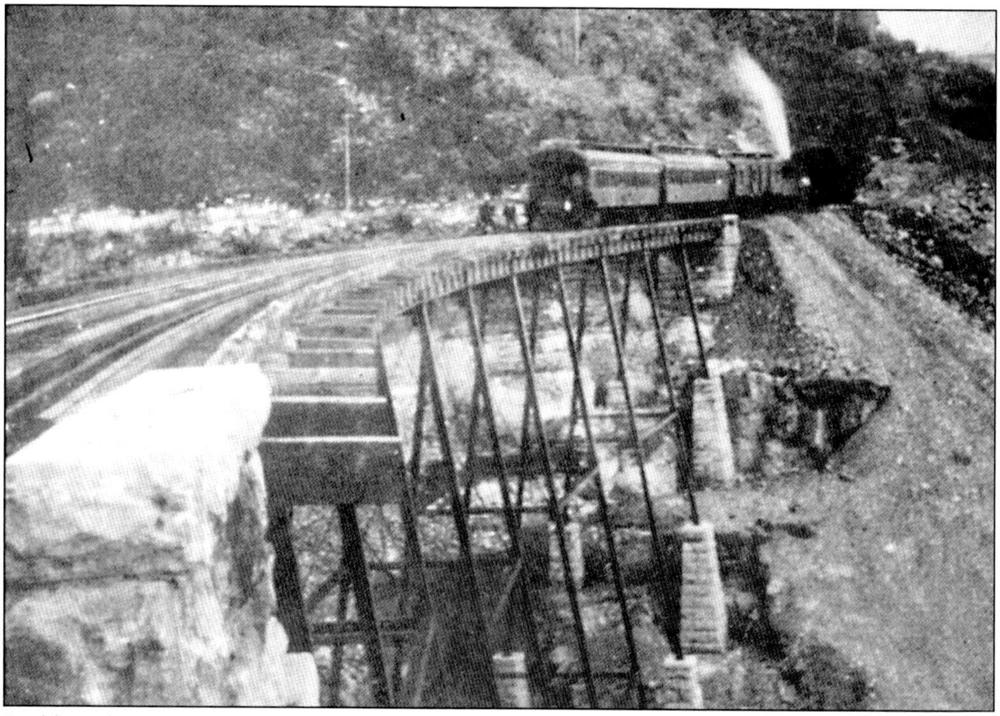

Building the tunnel was an epic construction project, and when completed, it removed the last serious obstacle of the Atlantic and Pacific Railroad as it crossed Arizona. In 1910, the Santa Fe built another single-track line above Johnson to provide a gentler grade for eastbound trains. During World War II, soldiers were posted at the tunnel and two adjacent trestles to prevent sabotage.

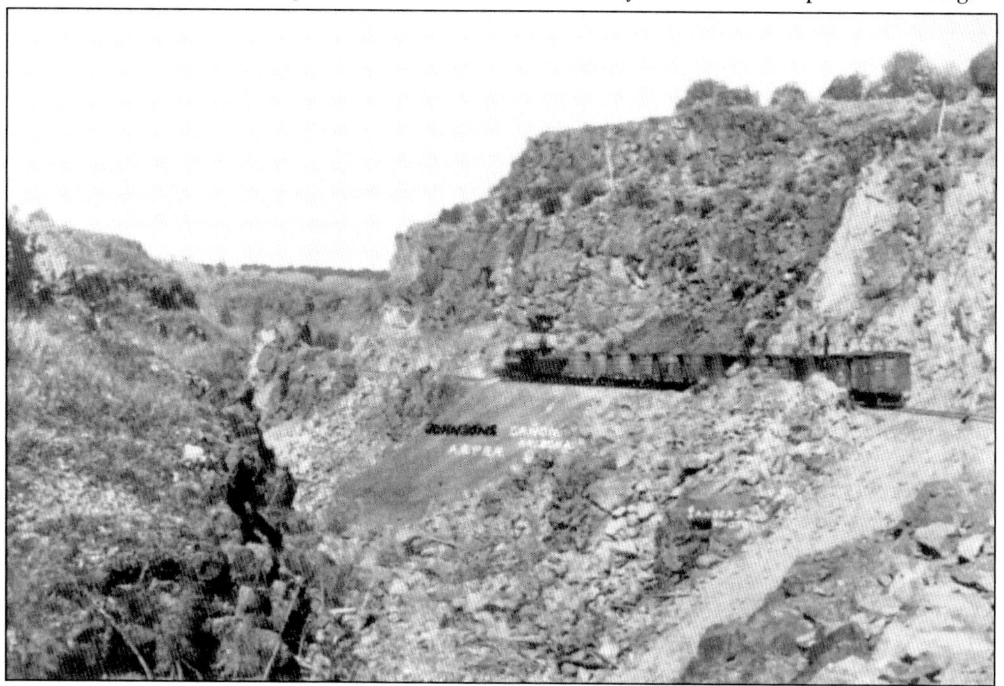

A train heads down Johnson Canyon on its way to Ash Fork.

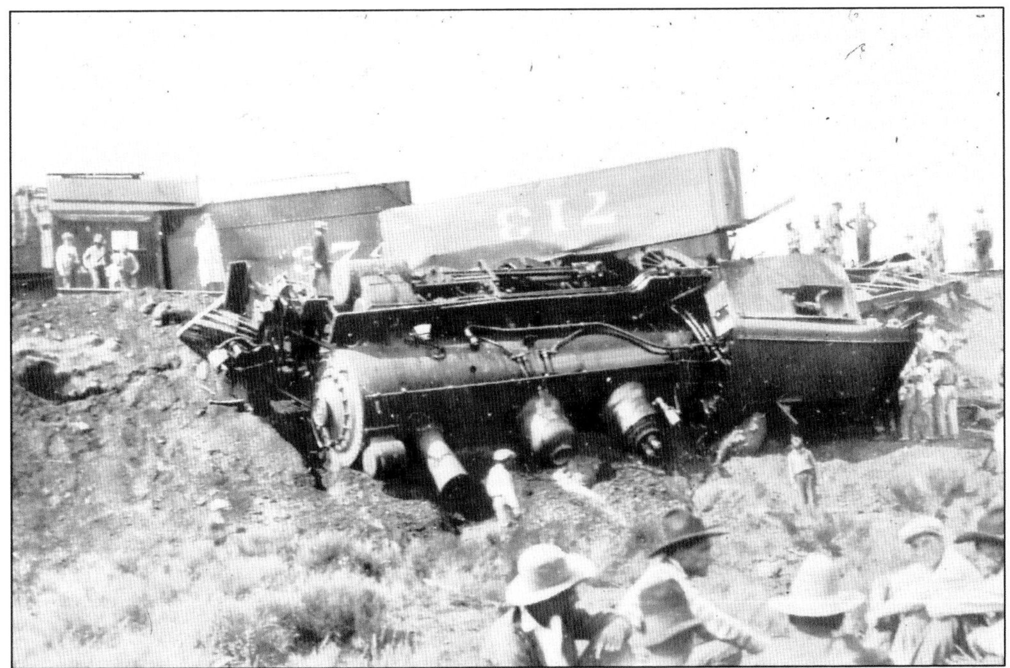

Going up the 1,000-foot climb at Johnson Canyon usually required two helper engines to assist the freight trains. Coming down the grade was another matter. Engineers had to brake hard when making the curve in front of the tunnel, and the pressure could cause the tracks to buckle, resulting in derailments and wrecks. The bottom of the canyon is still strewn with parts of wrecked trains.

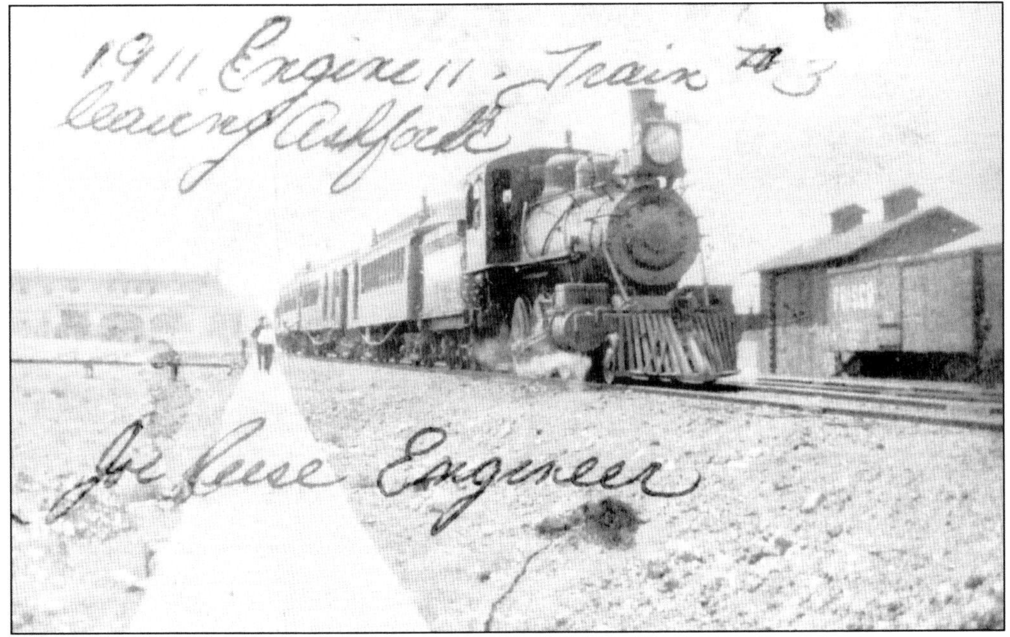

Engine No. 11, Train No. 3 pulls out of the yard at Ash Fork in 1911. In the background at center left is the Hotel Escalante. On the right of the engine is the original Ash Fork depot. (Courtesy Hume collection.)

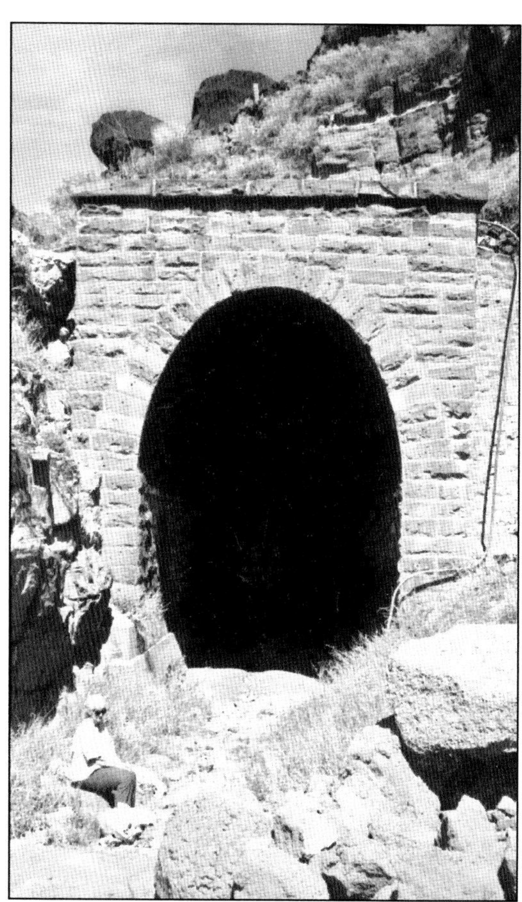

When the Santa Fe abandoned the line through Johnson Canyon in 1960, the rails were removed. (Courtesy Carol Popp.)

The usual price for a ticket to ride was about 10¢ a mile. For those lucky enough to be riding the Atchison, Topeka, and Santa Fe, the hospitality of Fred Harvey's famous restaurants and their comely waitresses awaited the weary travelers.

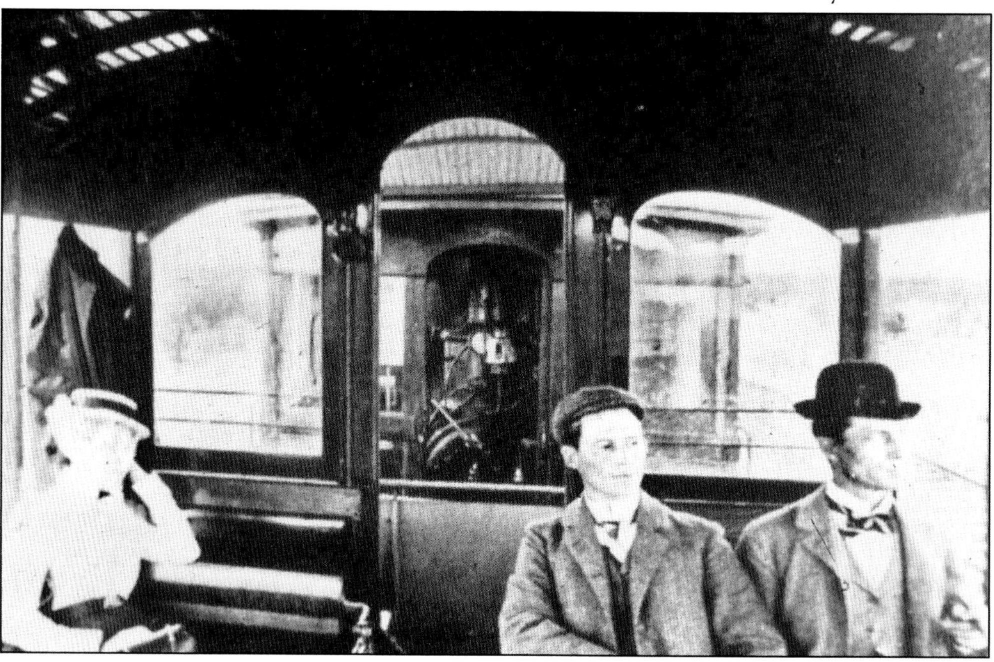

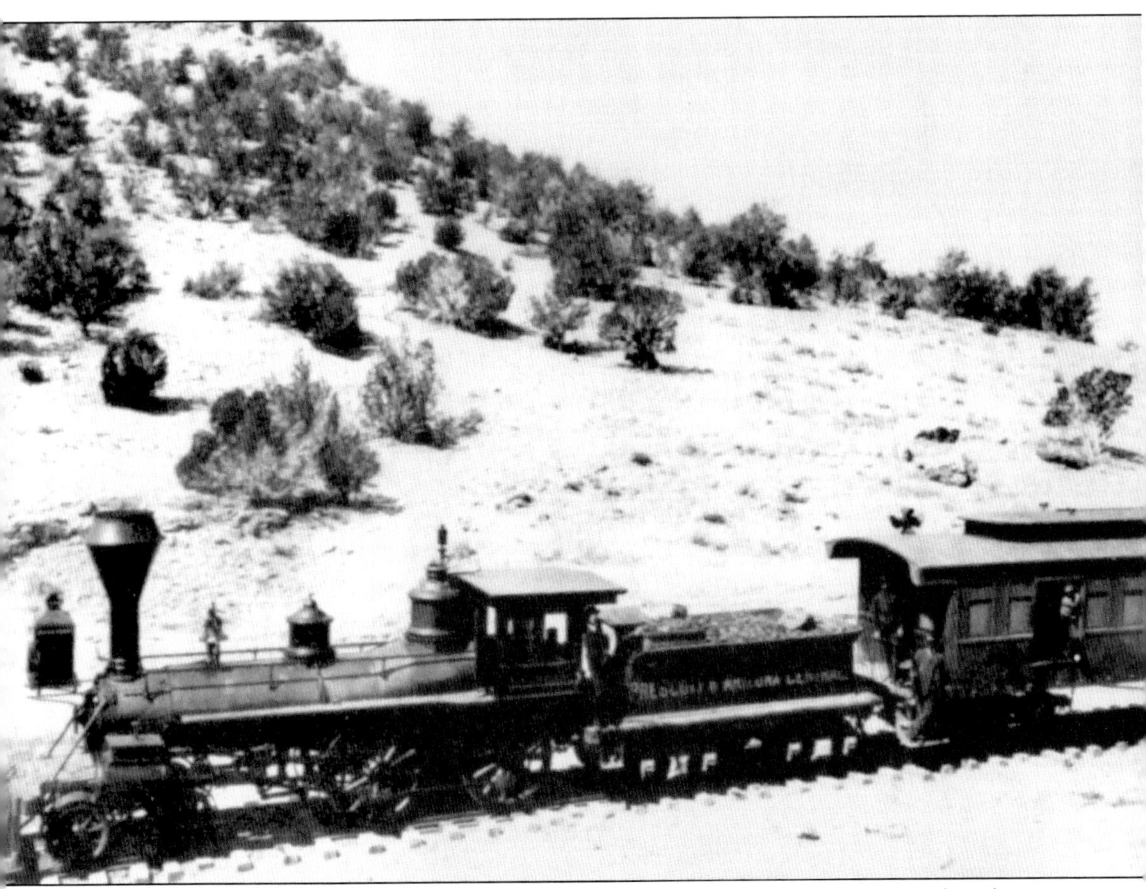

The citizens of Prescott raised $300,000 to construct the 72-mile Prescott and Central Railway from Prescott Junction (Seligman). They had to finish construction no later than December 31, 1886, or face a stiff $72,000 penalty. Construction crews working feverishly against the clock barely managed to drive in the last spike just before midnight on the 31st. Prescott was now linked to the main line. The Prescott and Central Railroad was in trouble from the beginning. The line had an erratic schedule, as the crews stopped for a beer and card game or to go hunting. During flash floods, the line was temporarily washed out. The final blow came in 1892, when Big Chino Wash flooded. The following year, the Prescott and Central closed down operations.

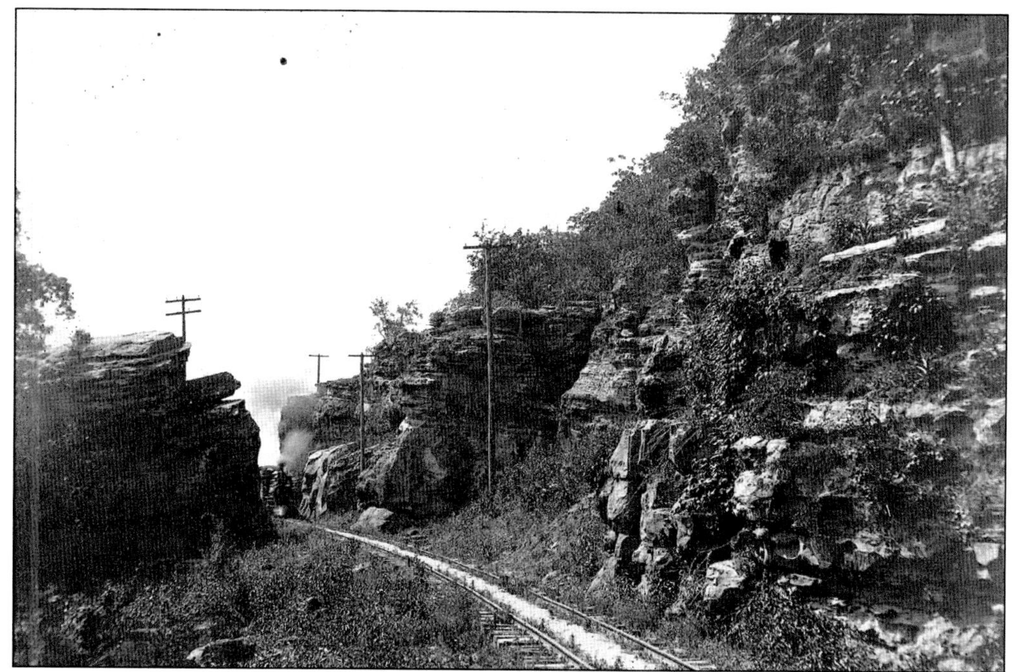

The Prescott and Central Railroad was built to link Prescott with the main line at Seligman, then called Prescott Junction. The line proved inefficient and went out of business in the early 1890s. A new line began from Ash Fork in 1893 called the Santa Fe, Prescott, and Phoenix Railway. This photograph shows a train passing through a cut south of Ash Fork.

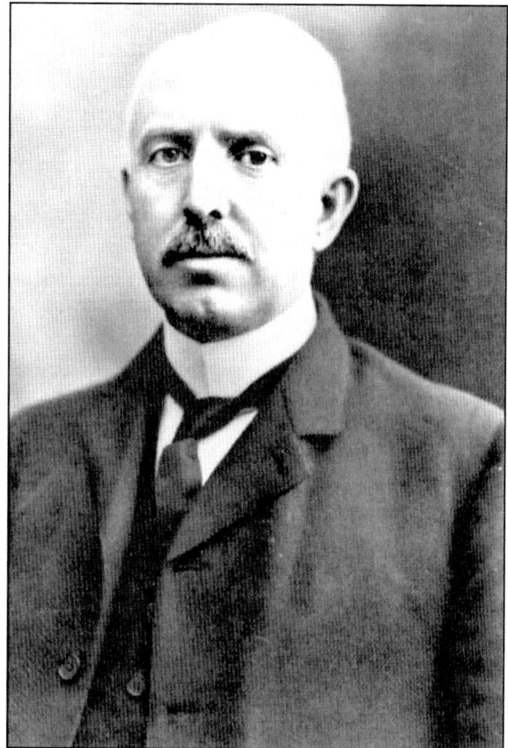

One of Arizona's greatest entrepreneurs, Frank Murphy, had a knack for being able to raise huge amounts of capital to fund mining and railroad projects in Arizona during territorial days. After completing the railroad linking Ash Fork to Phoenix in 1895, he began building the Prescott and Eastern through Mayer. The extension that zigzagged up the mountain to the rich silver mines near Crown King was called the Bradshaw Mountain Railroad.

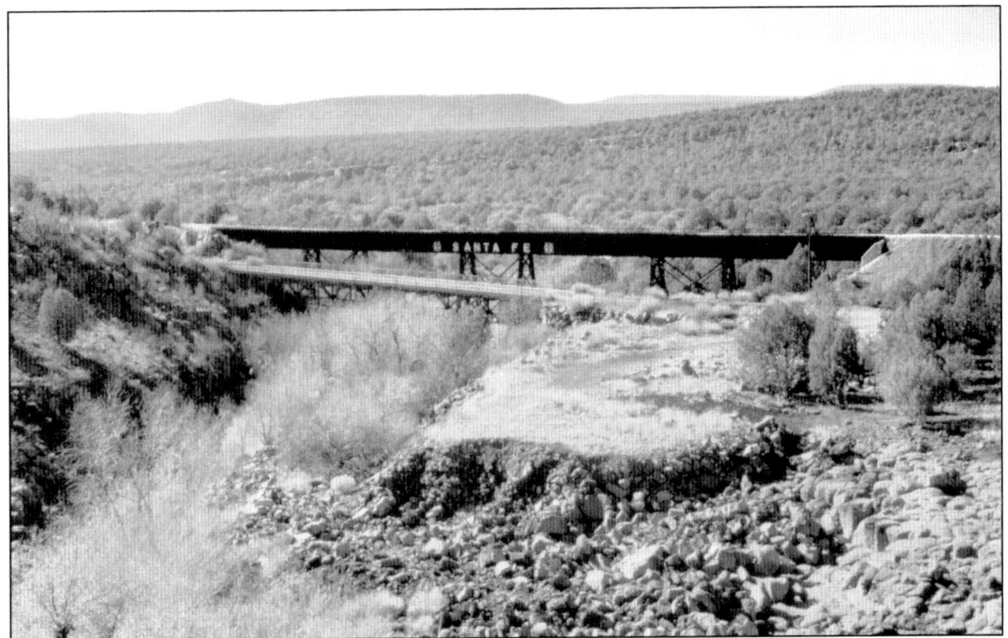

Frank Murphy's crew began construction in Ash Fork on January 23, 1892. The line wound through and around the rugged mountains of Central Arizona and reached Phoenix on March 4, 1895. The branch line was more commonly known as the Peavine for its many lazy loops, twists, and turns, causing one cowboy to suggest the line had "more kinks than a cheap lariat."

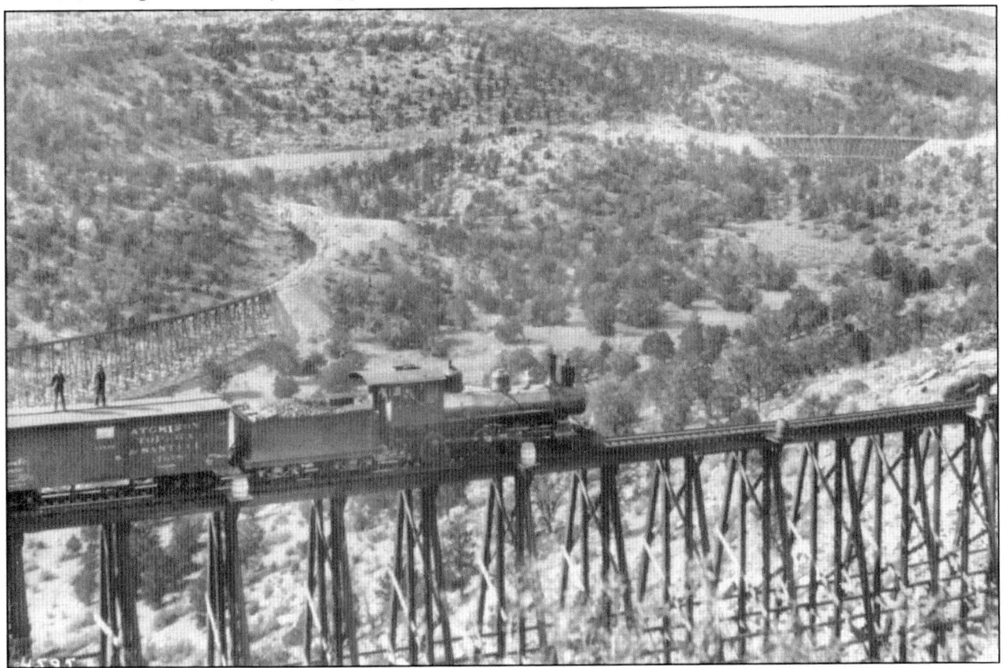

Limestone Canyon required several trestles. "If you can look out of the windows of the coach," said a passenger, "and you can see a railroad track both places, then my friend, you are on the Peavine! It may take you all day to get to Phoenix but you can see the country two or three times on one trip."

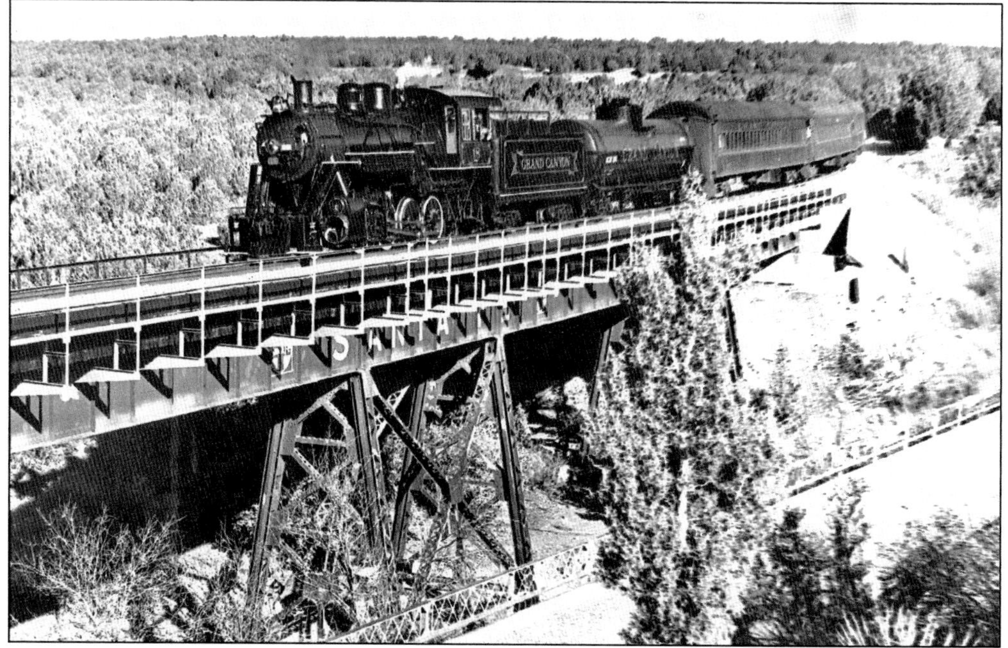

A Santa Fe passenger train chuffs across the bridge at Little Hell Canyon, 10 miles south of town. The Peavine still connects Ash Fork to Prescott and Phoenix. In the foreground is Highway 89. Before Interstate 17 opened in the late 1960s, U.S. 89 was Central and Southern Arizona's main link with the northern part of the state.

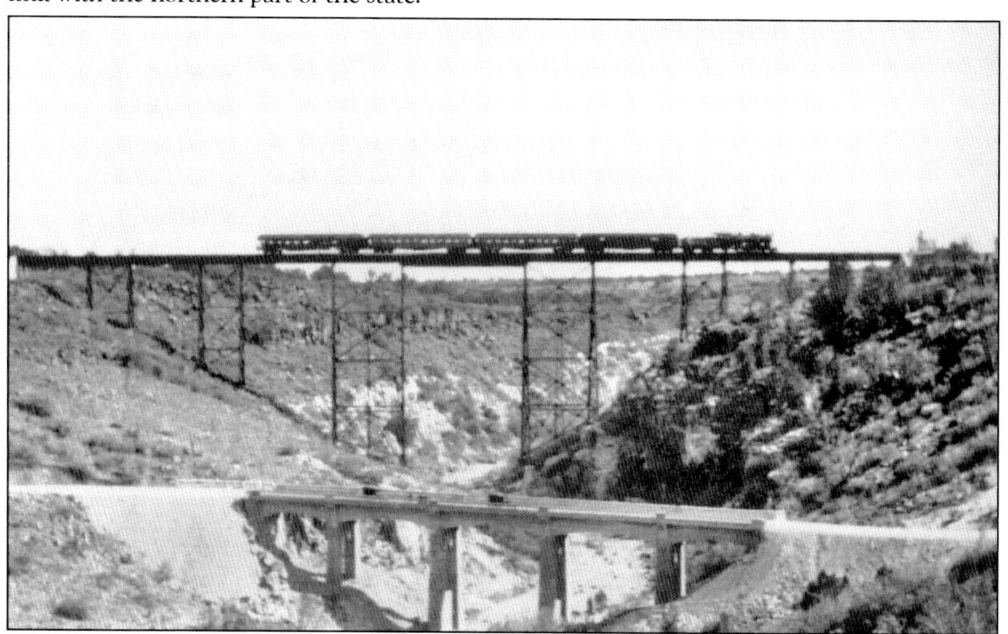

A new railroad bridge was erected over Hell Canyon in 1901, bypassing Limestone Canyon. This photograph was taken in the 1920s, with U.S. 89 in the foreground. A new highway overpass was constructed in the mid-1950s eliminating the dangerous curves in the canyon. During World War I and World War II, guards were posted at the bridge. (Courtesy Cornelius W. Hauck collection.)

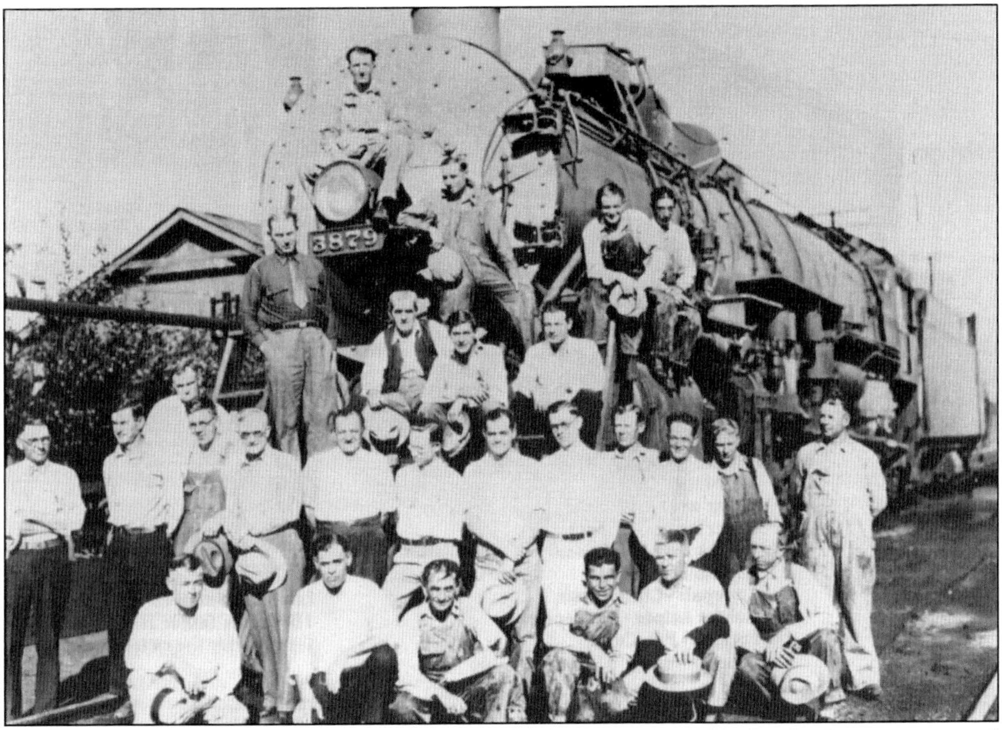

The roundhouse gang in 1925 gathers on and around Engine No. 3879. On the front row, second from left, is car inspector Jim Pena. He arrived in Ash Fork with his family from New Mexico in 1920. He and his wife lived in Ash Fork the rest of their lives, and when he died, he was one of the town's oldest residents. His daughter, Josie Martin, still makes her home in Ash Fork. Sitting on the headlight is hoghead (engineer) Lon Smith, another longtime resident.

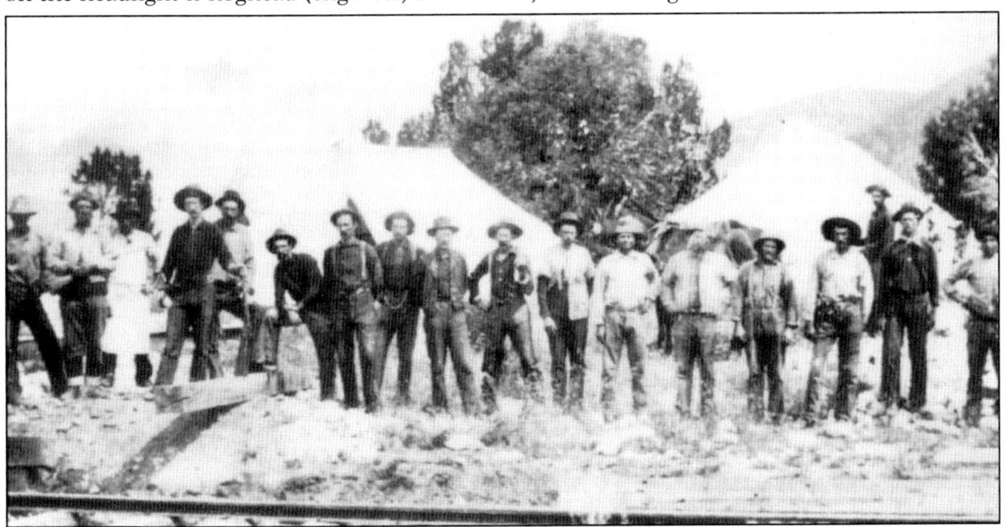

Injuries were common, as labor was cheap and safety standards were nonexistent. Tent saloons, stocked up with liquor, beer, women, and cards, sprang up along the construction area. On the average, a bottle of beer per man was consumed for each tie laid. Such camps sprouted to serve the crews then, like circuses, struck their tents and moved on down the line to the next end-of-track.

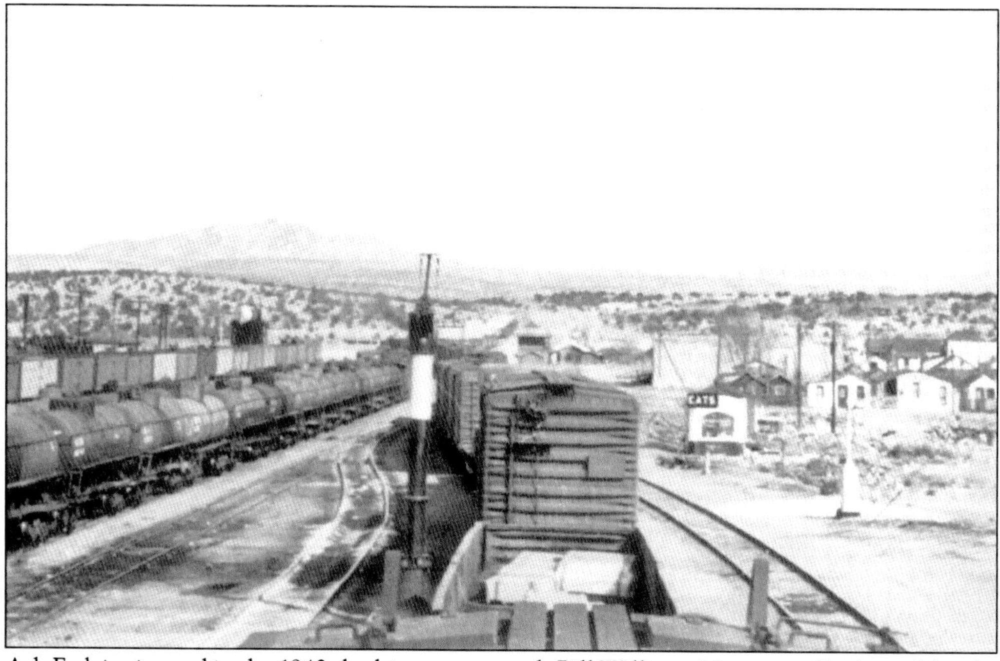

Ash Fork is pictured in the 1940s looking east towards Bill Williams Mountain. Eastbound freight trains had to climb the steep grade to Williams, a sharp 1,600-foot gain in altitude. Since the 1880s, railroad officials talked about another line to skirt the steep hills east of Ash Fork, and the new line was finally opened in 1960; Ash Fork's halcyon days as a railroad town were over.

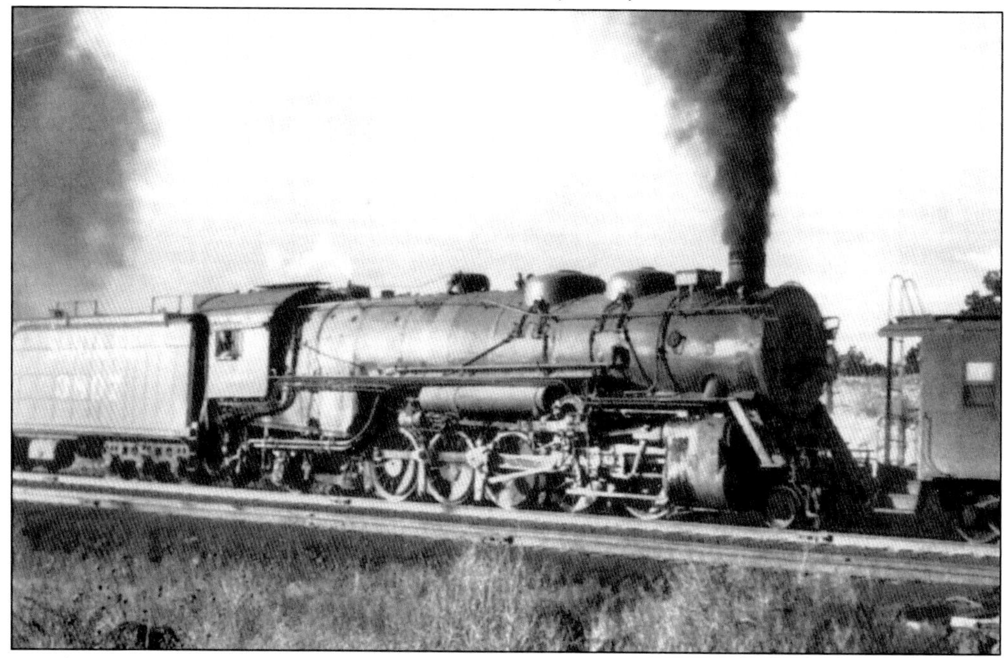
Freight trains heading up the steep grade towards Williams needed a boost from "helpers." A steam engine would literally provide a push. A helper is connected to the caboose of an eastbound freight train as it leaves Ash Fork. There were five helper crews standing by to give the long, heavy freight trains a boost up Johnson Canyon.

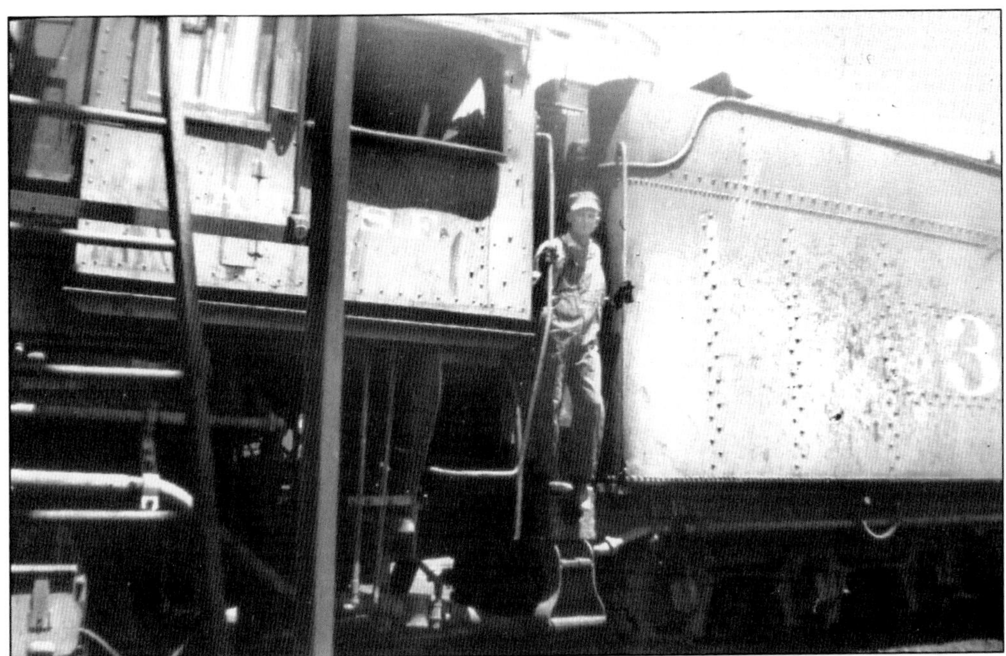

The author's father, Ira "Happy" Trimble, hired out for the Santa Fe in 1946. He started out as a fireman on the steam locomotives then made the transition to diesels in the early 1950s, when he became an engineer on the Peavine between Ash Fork and Phoenix for 25 years. This photograph was taken in the yards at Ash Fork.

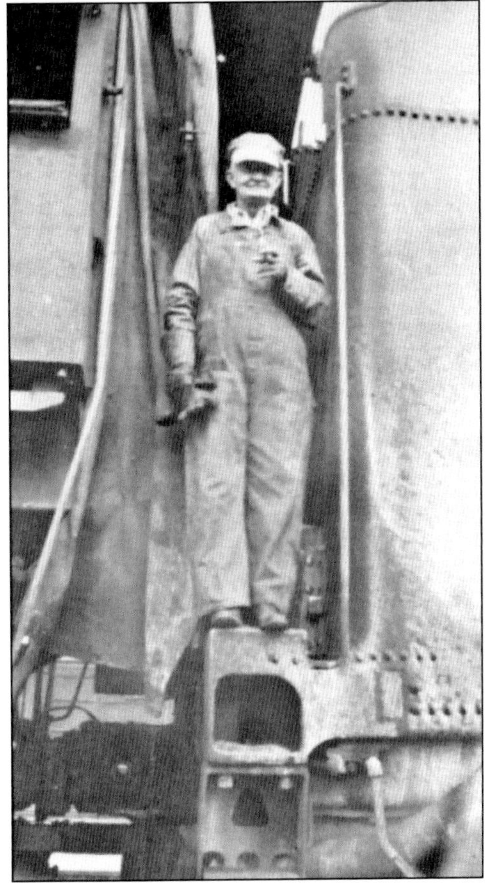

Leo Kelly arrived in Ash Fork in 1890. His father, Harry, was a tracklayer for the Atlantic and Pacific Railroad. For many years, Leo and his family lived in a house adjacent to the Harvey House. (Courtesy of Teeny Theroux.)

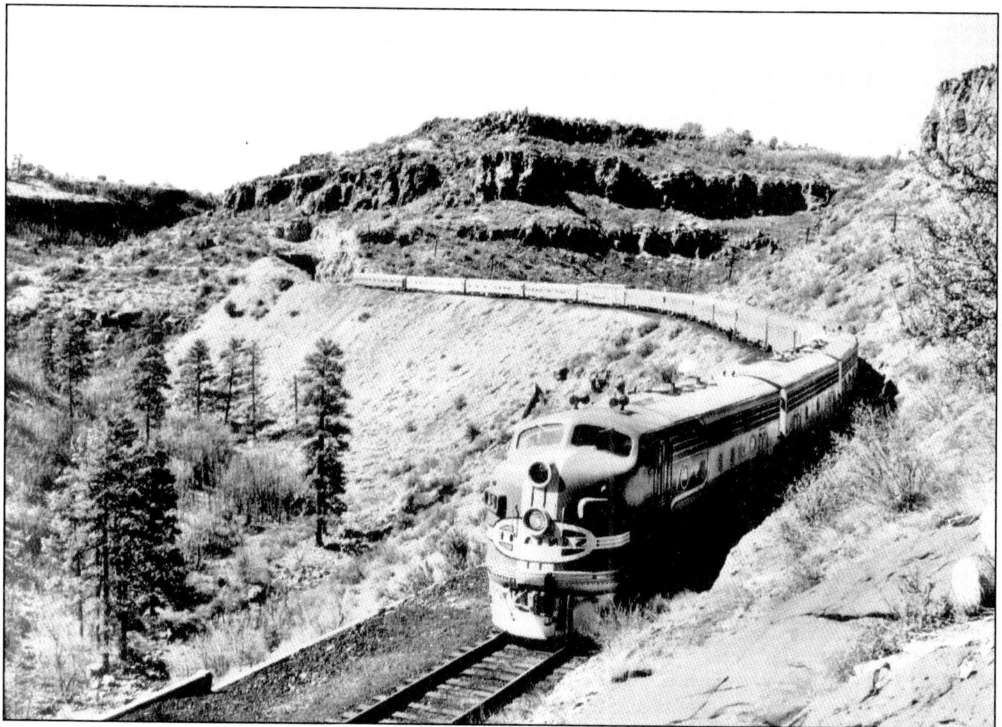

During the late 1940s, diesel engines began replacing the steam locomotives. A Santa Fe train, pulled by a diesel engine with the trademark war bonnet on its nose, heads down Johnson Canyon in the 1950s. During the age of the steam locomotives, rail lines, like wagon roads, had to follow watering places across the West. Diesel-fueled engines enabled the lines to bypass water-tank towns like Ash Fork.

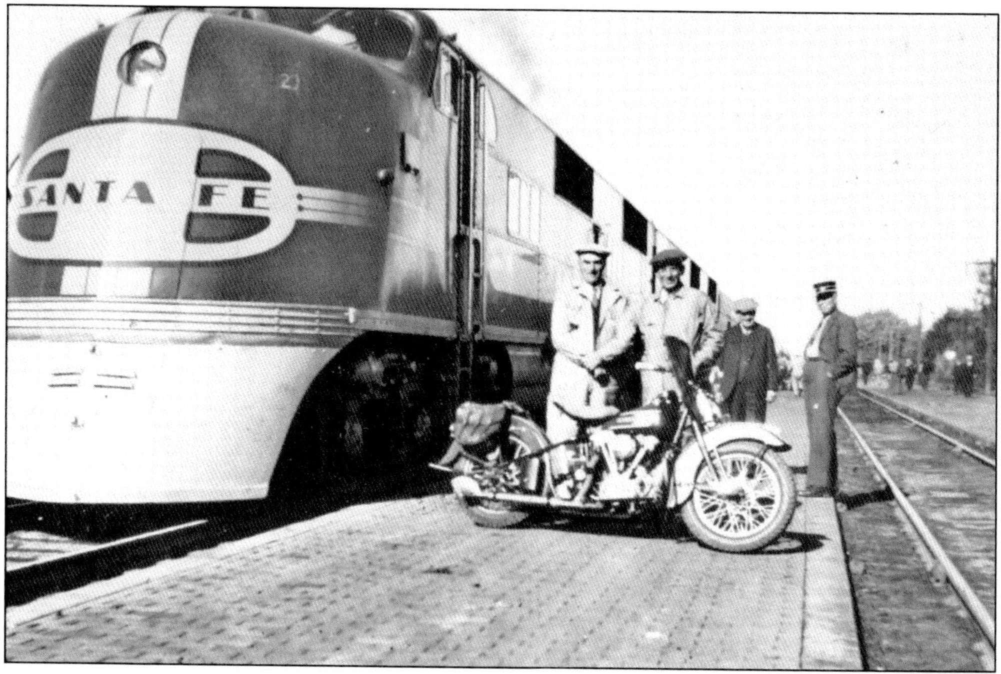

Three

THE EARLY YEARS
A TOWN IS BORN

Cooper Thomas Lewis was one of the town's first residents. The native of Illinois arrived in Prescott in 1872, and when the new town was born alongside the tracks of the Atlantic and Pacific Railroad, he decided to open a saloon, livery stable, and store on the south side of the tracks. When he arrived, the town was located on the north side of the tracks. He wisely bought some parcels of real estate on the south side of the tracks from the railroad and built rental houses on them. Lewis built the first structure using flagstone and declared prophetically that the colorful stone found north of town would one day make fine building material. His building still stands on Railroad Avenue. Lewis also acted as banker for the town, loaning money on a handshake, and found the time to run a small cow outfit.

There was another man in Ash Fork named Cooper Thomas Lewis, so he changed his name to Thomas Cooper Lewis. Lewis Avenue, Ash Fork's main street, which doubled as Route 66, is named to honor the town's "First Resident."

The arrival of the railroad in 1882 cut back on the area's dependence on stage transportation, but Ash Fork remained a center for travelers and freighters going north and south to Prescott and Jerome. It would be another 10 years before Frank Murphy would begin construction on the Santa Fe, Prescott, and Phoenix Railroad that would eventually link the territorial capital and Prescott to the main line railroad at Ash Fork.

For a few years, Ash Fork prided itself on being the gateway to the Grand Canyon. Billy Bass headquartered his Grand Canyon Stage Line in the new town on Ash Creek. His stagecoach hauled tourists from the train station at Ash Fork to nature's grandest architectural masterpiece.

Ash Fork would remain the "Gateway to the Grand Canyon" until 1904, when a new railroad line was built north from Williams.

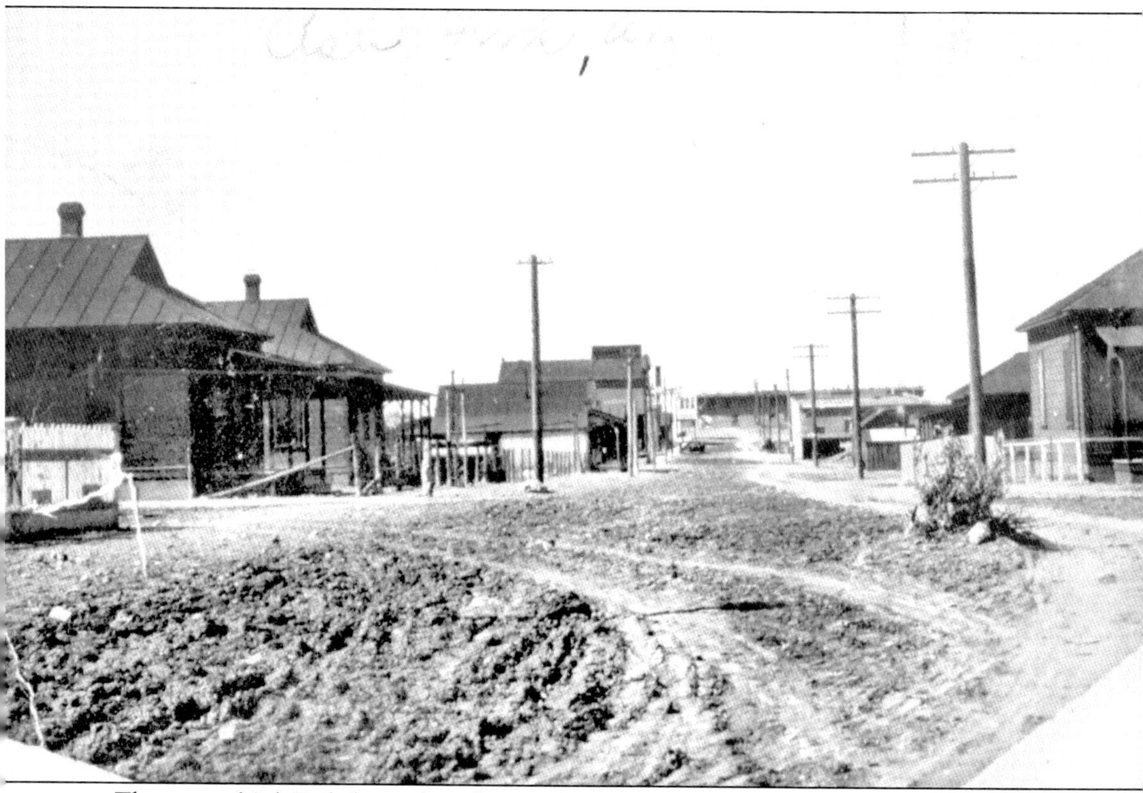

The town of Ash Fork, located on the west fork of Ash Creek, is a living monument to the sweat, tears, and the indomitable spirit of those early pioneers who would not give up and be driven out by such obstacles as disease, death, and fires. The town was an important junction for both the Santa Fe Railroad's branch line to Phoenix and U.S. 89's connection from Phoenix to Route 66. The new Harvey House, the Escalante, is at the far end of the street. During the 1920s, Route 66 would curve around the back side of the Harvey House and would make two more sharp curves before it headed west towards Seligman.

Cooper Thomas Lewis arrived in Prescott in 1877 and in Ash Fork when the railroad arrived in 1882. Lewis remained a bachelor until he was 50 years old; then, on November 14, 1899, he married Elizabeth Taylor of Prescott. Two years later, a daughter, Anna, was born. Anna's son, Lewis; his sons, Roy, Lewis, and Kurt; and their children still make their homes in Ash Fork, spanning five generations. Without a doubt, they are Ash Fork's "First Family." (Courtesy Hume collection.)

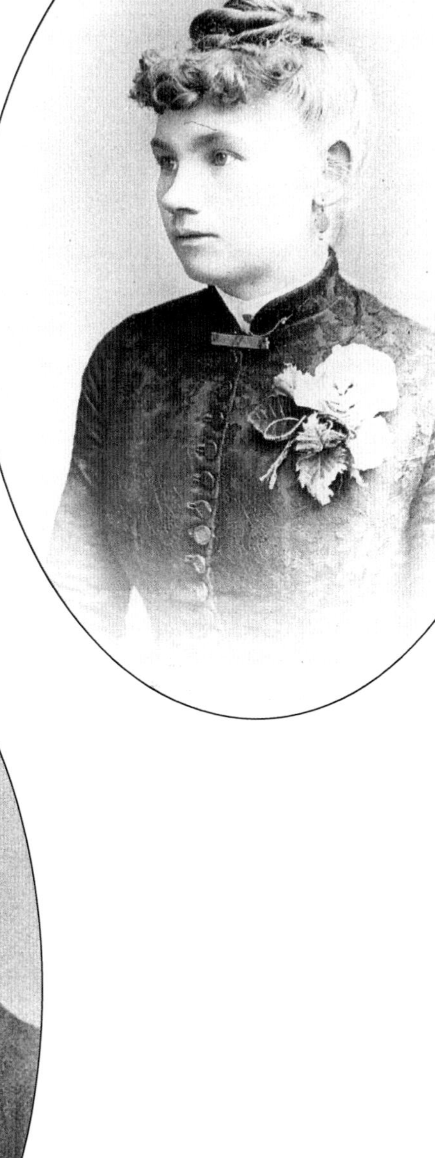

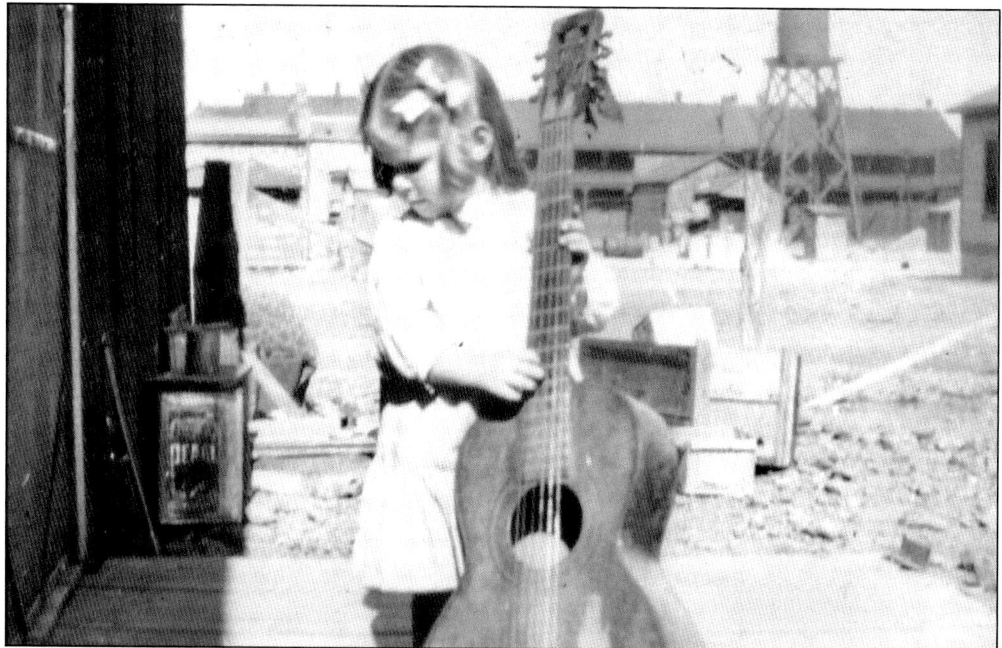

Anna Lewis Hume was born in 1901. The old depot and the Ash Fork House are in the background. The depot burned in 1905, and the hotel was moved up Lewis Avenue and became the White House Hotel. Anna lived her whole life in Ash Fork, raising four daughters and two sons. She died on January 13, 1967. In this photograph, taken around 1905, she's too small to strap on the guitar, so she's turned it into a standup bass. In the photograph below, Danny Taylor and Anna pose near the Ash Fork House on Third Street. In 1925, five years after her father died, Anna Lewis carried on her father's entrepreneurial spirit by installing the town's first power plant in the old flagstone building on Railroad Avenue. (Courtesy Hume collection.)

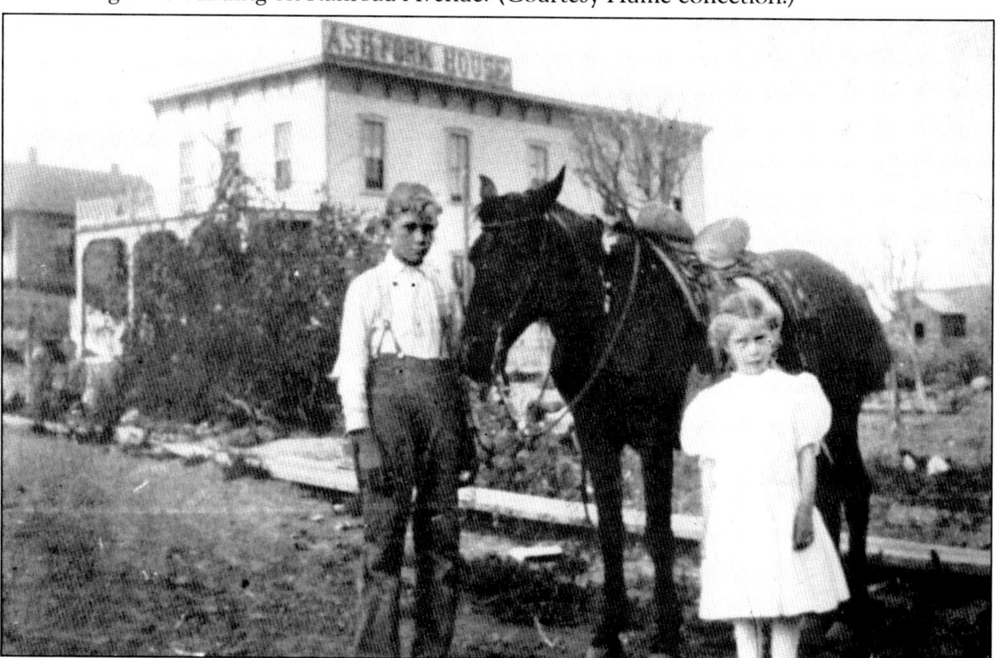

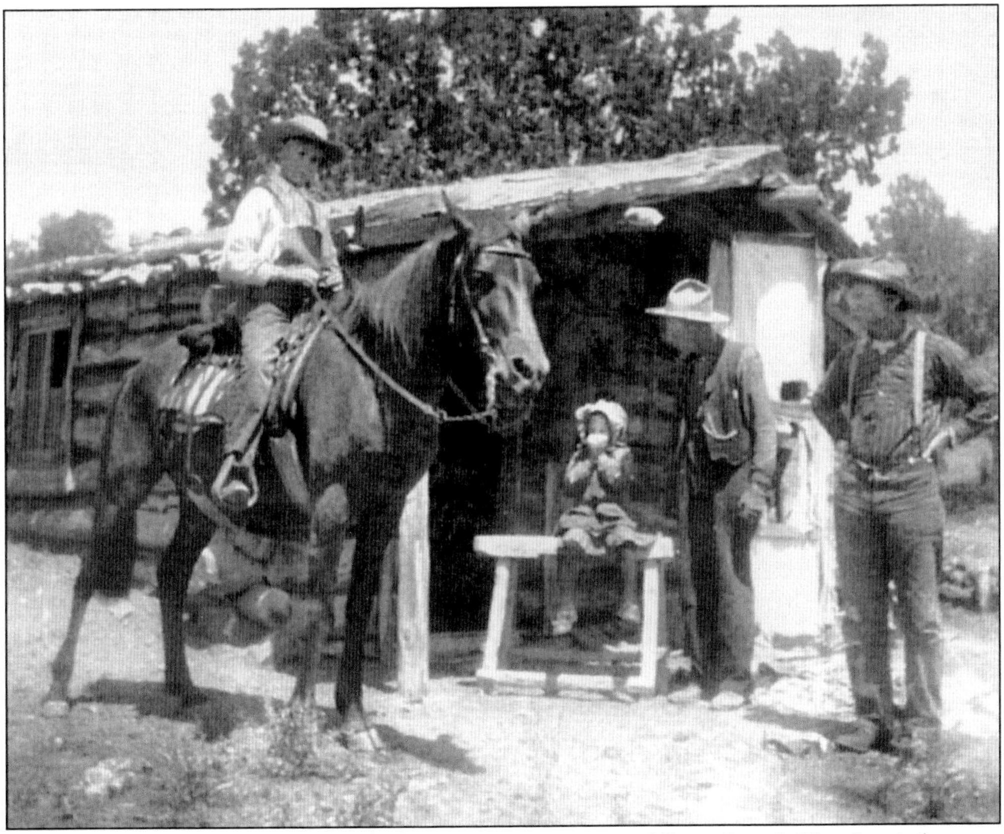

Danny Taylor is on horseback and little Anna is sitting on saddle rack with Tom Lewis (next to Anna) and Amos Chunning at the Chunning Springs Ranch. (Courtesy Hume collection.)

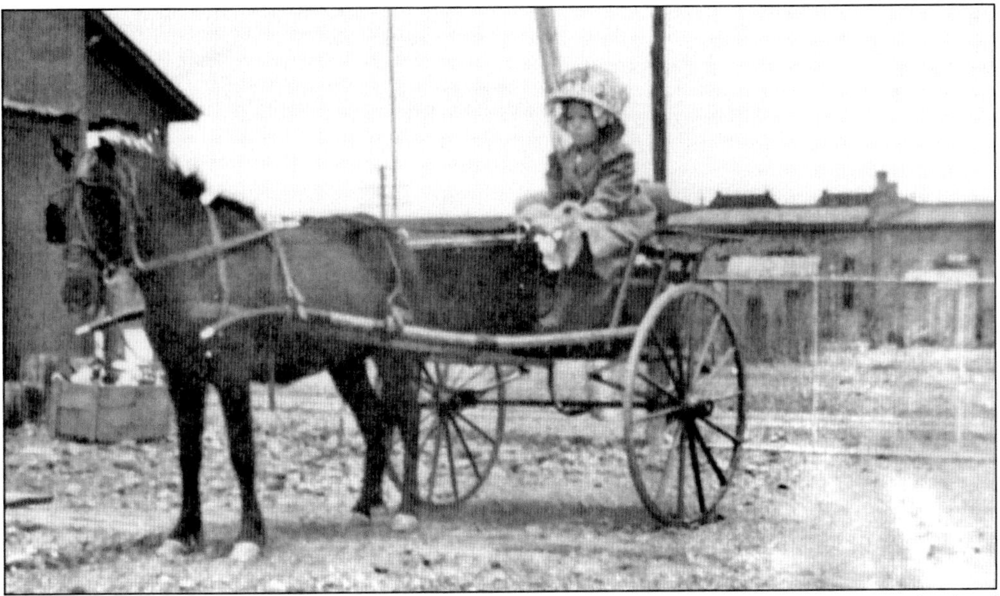

Old pioneers reminiscing about Ash Fork's early days fondly recall Anna exercising her Shetland pony with daily rides around town. (Courtesy Hume collection.)

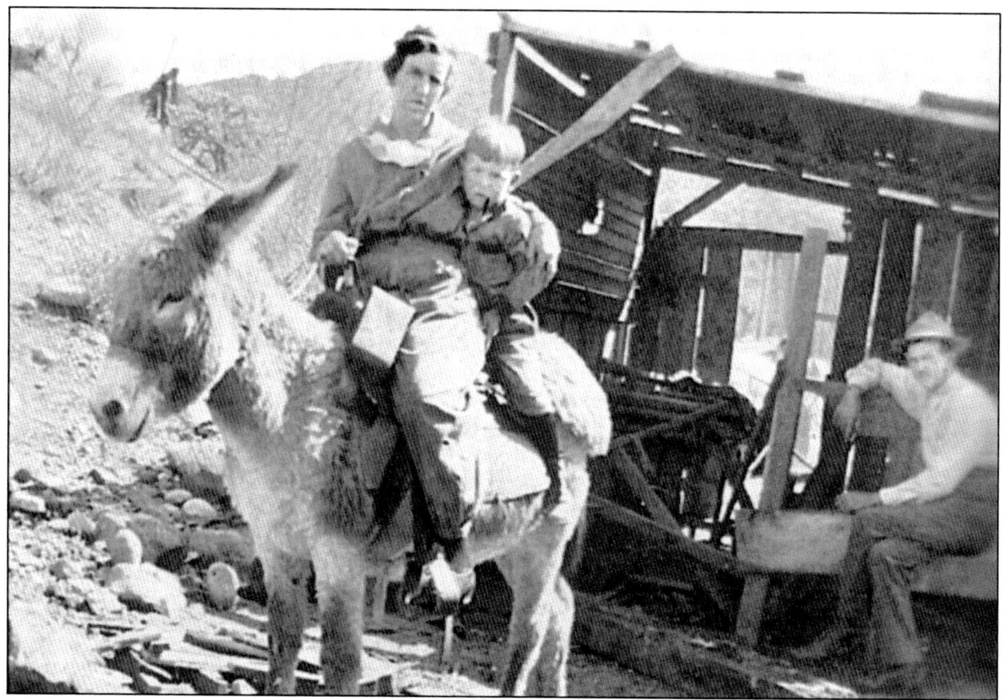

Mabel Kelly and her son, Charlie, sit on the hurricane deck of a donkey at a mine south of Ash Fork. (Courtesy Hume collection.)

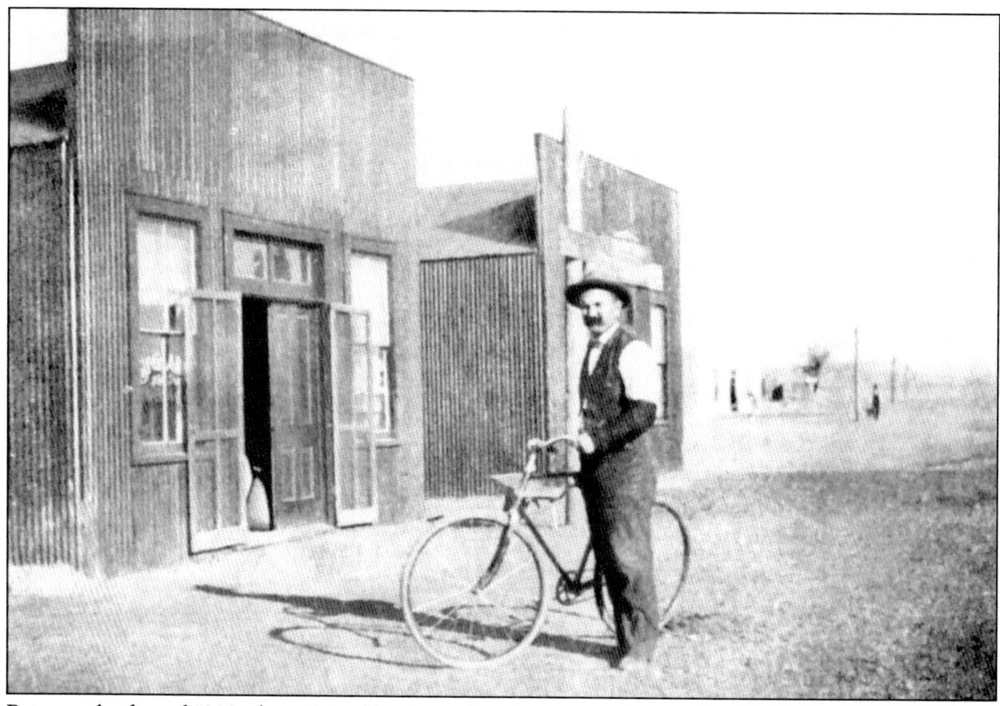

Prior to the fire of 1892, the original business district was on the north side of the tracks. Note the false-front buildings with tin siding. Bicycles had become a very popular means of transportation by the 1890s. (Courtesy Hume collection.)

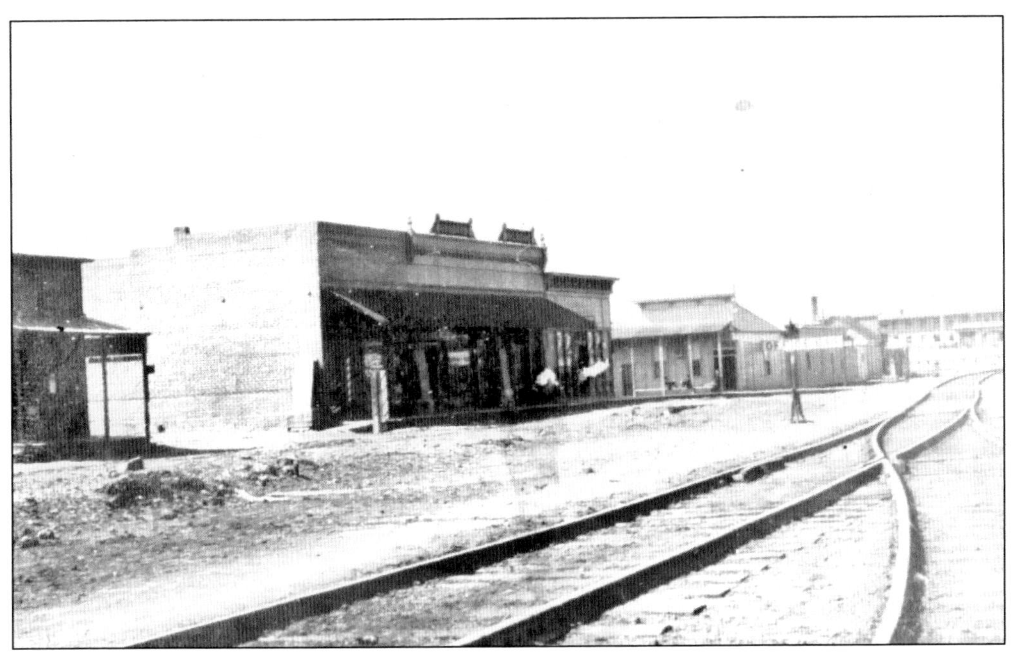

The Postal Telegraph, Store, and Parlor Saloon on Railroad Avenue and Third Street just south of the railroad tracks was owned by Tom Lewis. In 1892, practically the whole town was destroyed by fire. Railroad Avenue, adjacent to the south side of the tracks, was the town's main street. There were several saloons, boardinghouses, blacksmith shops, and restaurants. Along with the Lewis store, a Babbitt-Paulson general store and a business run by Winchester Dickerson made up Ash Fork's business district. (Courtesy Hume collection.)

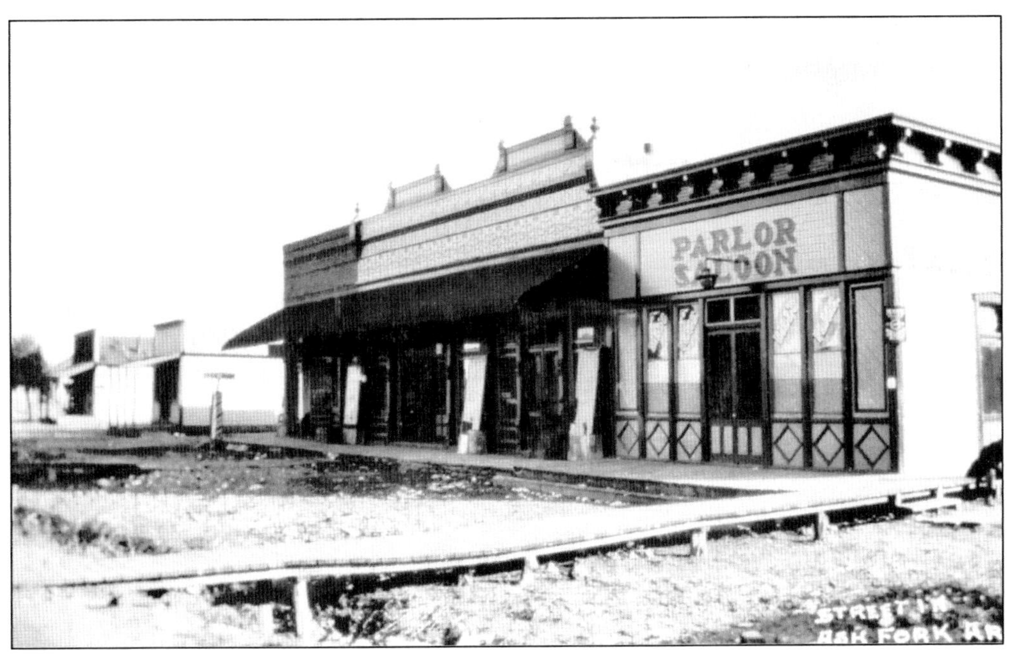

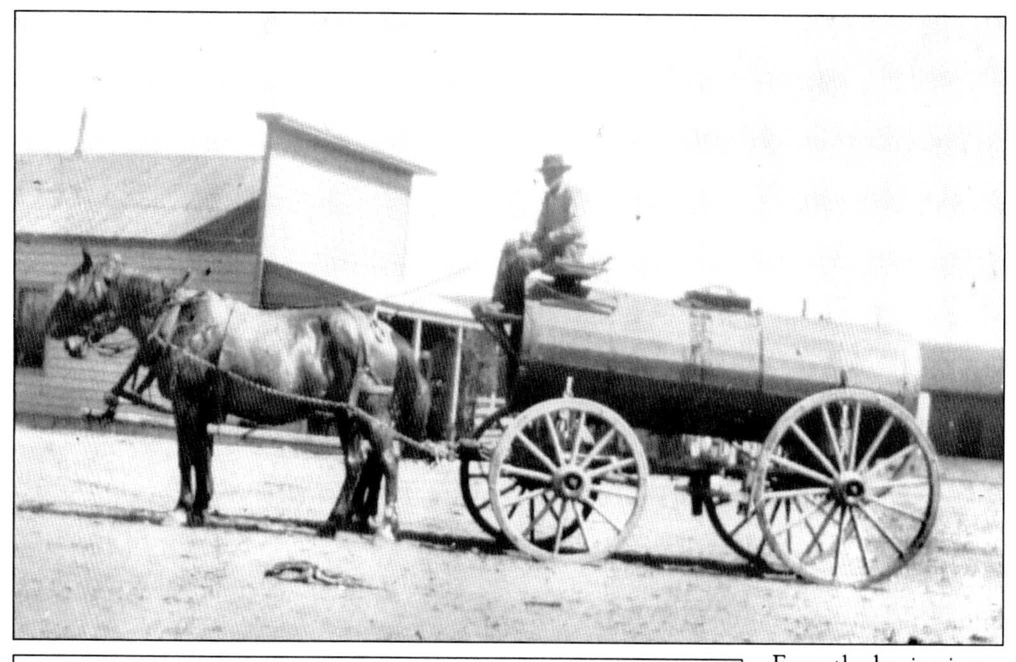

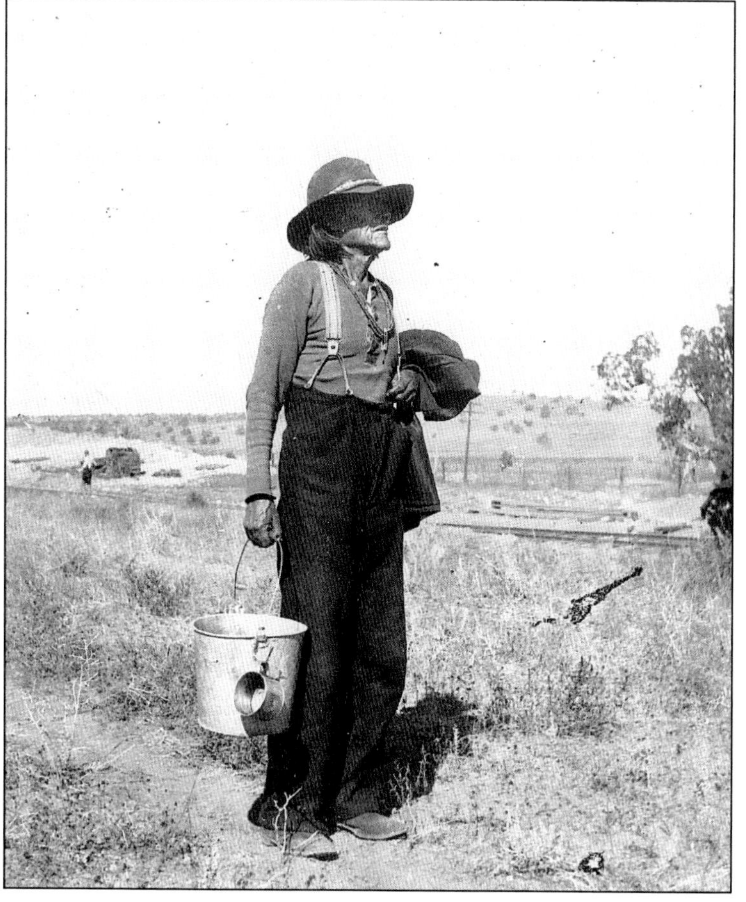

From the beginning, Providence seemed bent on testing the will of the early settlers. There were no springs nearby and no wells for water, so they hauled it in from sink holes along Ash and Johnson Creeks in barrels by wagon. Jack Bishop owned a water wagon and sold water for as much as 75¢ a barrel. The Santa Fe began hauling water from Del Rio Springs, a distance of 35 miles, during the 1920s. In the photograph on the left a water carrier provides liquid refreshment from a common cup to tracklayers. (Courtesy Hume collection.)

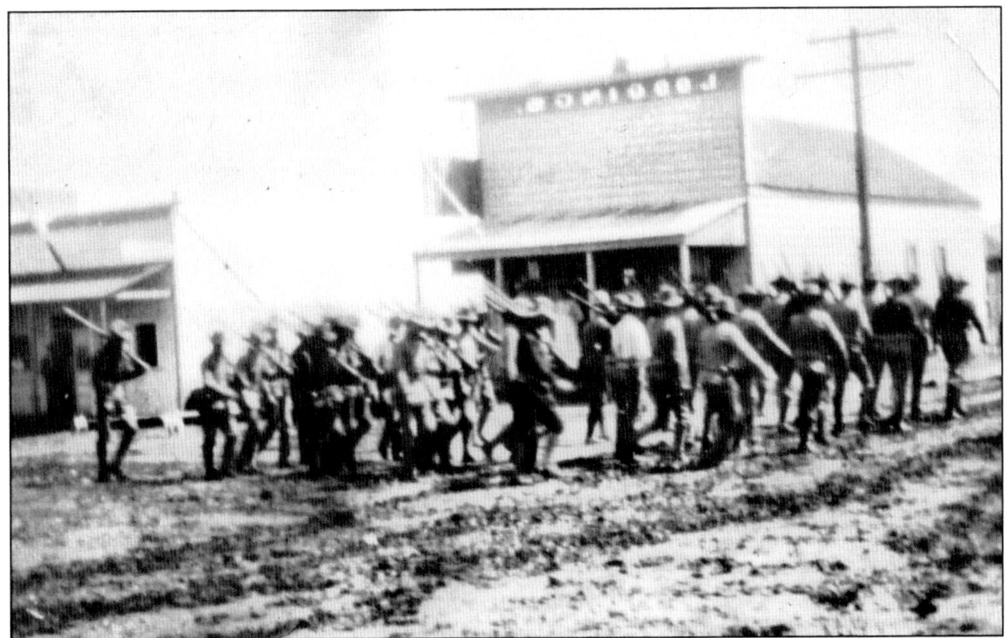

When the war with Spain broke out in 1898, Arizonans rallied around the flag, volunteering in droves to fight in Cuba. It was widely believed that their show of patriotism would enhance Arizona's chances of gaining statehood. Company A of the 1st U.S. Volunteer Cavalry, better known as the Rough Riders, was made up mostly of men from Northern Arizona. On their way by rail to a training camp at San Antonio, Texas, the Rough Riders took advantage of a stop in Ash Fork to drill. Their commander was the storied William O. "Buckey" O'Neill of Prescott. The popular O'Neill had been both sheriff of Yavapai County and mayor of Prescott. Captain O'Neill would be the only Rough Rider officer to die in combat, just prior to the charge up San Juan Hill.

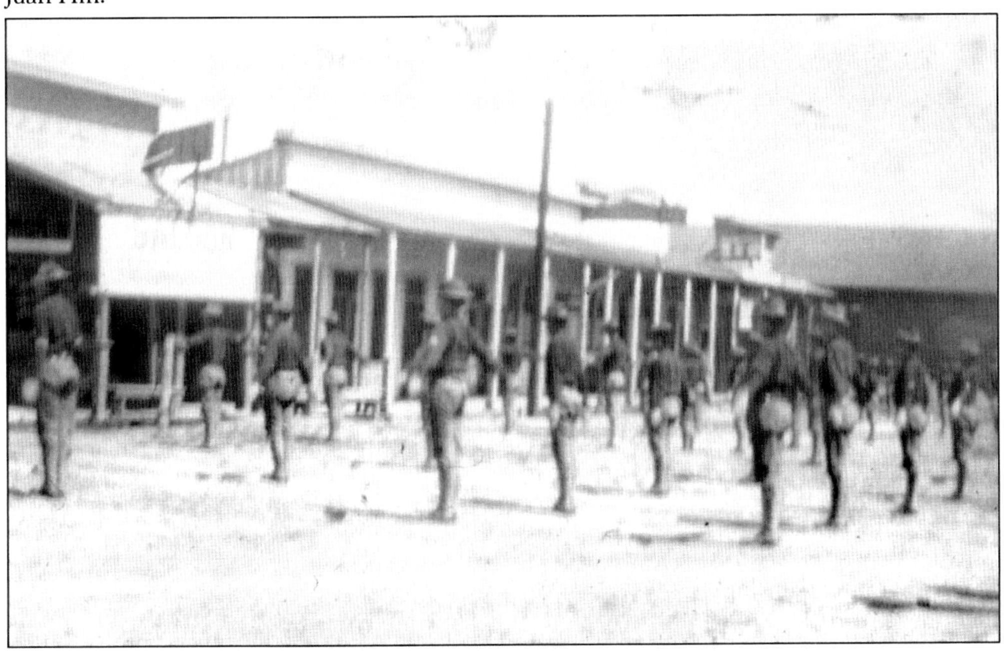

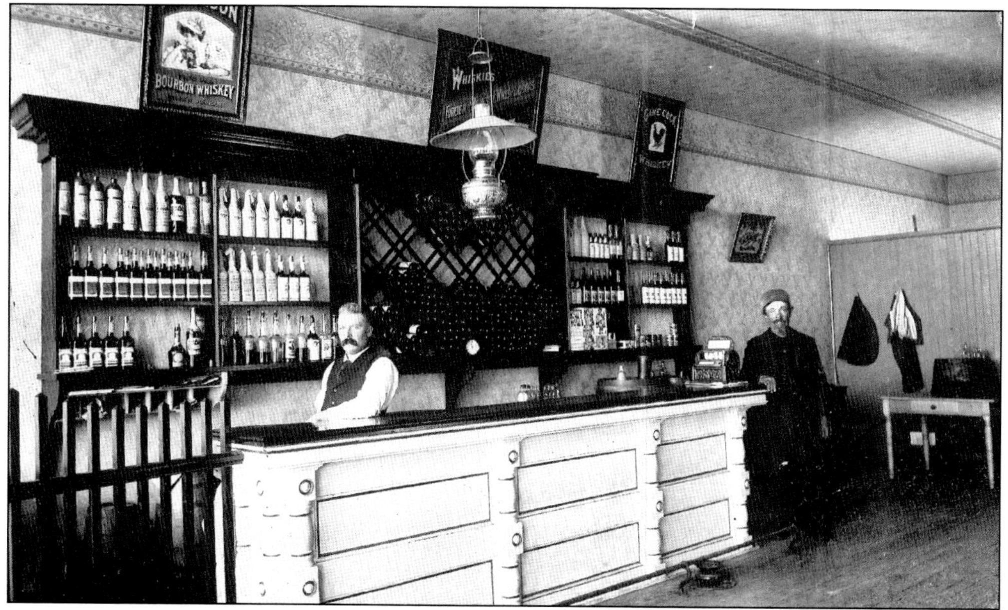

Saloons were among the first businesses to appear on the scene. They provided a social gathering place for men to imbibe, catch up on the latest news, play cards, and smoke cigars. Saloons often stayed open 24 hours a day, seven days a week, to squeeze the last dollar out of the cowboys, freighters, and railroaders. Pictured is the interior of Ed Sheivley's new Palace Saloon. (Courtesy Hume collection.)

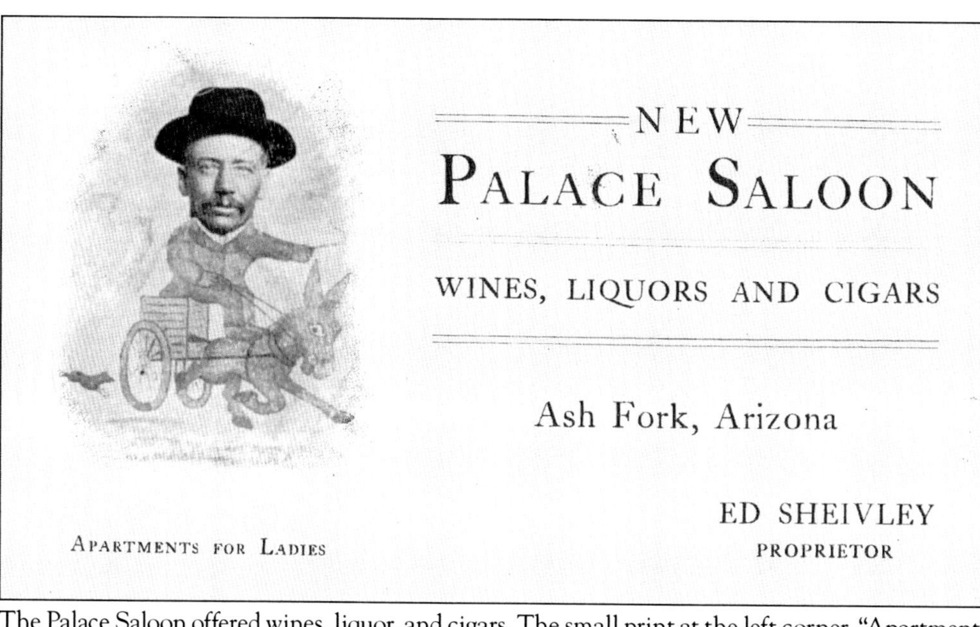

The Palace Saloon offered wines, liquor, and cigars. The small print at the left corner, "Apartments For Ladies," seems to suggest a lonely railroader, mule skinner, or cowboy could also find female companionship nearby. (Courtesy Hume collection.)

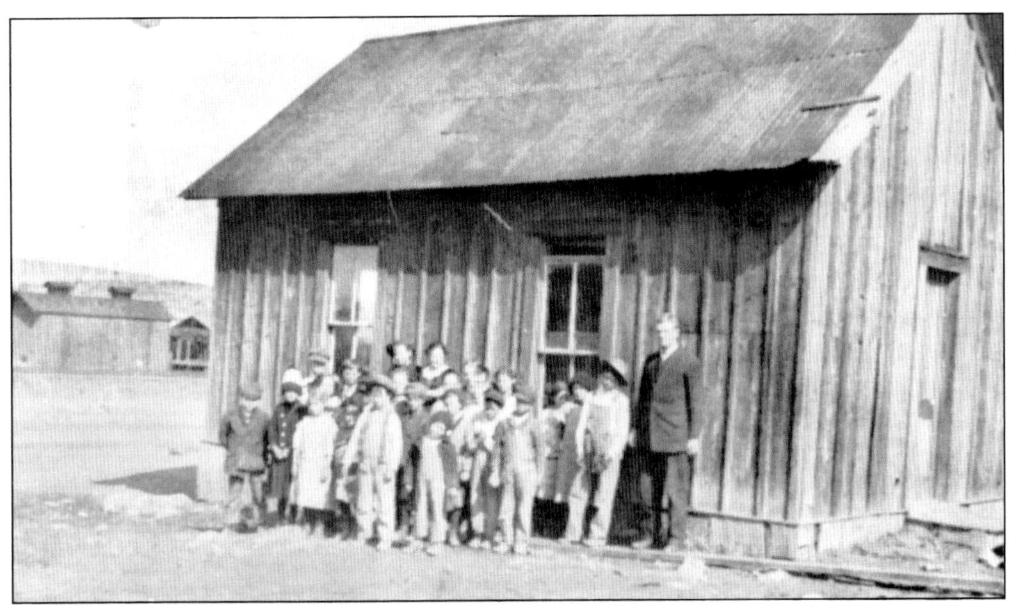

Schools were always high on a new town's priority list. Ash Fork's first school was a wood-frame building. Most of the time, students were buried in McGuffey's Readers, which were literary anthologies celebrating hard work, honesty, and piety. A one-room schoolhouse and one lone teacher had to serve most small communities. Teachers were both men and women and served as school janitors in addition to their instructional duties. The standard offer was free room and board at the homes of students and $10 to $35 a month in wages. Once a woman got married, she usually had to relinquish her teaching job. Early reports say there was a small one-room school on the north side of the railroad tracks. The wooden structure was later moved near where the fire station is located today. (Courtesy Hume collection.)

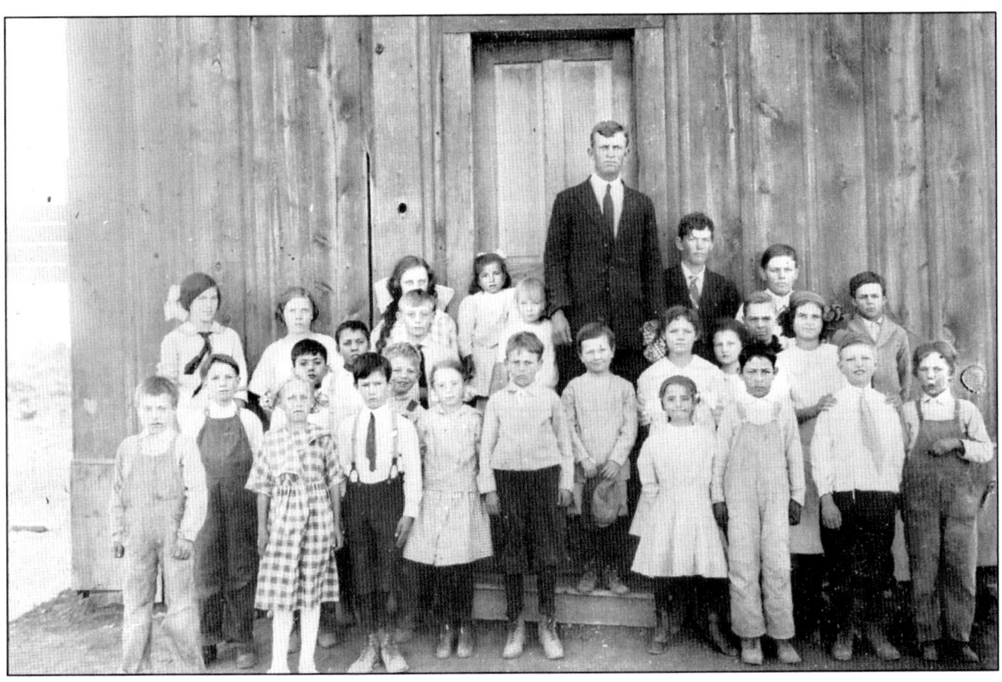

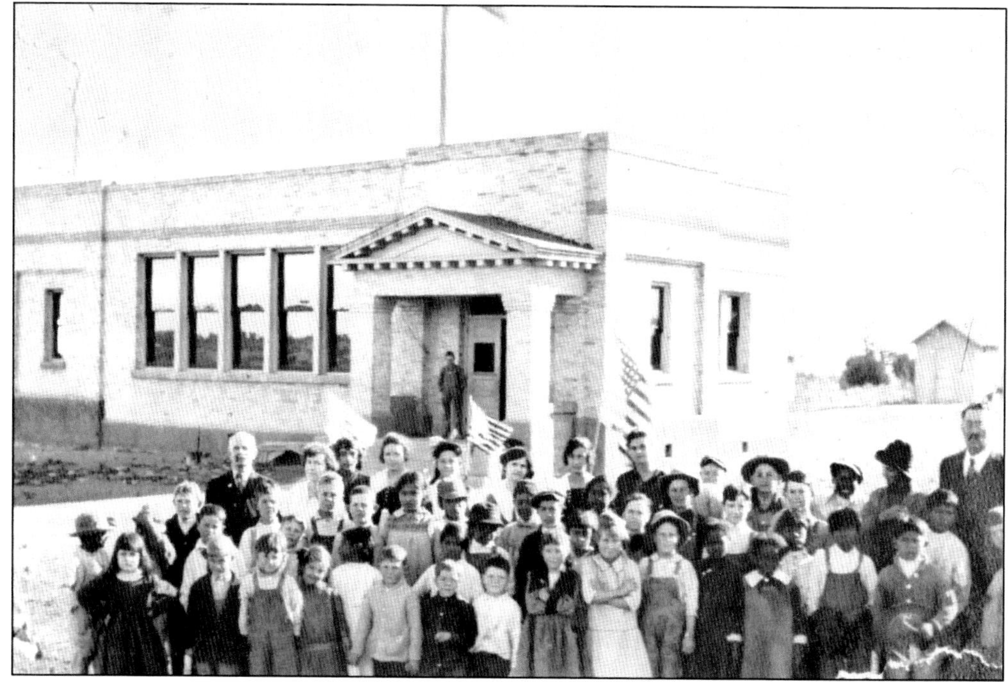

Students organized a patriotic gathering in front of the new school building in this photograph taken in 1915. (Courtesy Hume collection.)

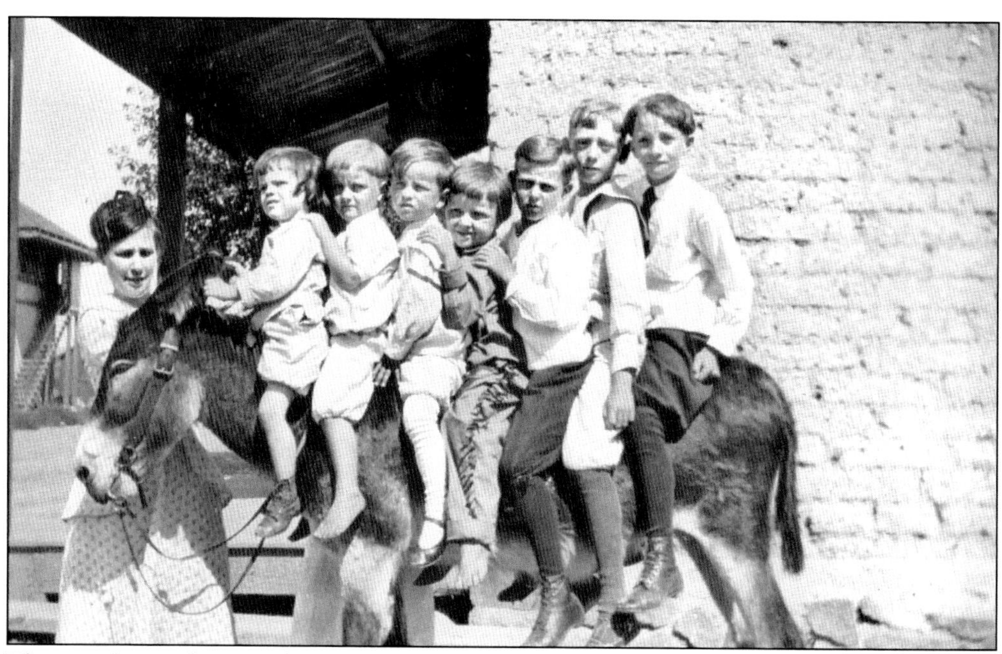

These students ride in tandem on their way to school on Ash Fork's mule-powered rapid transit authority. (Courtesy Hume collection.)

Four

The Escalante Hotel
Fred Harvey's Crown Jewel

Ash Fork's first Harvey House was a wooden structure located on the north side of the tracks facing Cooper Thomas Lewis's Parlor House Saloon and the Postal Telegraph Store.

On June 17, 1905, a fire destroyed the depot, hotel, restaurant, and water tower in the heart of the business district. It started in the kitchen of the original Harvey House, doing $20,000 worth of damage. Railroad officials promised they would build a new Harvey House of steel and concrete much better than the original. Despite this, some of the residents were upset, because the new building would be 500 feet west of the old one.

The result was the luxurious Escalante, named for the 18th-century Spanish padre-explorer Silvestre Escalante, who journeyed into Arizona in 1776. The name was in keeping with the Harvey tradition of naming their establishments after Spanish explorers.

The Escalante, at a cost of $115,000, opened in March 1907. It was built in an *L* shape with a restaurant serving meals in a beautiful, crystal chandelier–lighted dining room. Silver, linen tablecloths, and crystal were used as table settings. No man was allowed to enter the dining room in shirtsleeves, but the manager kept a supply of coats on hand to loan. An open balcony was extended along the front of the building, and a covered screened porch stretched across the back. The grounds were beautifully landscaped with fountains and flowers. On the east side was a cactus garden. A brick walkway lined the front of the building. Along with the luxurious hotel and restaurant were a newsstand, curio shop, barbershop, and depot. It was billed as the best Harvey House west of Chicago.

The Escalante had all the opulence and conveniences of a first-class hotel in an Eastern city, including telephone, hot and cold running water, electric lights, baths, and steam heat.

A familiar landmark since 1907, competition from roadside ventures along Route 66 caused it to close down its hotel operations in 1951. Two years later, the restaurant closed. Despite local residents' efforts to save it, the stately Escalante was demolished in 1968.

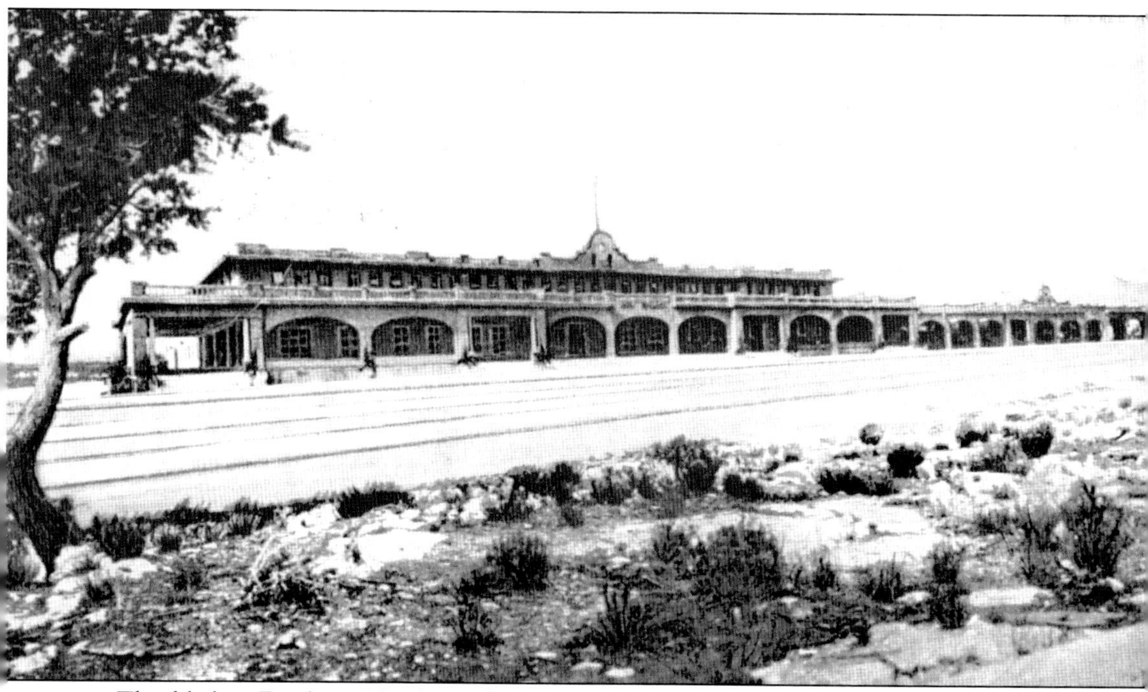

The fabulous Escalante Hotel was the crown jewel of Harvey Houses along the Santa Fe main line between Kansas City and Los Angeles. In operation for almost 50 years, it was built to accommodate both passengers and employees. The hotel's accommodations included a dining room, reading room, curio shop, newsstand, barbershop, and depot. It closed in 1951 and was demolished in 1968 in what can only be described as a tragic loss of an important piece of Western history. The original Harvey House in Ash Fork, built in 1894, was a wood-frame hotel across the tracks from the flagstone depot. A year later, a contract was signed with the Fred Harvey Company to run it.

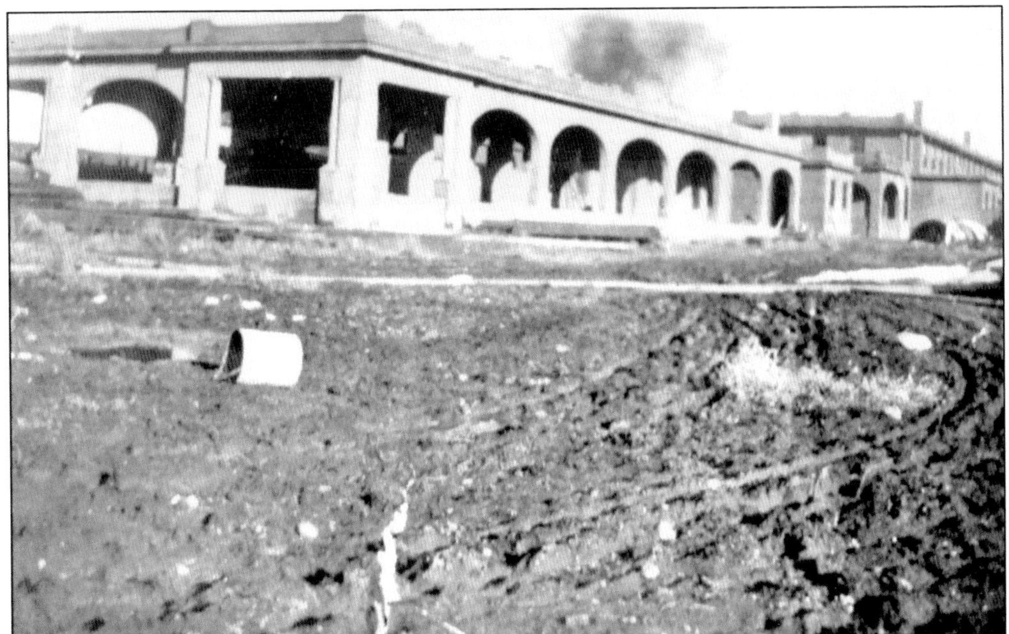

The original Harvey House burned down on June 17, 1905, and railroad officials promised to build a beautiful new structure 500 feet west of the old one, also replacing the depot. True to their promise, the fabulous new Escalante opened for business in March 1, 1907. This photograph shows the hotel near the end of construction.

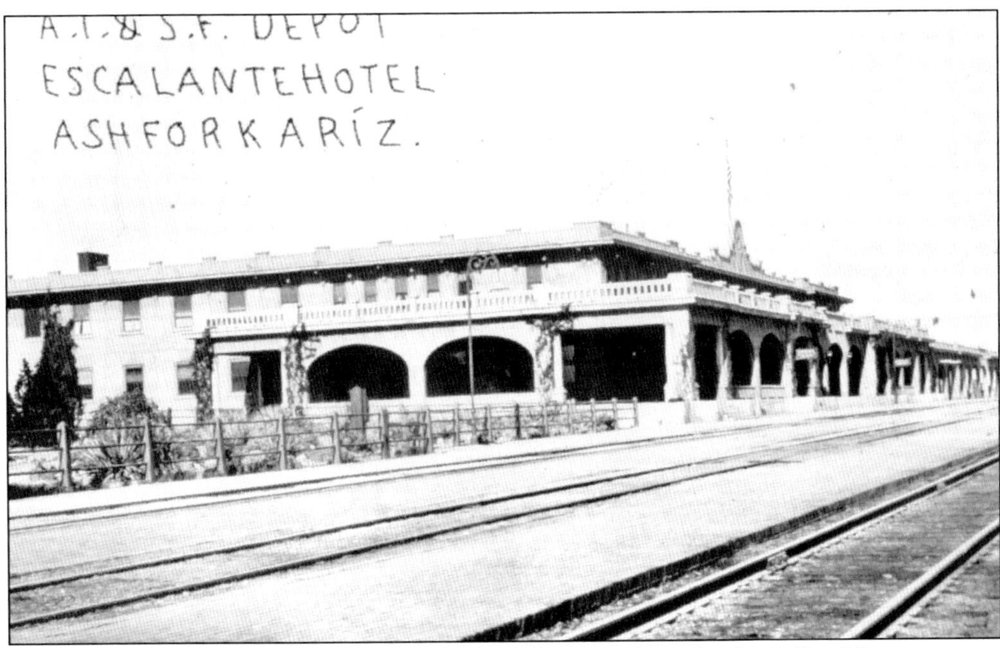

Soon after the opening, excitement prevailed briefly when the wife of an official became angry and chased him around the place for more than an hour with a loaded revolver. Deputy John Foley was able to take charge of the event and disarm her "in as gentlemanly way as possible," (according to a Prescott newspaper article) and marital bliss was apparently restored.

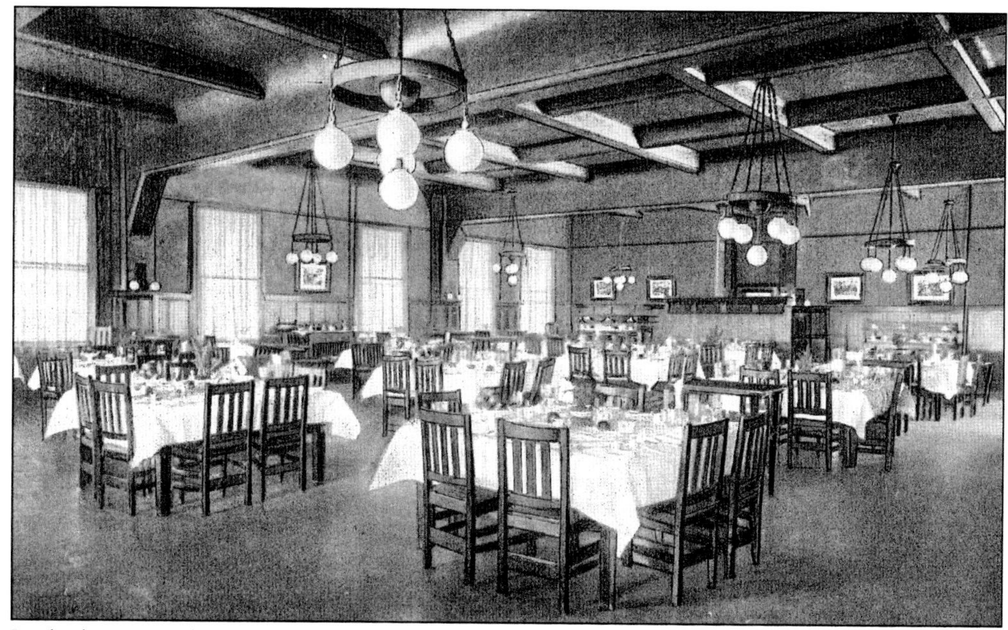

In the luxurious dining room around 1900, one could be served a breakfast consisting of cereal, fruit, eggs atop a steak, hash browns, and six large hot cakes with butter and maple syrup, topped off with apple pie and coffee for 50¢. Dinners went for a quarter more and included a fancy gourmet dish or wild game. For men, a jacket was required in the dining room.

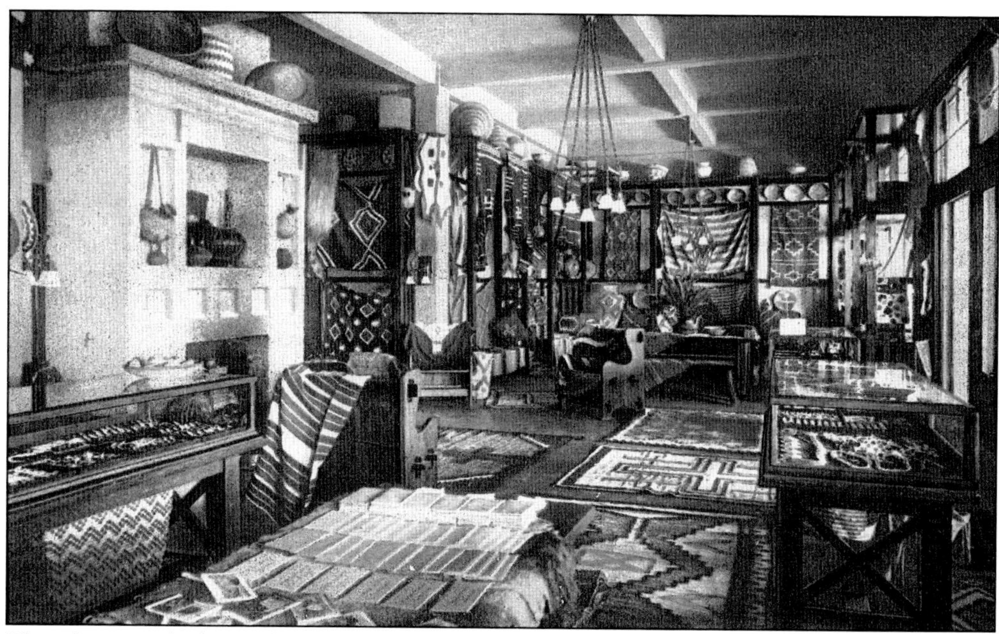

This photograph shows the curio shop with its authentic Navajo rugs and Hopi pottery and baskets, along with other Native American arts and crafts. Passenger trains usually paused in the station long enough to give the tourists a chance to shop.

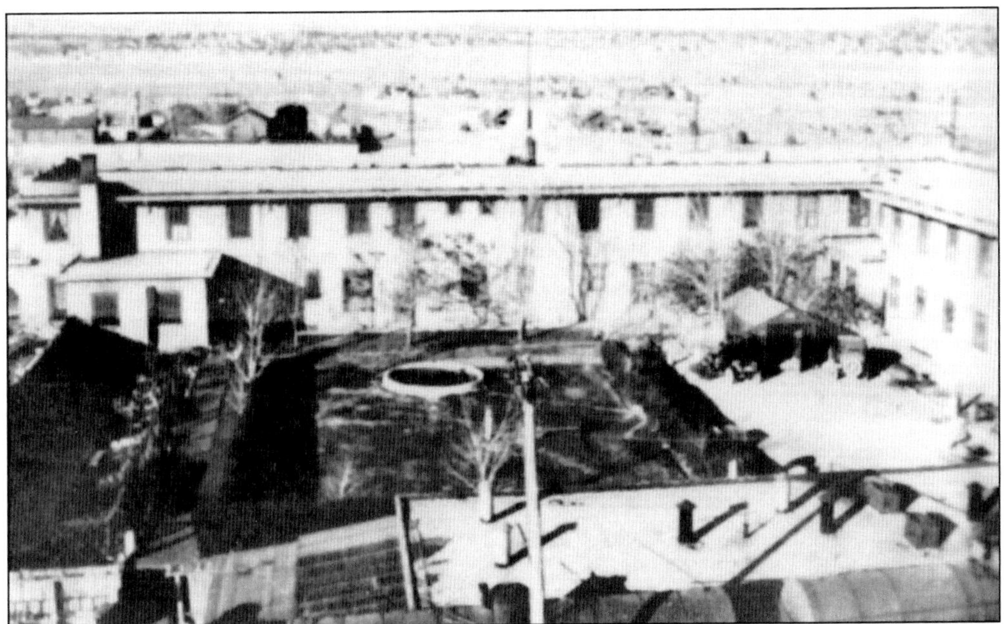

This is a seldom-seen view of the back side of the Escalante. There was a water fountain and the only lawn in the town. Ash Forks ball fields were notorious for their rocks and tumbleweeds, so the grass park was a natural attraction for the author and his friends, who often sneaked in to play football. The games were usually brief, as hotel officials frowned upon kids playing on their grass. On the right was the dormitory for the Harvey Girls, where a thick growth of vines concealed a ladder leading to the second floor. This allowed the ladies and their friends to come and go without the dorm mother's knowledge. Passengers stretch, grab a bite to eat, shop in the curio store, or visit the newsstand during a train stop in front of the Escalante around 1910. In the background is the original flagstone depot.

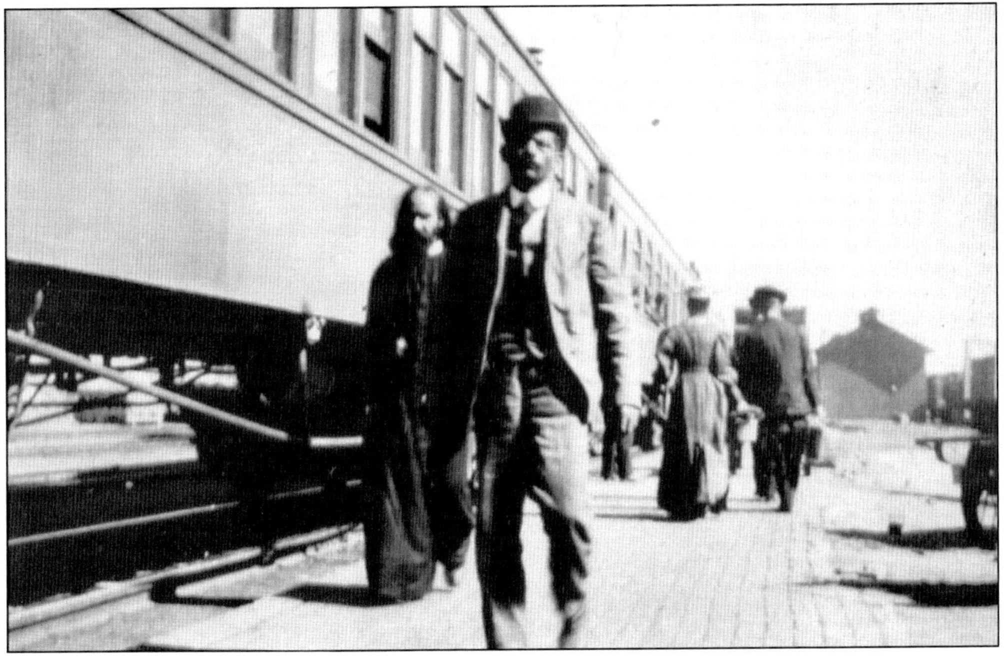

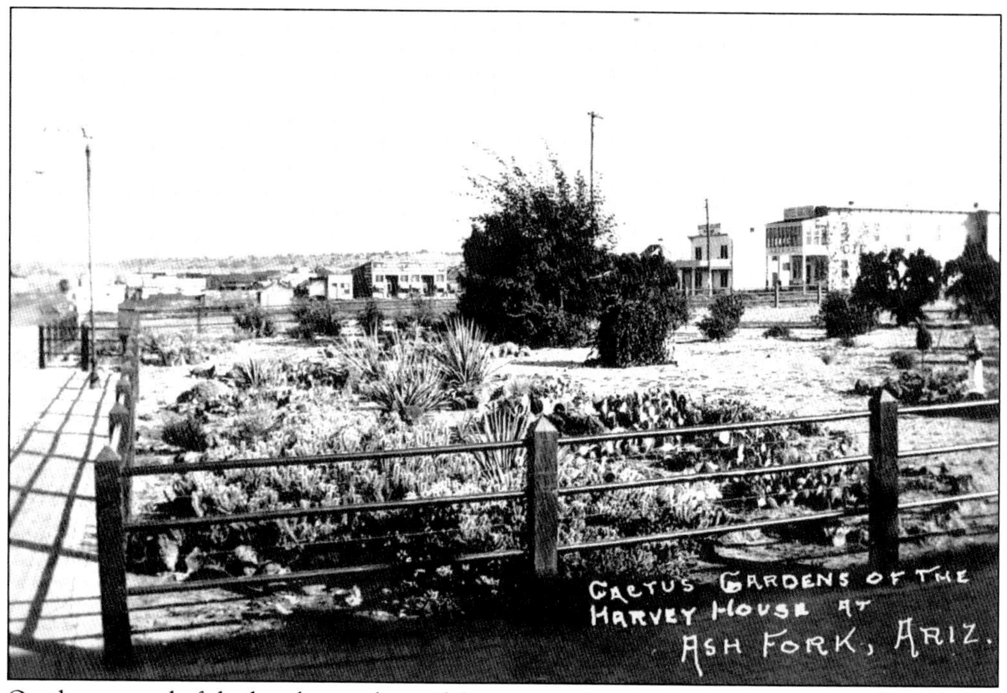

On the east end of the hotel was a beautiful cactus garden. In the background on the right are the Arizona Hotel and White House Hotel on Lewis Avenue.

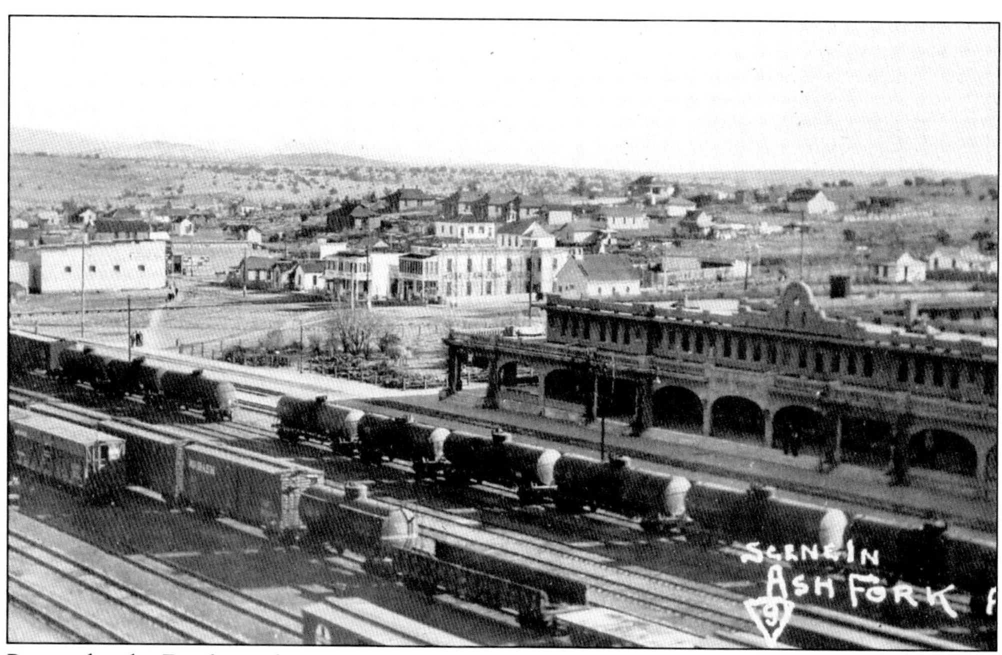

Pictured is the Escalante during the 1940s. In the foreground are tanker cars loaded with water for the town. Every day, a train delivered water from Del Rio Springs at Puro in Chino Valley.

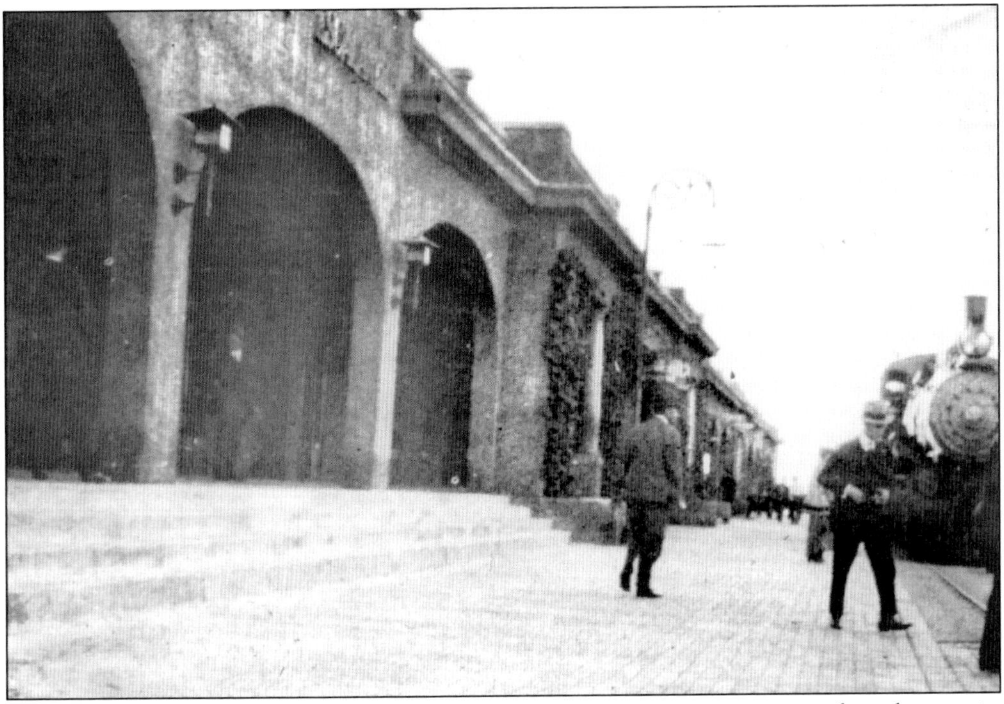

Before the days of railroad dining cars and Harvey Houses, passengers were forced to eat in local hash houses wherever the train happened to stop. The food was terrible, and the service was slow. The same meal could be sold two or three times, because just as the food was served, the conductor would yell, "All aboard," and the passengers would have to leave without eating. Conductors would get a kickback from the restaurants.

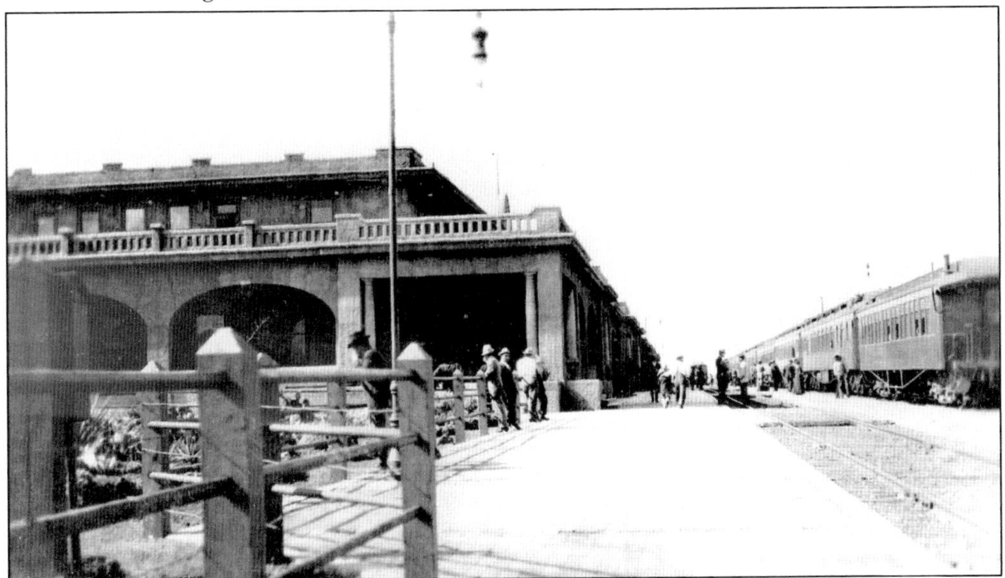

Traveling salesmen and businessmen had to endure these conditions on a regular basis. Among them was an Englishman named Fred Harvey. One day in the early 1870s, he approached the Santa Fe Railroad with a novel idea of providing passengers with attractive surroundings, superior service, and good food. The company accepted his proposal, and the rest is history.

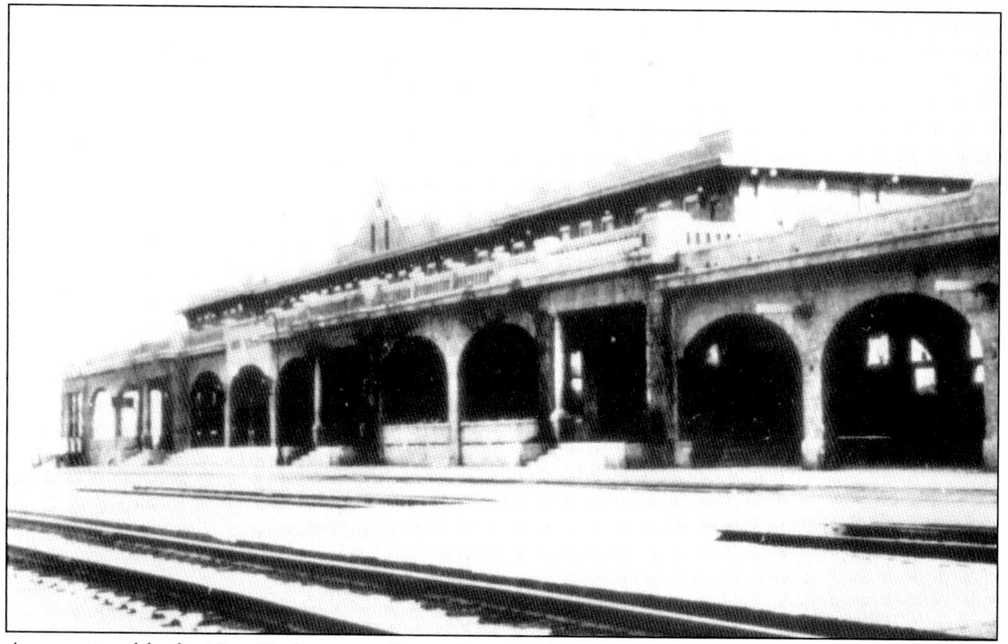

A story is told of a New Yorker, president of one of the most valuable railroad properties in the country, who was traveling out West. Upon his return, he wrote to the head of the Fred Harvey Hotels in Kansas City: "Can you arrange it so that I can get at my club here beefsteaks just like the one I had at your eating house in Ash Fork, Arizona." The club was one of the most exclusive in downtown Manhattan.

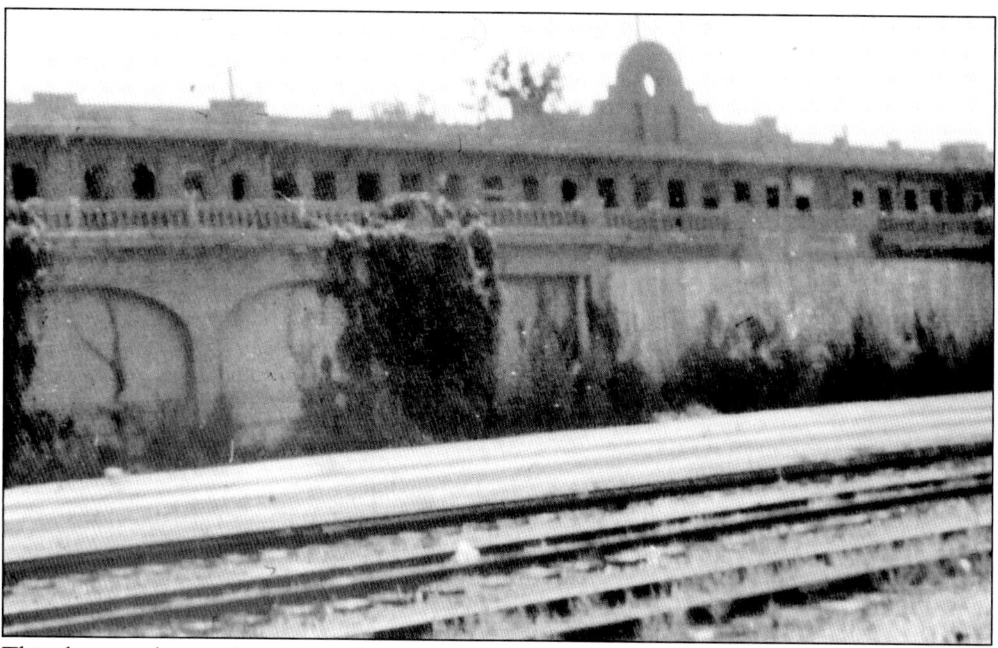

This photograph was taken during the 1960s, when the old building was abandoned and its gracious entrances were boarded up. The railroad and Harvey House were for many years the town's major employer and main source of income. Spanning almost 50 years, thousands of travelers visited the famous hotel while changing trains or enjoying the ambiance of the grand hotel.

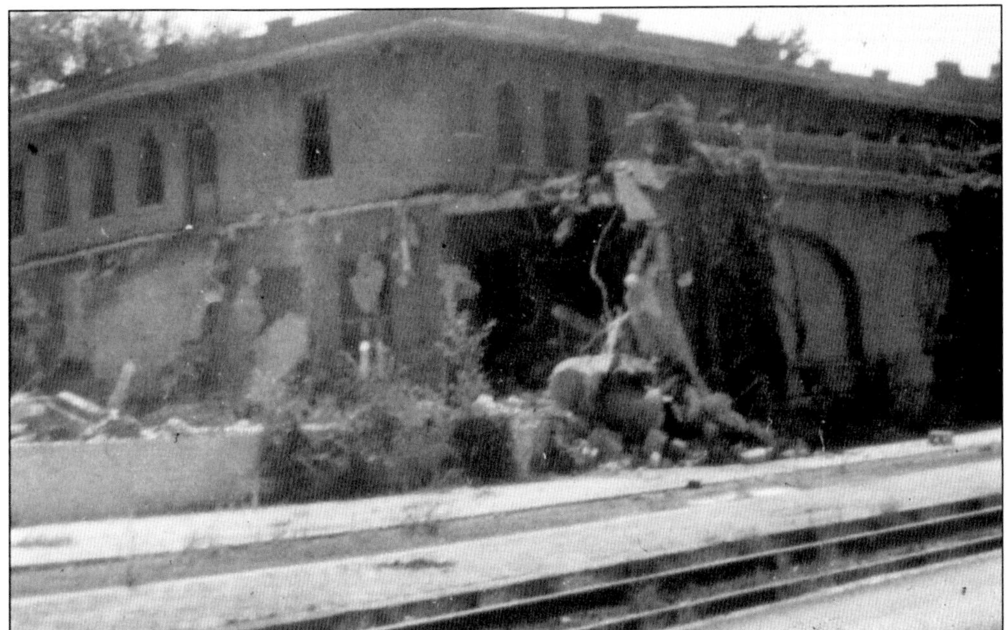

Demolition of the Escalante took place in 1968. A desperate call to Gov. Jack Williams, whose father had once worked at the depot, went to no avail, and the wrecking ball went into action, turning the once-luxurious building to rubble. (Courtesy Hume collection.)

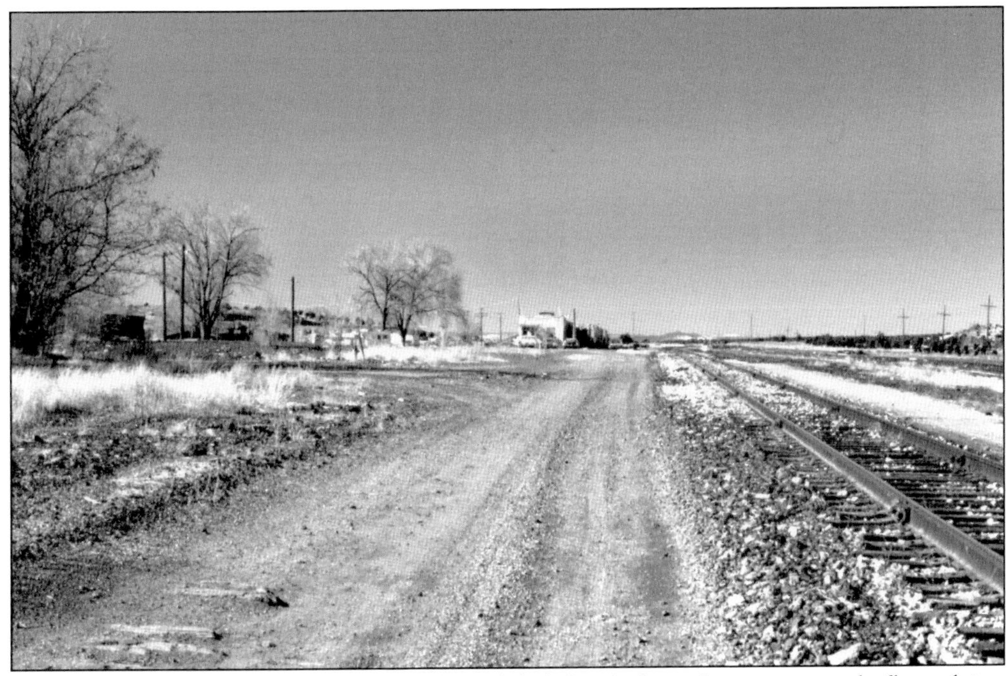

All that remains of the grand old hotel are faded shards from the exquisite tile floors lying scattered on the ground.

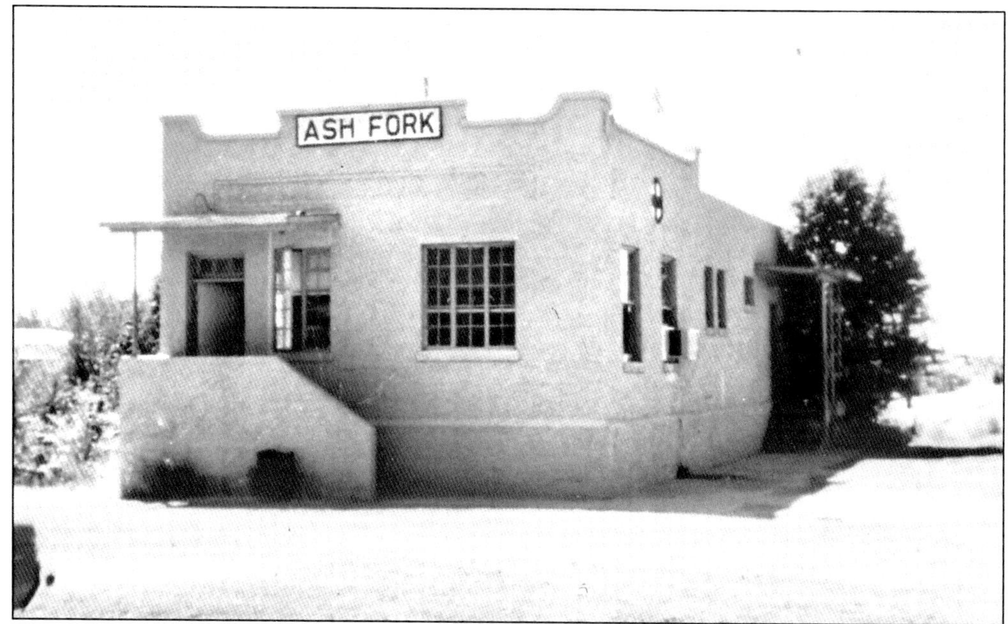

The old freight depot serves today as the depot for the Burlington Northern–Santa Fe Railroad. For several years, there wasn't anything to identify the town. Local historian and civic leader Fayrene Hume petitioned the railroad company to honor the old location with a sign. (Courtesy Hume collection.)

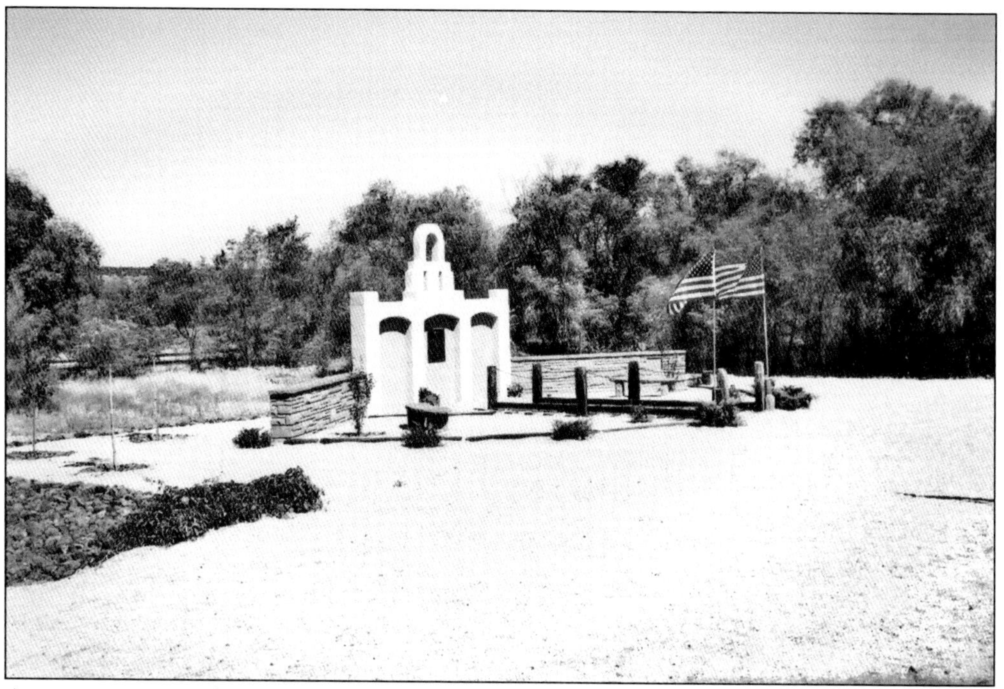

A monument near the site of the old Escalante Hotel was erected on September 8, 2001, that commemorated Ash Fork's historic link with the railroad. The arch on top pays tribute to the famous arch on the Harvey House.

Five

BISCUIT SHOOTERS
THE HARVEY GIRLS

In 1876, Fred Harvey opened the first of his elegant Spanish-style restaurant-hotels at 100-mile intervals along the Santa Fe Railroad. It was later claimed that they were spaced at those intervals to keep Western people from all settling in one place "where Harvey served his meals."

It wasn't just the excellent food that attracted people to his restaurants. Harvey hired a wholesome group of young women to come West to work as Harvey Girls. They were all young women hoping to escape their hometown for romance and marriage.

The restaurants were models of efficiency. Before reaching the station, the brakeman would take orders and wire them ahead to the Harvey House. When the train was a mile away, the engineer would blow his whistle and a uniformed employee would ring a gong, signaling the Harvey Girls to spring into action. By the time the train pulled up and the customers were ushered in, the meal was ready to serve.

The women signed a one-year contract promising not to get married until the contract was up, but no sooner had one stepped down from the train than the marriage proposals came rolling in. It was claimed the pretty ones took less than a day, while the ugly ones took three days at most.

A Harvey Girl could usually have her pick of the most prosperous gentlemen in town. Harvey never held them to the non-marriage clause; in fact, like a proud father, he'd even throw wedding parties in their honor. The turnover of help was never a problem, as there was always a long waiting list of applicants anxious to go West and work as a Harvey Girl. It was said Harvey tried to hire plain-looking girls, because they were more likely to fulfill their contracts. Also according to one, "the plain ones seemed to get in less trouble."

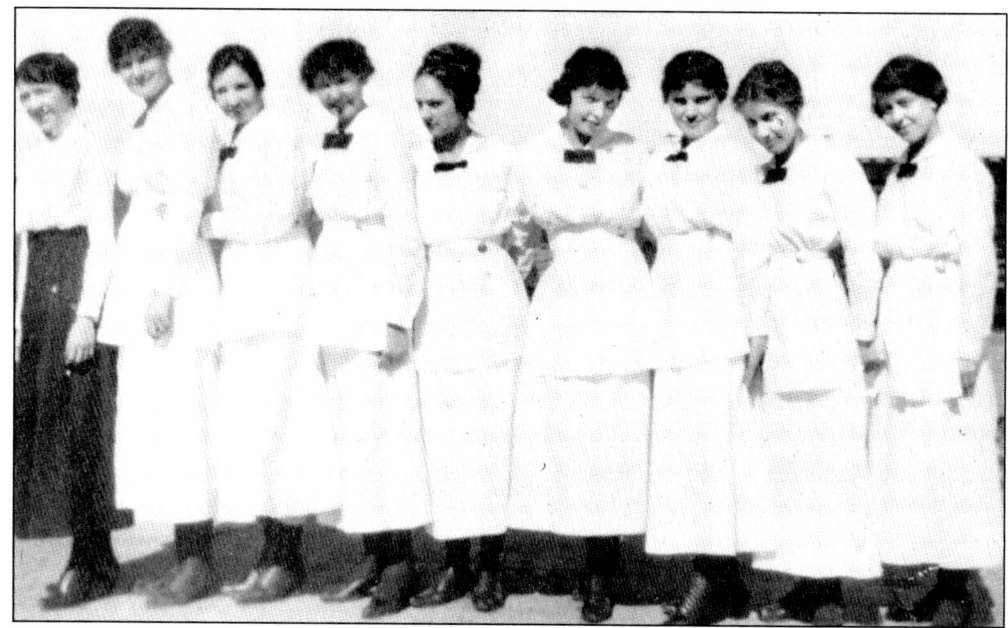

Fred Harvey recruited young women from back East to work in his restaurants along the Santa Fe line. The recruiting advertisement called for "young women of good character, attractive and intelligent, between 18 and 30." Women had few career choices in the latter part of the 19th century, and Harvey's restaurants offered them a chance to seek adventure and matrimony in the West.

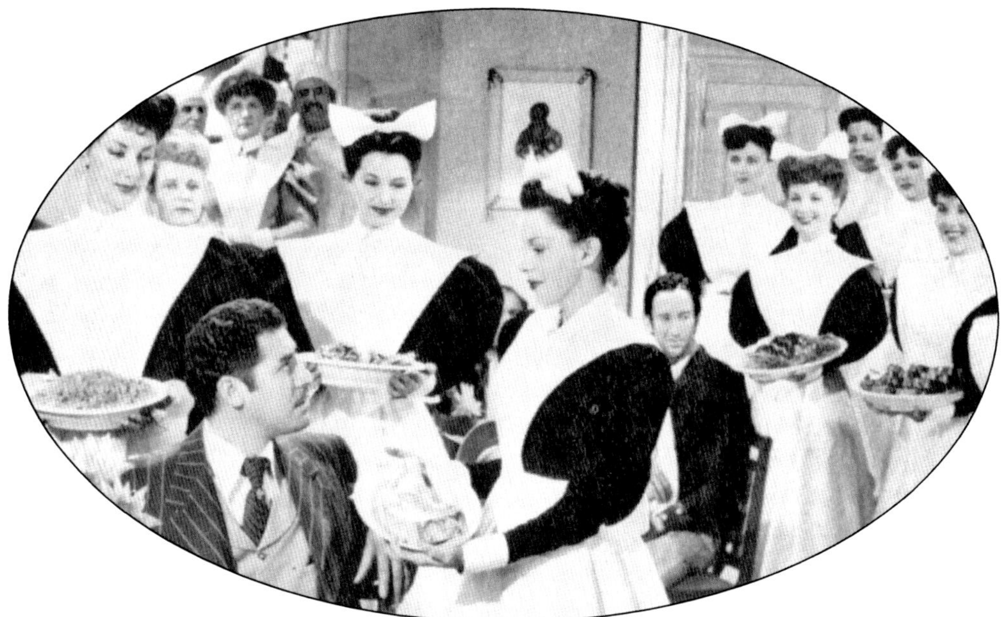

They were known as Harvey Girls, but the cowboys preferred to call them "biscuit shooters." They would be romanticized in a 1946 film, *The Harvey Girls*, starring Judy Garland. The musical comedy told a fanciful story of how the Wild West was tamed by the waitresses of the Fred Harvey restaurants. One of the songs, "The Atchison, Topeka, and the Santa Fe," won an Oscar for best song.

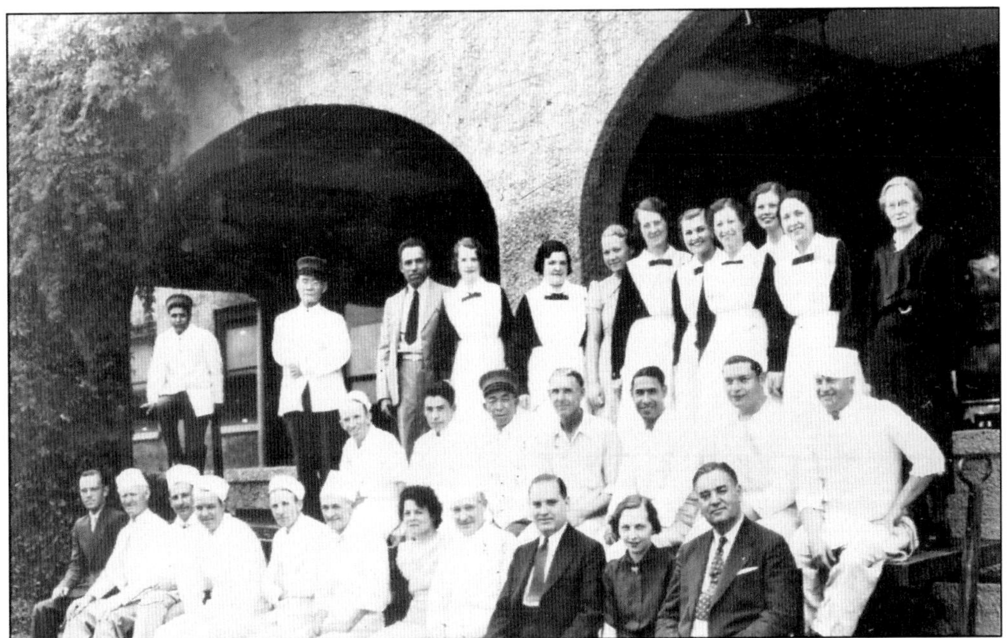

The Harvey House crew poses in front of the Escalante in 1937. Harvey Girls earned a salary of $17.50 a month plus room, board, and tips. Lonely Westerners were dazzled by the crisply aproned lasses who married some 5,000 of them. "Fred Harvey kept the West in food and wives," said humorist Will Rogers.

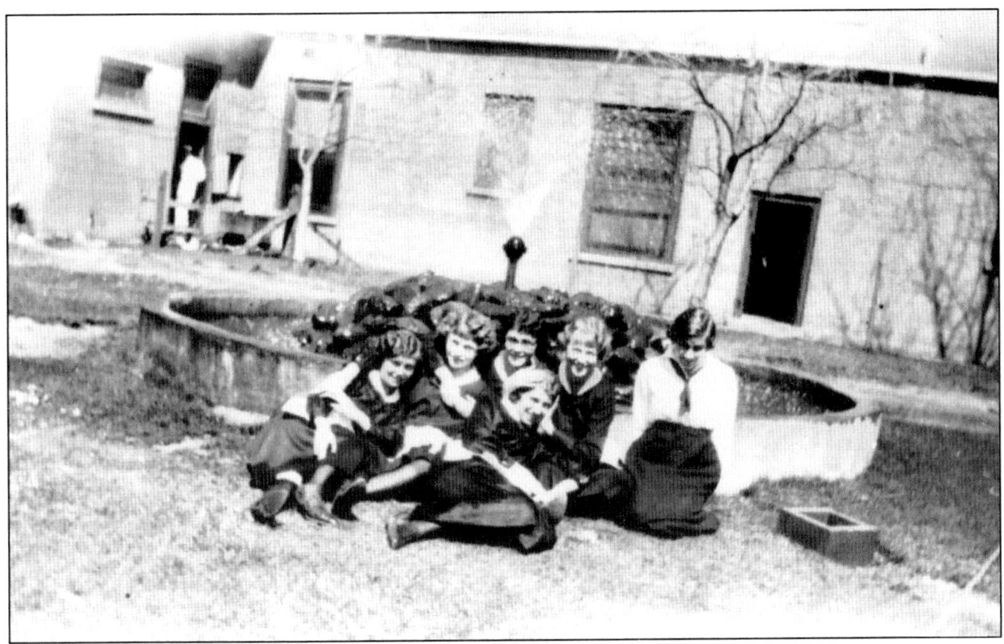

A former Harvey Girl wrote of her experience: "They were very particular about the girls they hired. They trained you for six weeks. They could tell then whether you stayed or got a pass back home. We lived upstairs in dormitories and normally you had to be in by ten o'clock at night. If there was a dance you had to ask the manager for permission to go."

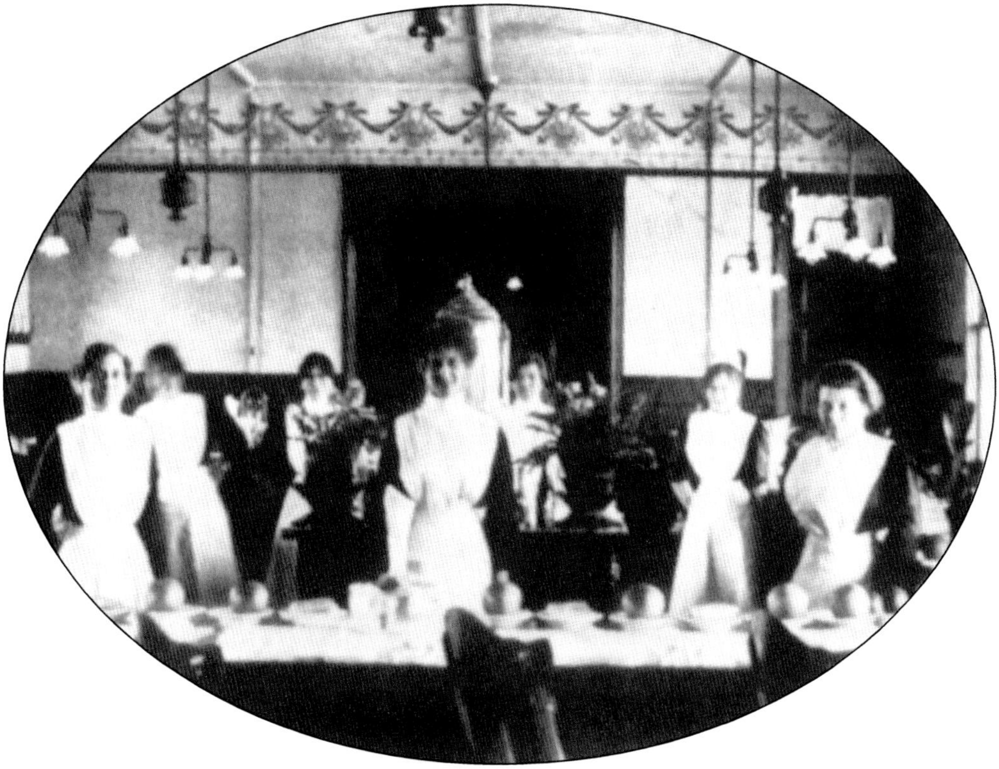

Conversation between the Harvey Girls was forbidden while customers were in the station. They used signals and codes. When the customer's cup was turned down it meant tea; when turned up, bring coffee. If the cup was gone, the customer wanted milk. Company inspectors were always passing through to make sure Harvey's strict rules were enforced. Many times it was Harvey himself.

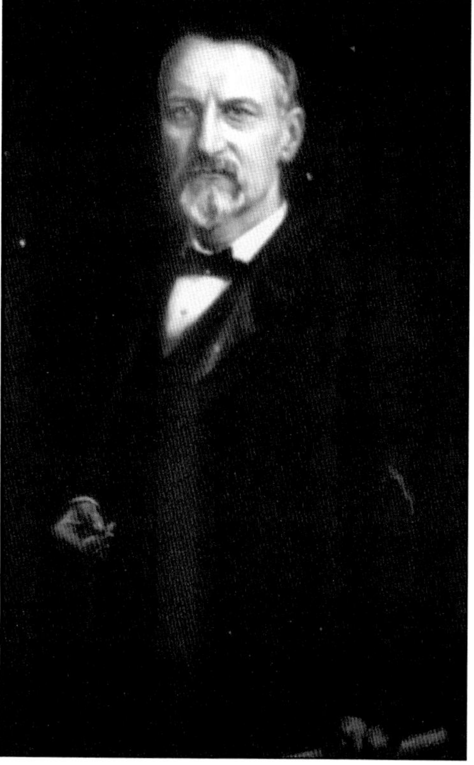

Fred Harvey came to America in 1850 at the age of 15. In 1876, he began managing the depot in Topeka and was an immediate success. During the next 20 years, Harvey opened his Spanish-style restaurant-hotels, becoming the concessionaire for all the meals served along the Santa Fe line. Eventually he commanded a catering empire of 47 depot diners and restaurants, 15 railroad hotels, and 30 dining cars.

Six

High, Wide, and Handsome Cattle Country

The railroad opened up thousands of square miles of grazing lands to both cattle and sheep. At Ash Fork, stockyards were built north of town. Cattle buyers arrived in town, looked over the stock, made a deal, sealed it with a handshake, and shipped the cows to market on the railroad. The stockyards at Ash Fork shipped more cows and sheep than any other between Kansas City and Los Angeles.

Colin "Cole" Campbell had been a sheep man in the territory for 10 years around Winslow but found the country around Ash Fork ideal for running sheep. He arrived in Ash Fork around 1900, and soon he was known as the "King of the Sheep Industry," running one of the most successful sheep operations in the territory.

Cole and his sons Gene, Frank, and Hugh established the Ash Fork Livestock Company in 1906, and during the first half of the 20th century, the outfit was one of the biggest in Northern Arizona. It was hard to guess just how wealthy Gene and Frank Campbell were, but colorful stories about the two became legend. Unpretentious, they never wore anything but faded blue jeans, old slouch hats, and work shirts. A stranger might easily mistake them for saddle bums or poor, greasy-sack cowmen. Once, while on a cattle-buying trip back to Chicago, dressed in their customary fashion, the two were arrested by the Windy City's police for vagrancy.

One day, Frank and his wife, Floye, were returning from a business trip to Prescott in her new Cadillac when Frank chanced to see one of his sheep outside the fence. He stopped the car, got out, and chased it down. Picking it up, he carried it over to the car and started to put it in the back seat. "That sheep can't ride in my new car," his wife proclaimed.

"He can if he wants to," Frank replied indignantly, "he helped pay for it." And the sheep rode into town sitting proudly in the back seat.

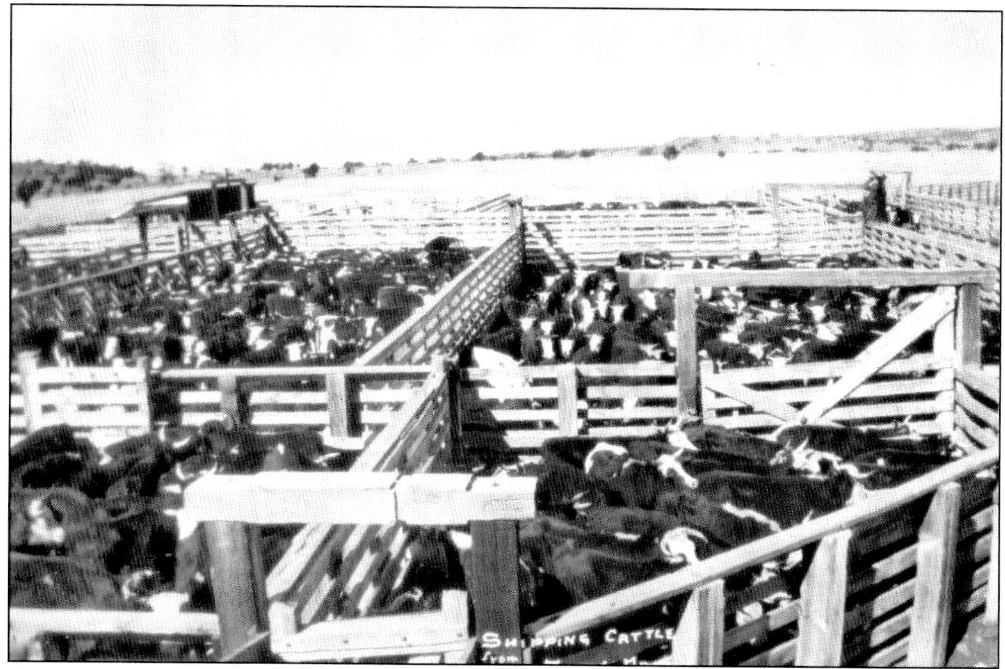

The arrival of the railroad in 1881 not only opened up the cattle business in Northern Arizona, but it also gave sheep and cattle ranchers access by rail to California and Eastern markets. When the Atlantic and Pacific Railroad crossed Northern Arizona in the early 1880s, cattlemen discovered pristine rangelands where grass grew "stirrup high." At the same time, a severe drought struck Texas, causing cattlemen to drive their cattle to the new areas. (Courtesy Hume collection.)

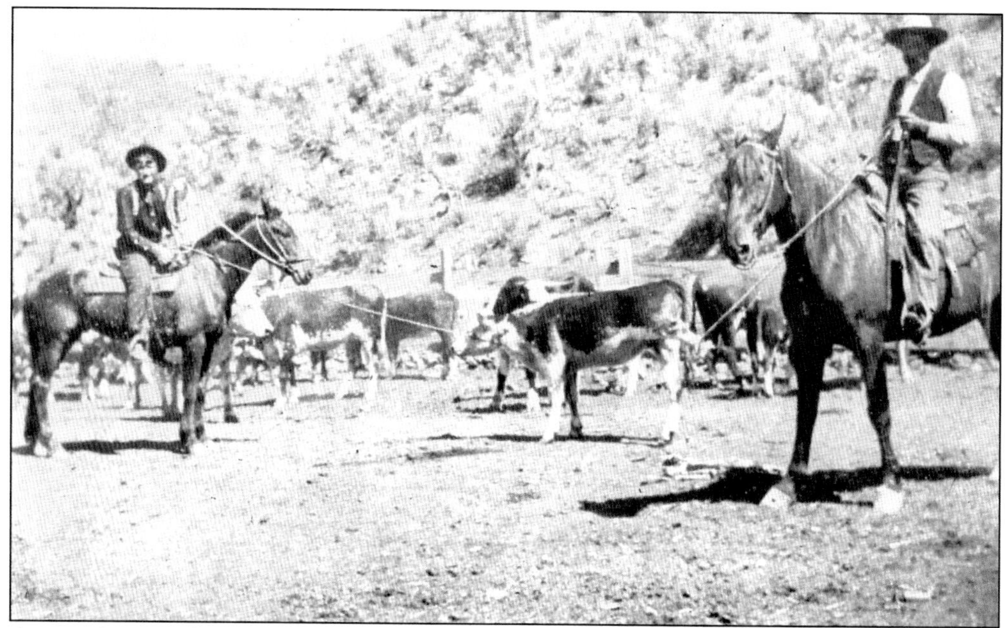

Among the arrivals were the legendary Hashknife outfit and the Babbitt brothers' CO Bar. Before the decade ended, tens of thousands of cattle and sheep were ranging across Northern Arizona. (Courtesy Hume collection.)

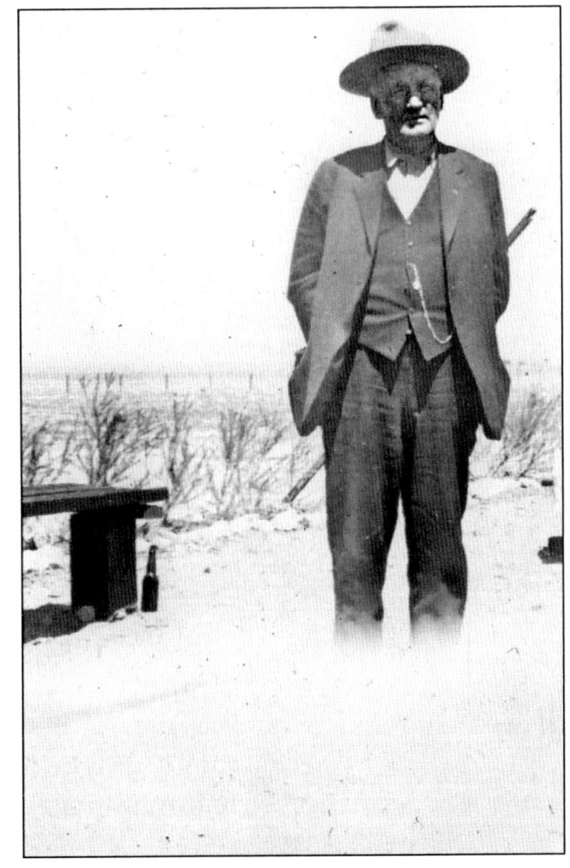

Cole Campbell lived at the Harvey House and one day was relaxing under the huge veranda. He removed his hat, placed it on the deck upside down cowboy-style, and fell asleep. When he awoke, the hat was full of money. Sympathetic train passengers, believing he was a down-on-his-luck cowboy, had contributed generously to the wealthy cattleman's welfare. (Courtesy Hume collection.)

Cole had three sons: Hugh, Gene, and Frank. The oldest, Hugh, died of injuries during World War I. When Gene returned from France after the war, he took over management of the outfit and in 1919 built his home in Ash Fork. Cole died in 1927, leaving the bulk of his estate to Gene, who later partnered the outfit with Frank. For several years, Gene served as president of the National Wool Growers Association.

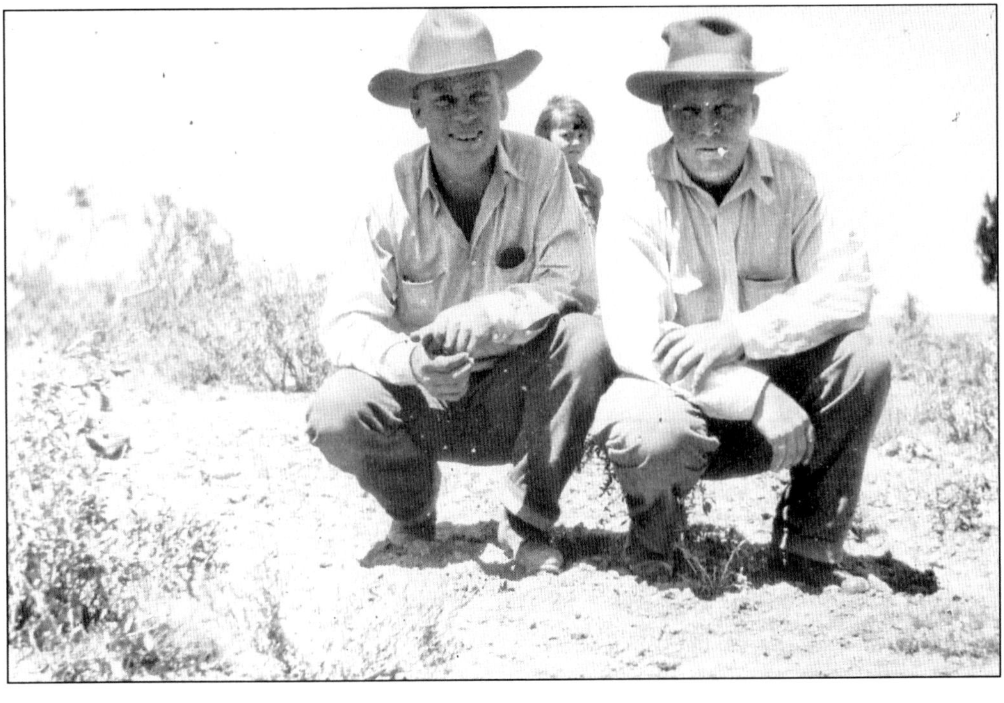

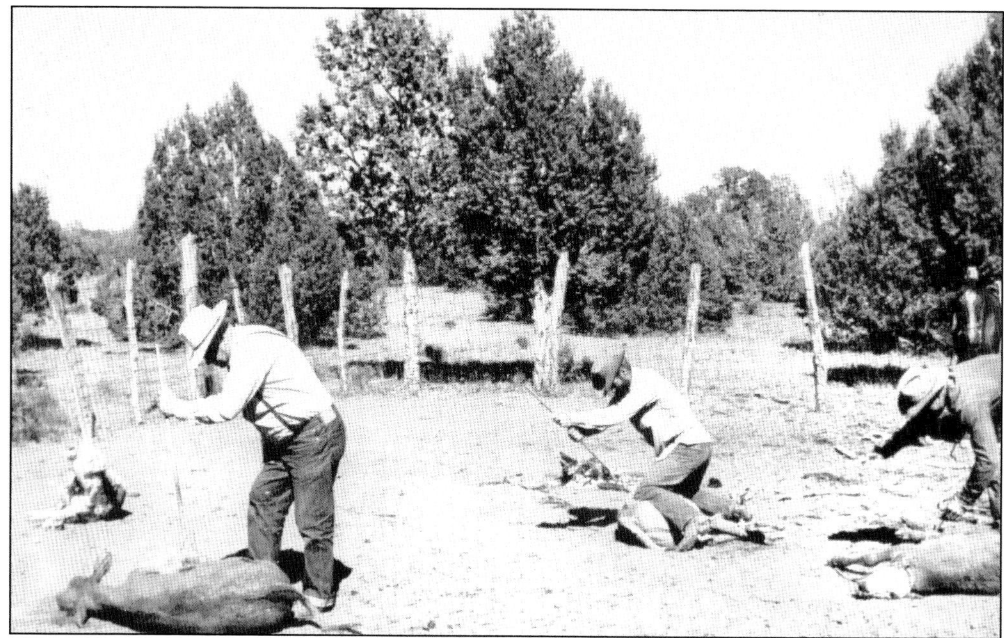

Frank Campbell, commenting on the changes in cattle ranching, said "Pushbutton ranching—my Lord—a cowboy today wants to jump into a pickup or car if he has to go only fifteen or twenty miles." (Courtesy Hume collection.)

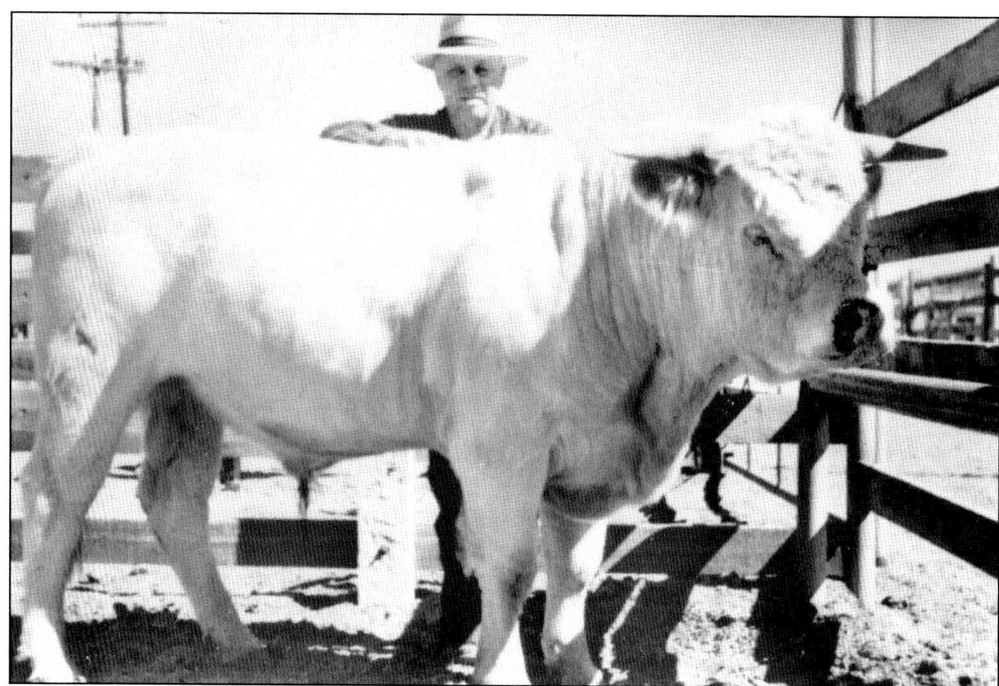

In 1939, Frank and Gene Campbell became the first cowmen in Northern Arizona to introduce Charolais cattle from France. They crossbred the French cows with their white-faced Hereford cattle to produce a heavier stock. (Courtesy Hume collection.)

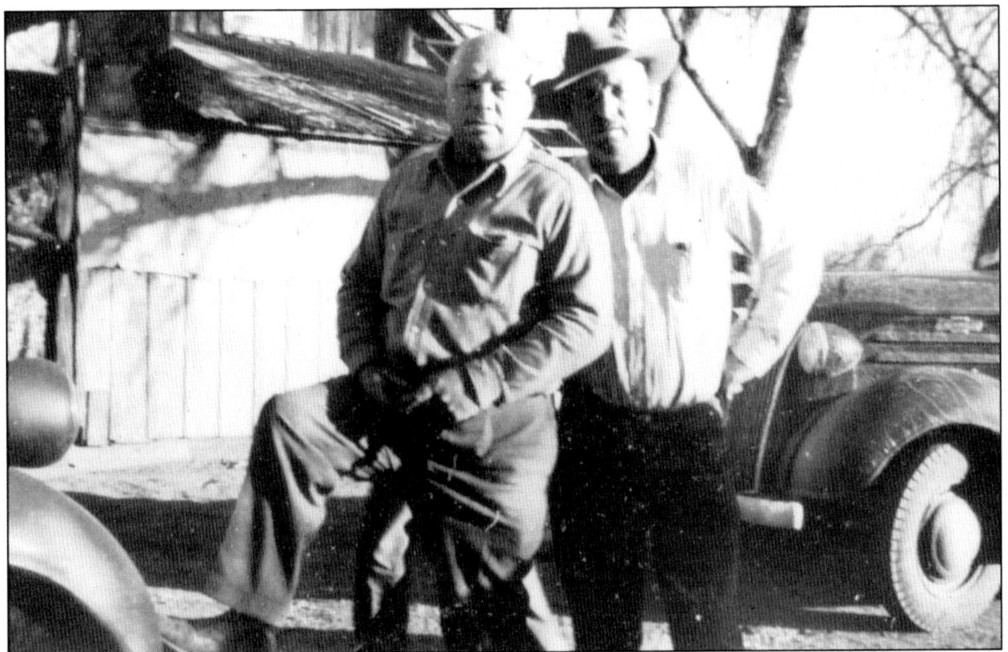

Gene and Frank Campbell divided the outfit in 1962. Gene died in 1968, and Frank passed away in 1980. Gene's sons, Gene Jr. and Jack, managed the Ash Fork Cattle Company until they sold a major portion of the ranch in 1971. It became Juniperwood Ranch, but the Campbells retained the grazing rights. However, due to a prolonged drought, a large part of the herd was also sold. (Courtesy Hume collection.)

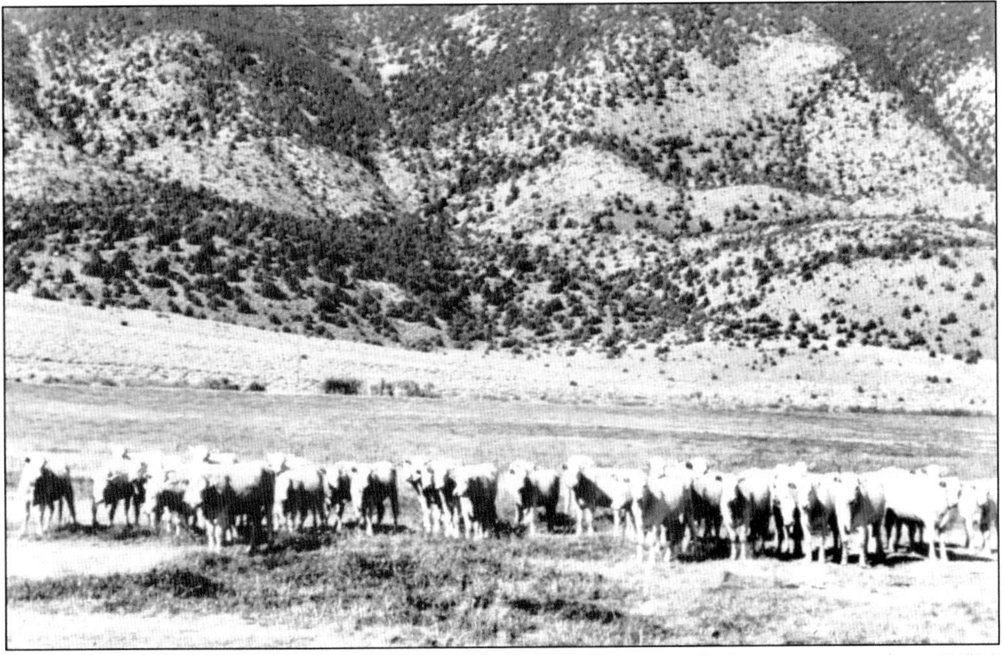

During its heyday in the 1940s and 1950s, the Ash Fork Livestock Company ran about 2,500 head with the Bar Z Bar brand stamped on their hides ranging over 177,000 acres of grassland and more under forest permits. (Courtesy Hume collection.)

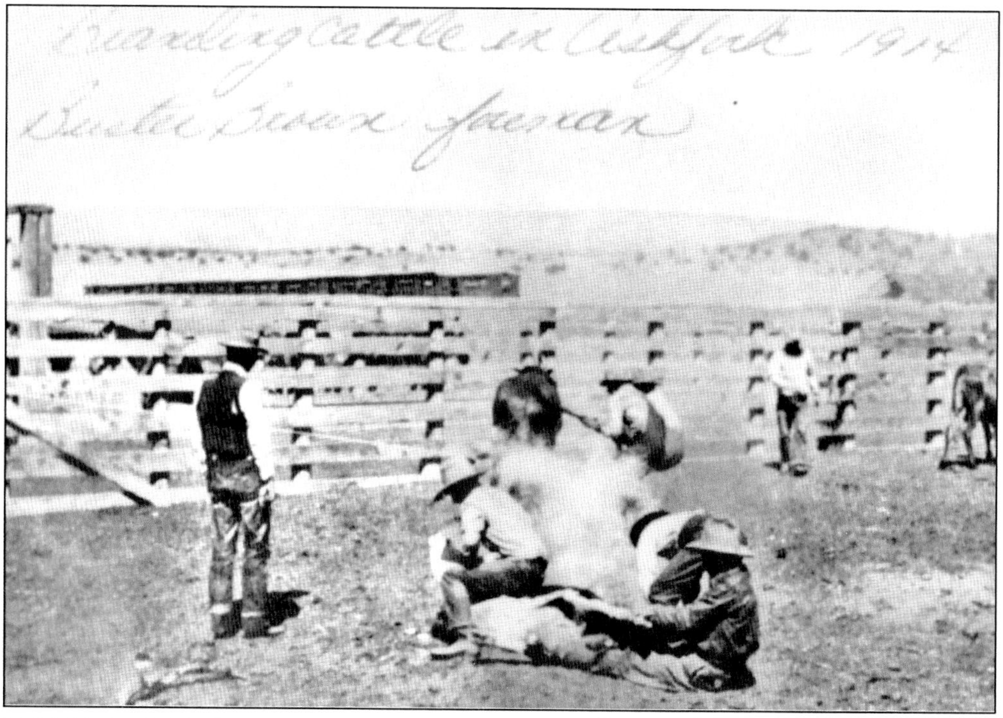

Cowpunchers with Buster Brown's outfit brand calves north of Ash Fork in 1914. Other ranches around Ash Fork included the Double AA, Tom Foley, Black Tanks, Babbitt brothers, Frank Dickerson, Goldtrap, and the Sevens Ranch. (Courtesy Hume collection.)

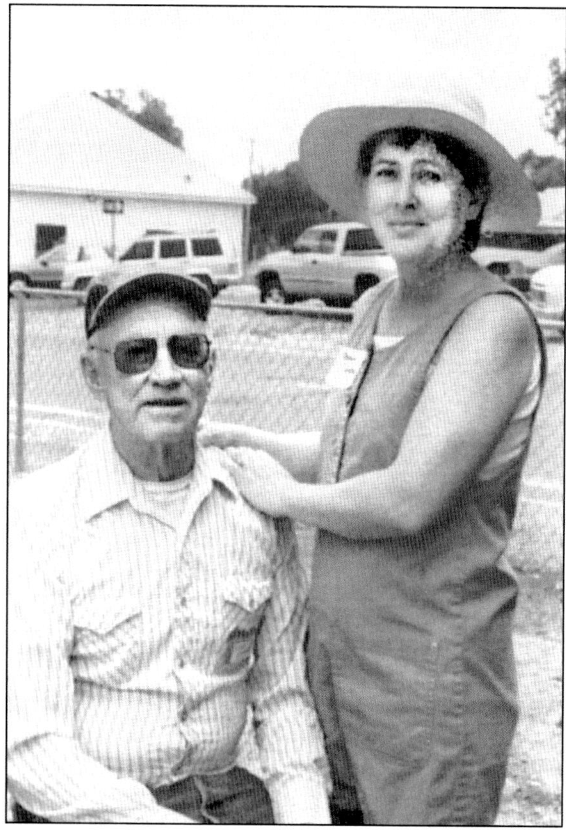

Jack Campbell, with his wife, Bonnie, still runs the Bar Z Bar outfit and headquarters in Ash Fork. A severe drought hit Northern Arizona in the 1950s; the region experienced its driest year on record in 1956. That New Year's Eve at midnight, Jack stepped out on to his front porch and with a forthrightness that typified the breed shouted, "Good bye 1956, you dry son of a bitch." (Courtesy Jack Campbell.)

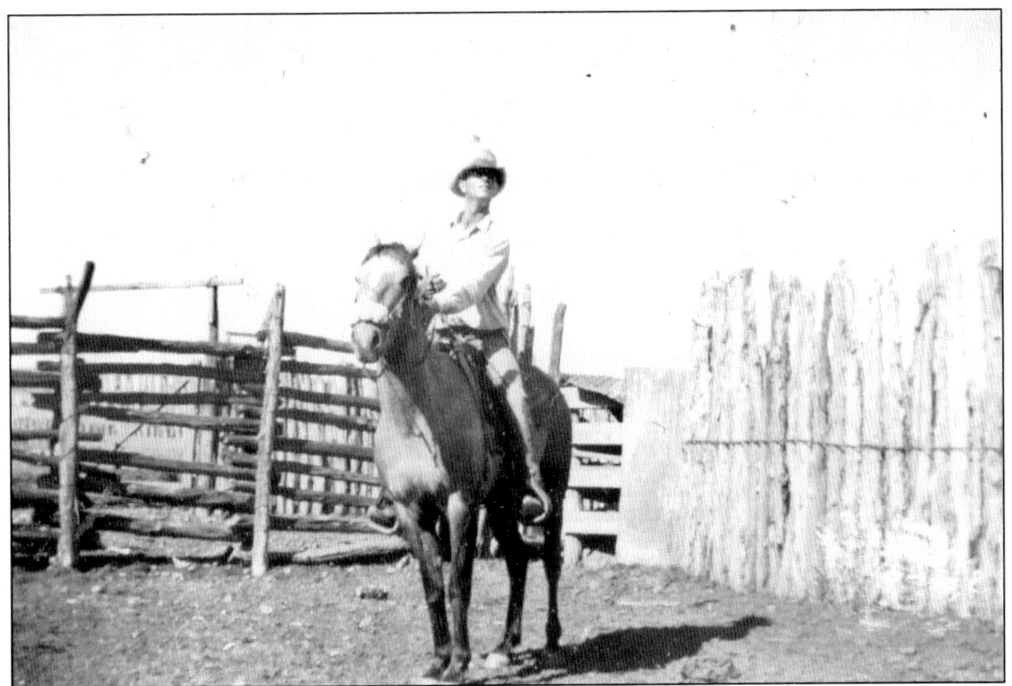

Frank Dickerson, a son of early merchant-rancher Winchester Dickerson, was a star athlete and graduated with Ash Fork's first high school class. He was also a cowhand from his boot heels to the top of his hat.

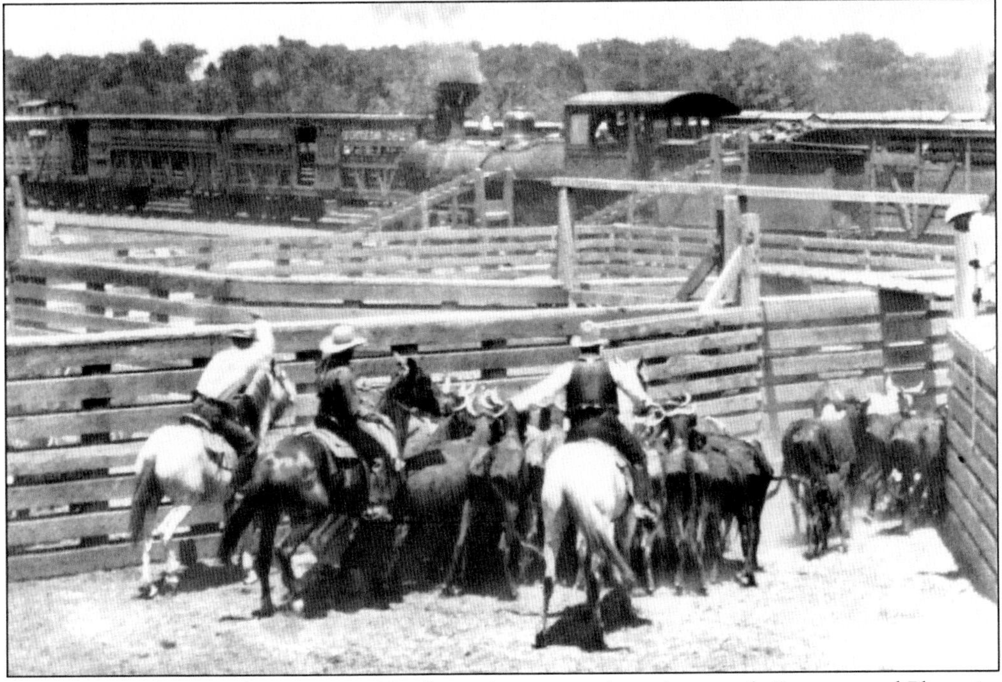

As the railroads moved west across Northern Arizona and south towards Prescott and Phoenix, the cattle business followed close behind. Ranchers could ship their cattle to California and Eastern markets without having to make the hazardous long drives over land.

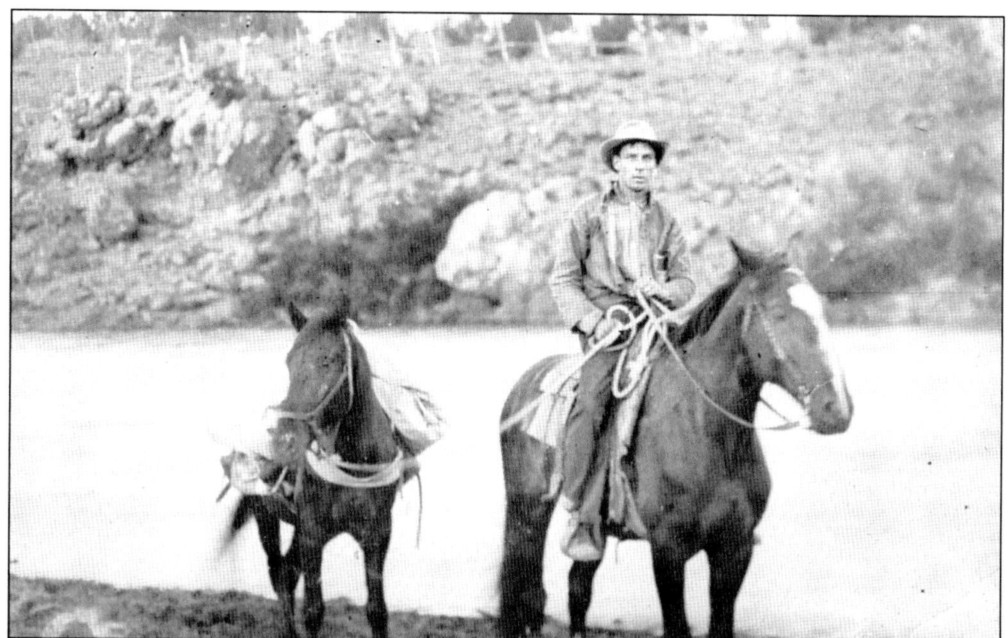

The heyday of the open-range cowboy lasted a little more than a generation, from the end of the Civil War to the end of the 1890s, when bad weather, disastrous market prices, and poor range management forced an end to the freewheeling days. Cowboys were young men of a particular time and place, performing body-punishing and hazardous jobs and living by a code of rugged, free-spirited independence, self-reliance, and resourcefulness. It was said that the breed was so independent that if one was thrown into a river he'd naturally float upstream.

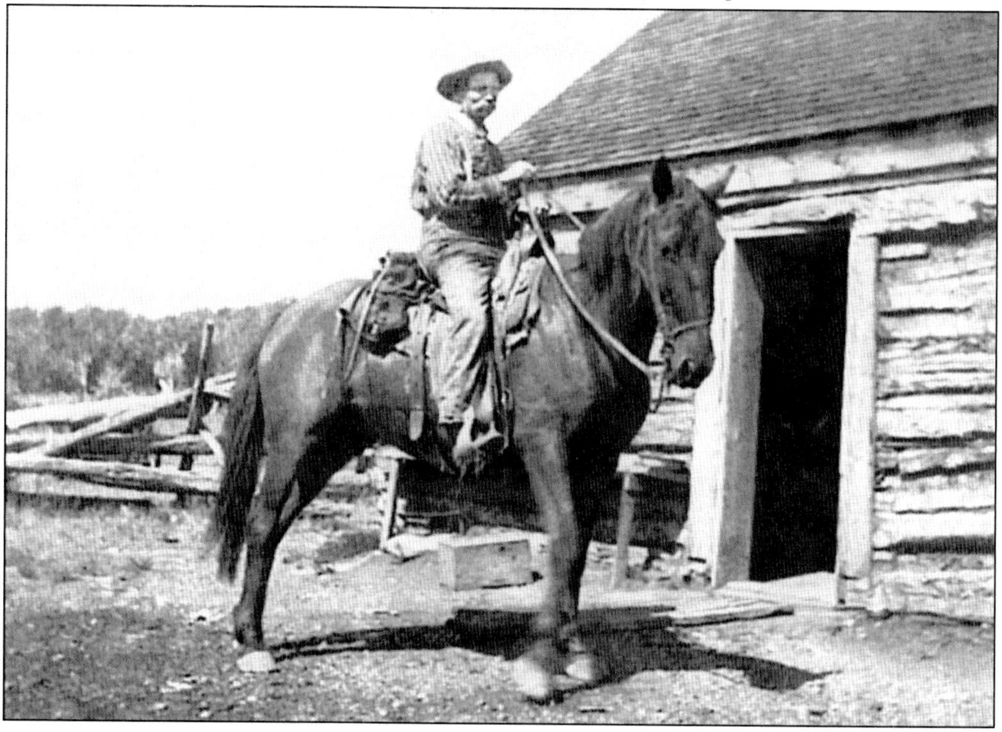

Seven

The Mother Road
Route 66

Of all of America's great highways, none epitomized American pop culture more than Route 66. Stretching across the heart of the country from Chicago to Los Angeles, it rambled nearly 2,500 miles through Missouri, Oklahoma, Texas, New Mexico, and Arizona. Route 66 was the 20th-century rendition of the golden road to the Promised Land. It was America's Main Street, the Cumberland Gap, Gila Trail, Beale Camel Road, Oregon Trail, California Trail, and the Yellow Brick Road all rolled into one.

The Beale Camel Road along the 35th parallel eventually evolved into the National Old Trails Highway, established in 1912, also known as the Ocean-to-Ocean Highway. Some of it followed the old National Road that began in 1806 at Cumberland, Maryland. Other parts followed Marcy's Road and the old Santa Fe Trail.

Route 66 was one of the original federal routes in the U.S. highway system established on November 11, 1926. At the time, only 800 miles were paved. By 1938, the rest of it would be paved. During the Great Depression of the 1930s, Route 66 would be a major path for the migrants who headed for California.

America embarked on a program of building freeways in the years following World War II, and highway construction crews began widening Ash Fork's Lewis Avenue in 1954. The town's main street became a one-way westbound avenue, while eastbound traffic was channeled along Park Avenue.

The death knell for Route 66 came with the passing of the Federal Highway Act of 1956. Signed by Pres. Dwight D. Eisenhower, it provided for a 66,000-kilometer national system of interstate and defense highways to be built over 13 years. The president later wrote, "More than any single action by the government since the end of the war, this one would change the face of America."

It did, and soon Route 66 would pass into the pages of history along with the wagons, stagecoaches, and even camels when, on June 27, 1985, the venerable old highway was officially removed from the U.S. highway system.

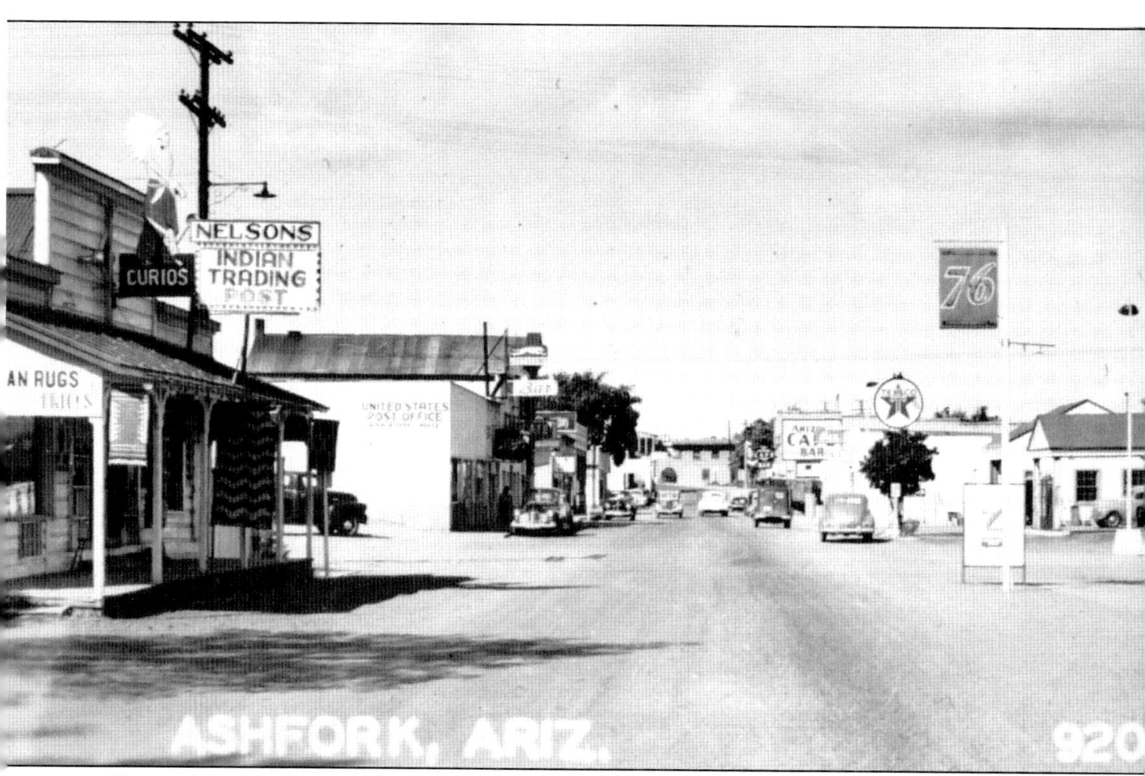

Route 66 opened in 1926, and Americans took to the highways in increasing numbers. It ran parallel to the railroad and passed through Ash Fork a block south of Railroad Avenue. The paving of Route 66 was finished in 1937. This photograph of downtown was taken about 1946. On the left, looking west on Lewis Avenue, is Fred Nelson's Indian Trading Post. The next few buildings have common walls: the post office, barbershop, Gummies Buffet, the drugstore, and the opera house. Common walls join O'Brian's Café, O. B. Farmer's barbershop, and Slamon's Variety Store. The only brick building is the Big Store. The only businesses west of Fourth Street are the White House Hotel, 66 Café, and Arizona Hotel. Dead ahead on Route 66 is the Harvey House. On the right side of the highway are Zettler's Market, Charlie Clingman's Pool Hall, Louise Mena's Union gas station, McMahan's Texaco, and Shea's Place. West of Fourth Street is the Arizona Café and Bar and a Standard Oil service station.

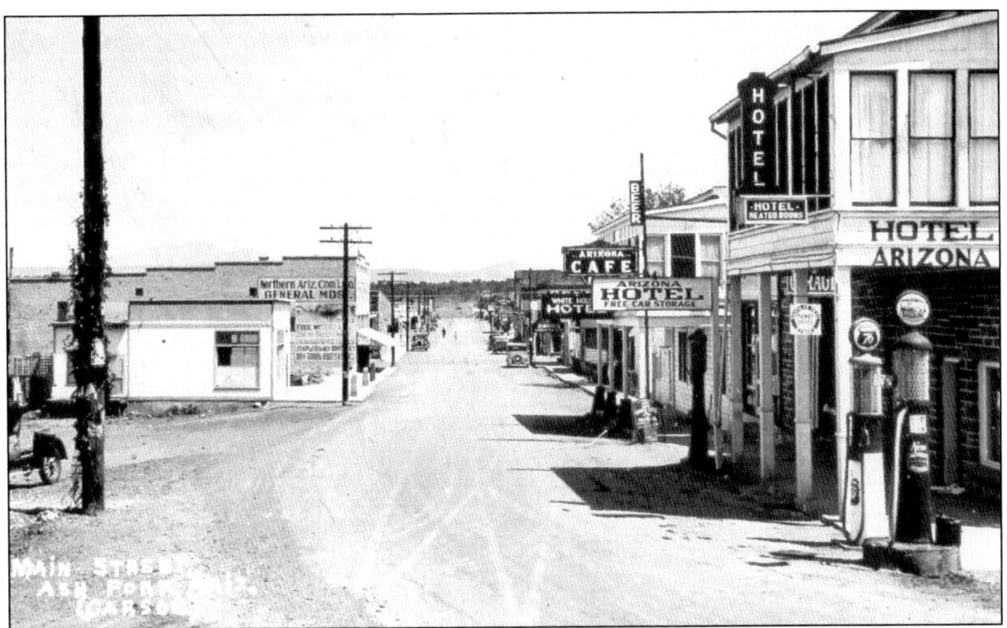

When Route 66 opened in the mid-1920s, the business district shifted from Railroad Avenue south to Lewis Avenue. The tall building on the left is Winchester Dickerson's general store. During the 1930s, it became the Arizona Café and Bar. On the right is the historic Hotel Arizona.

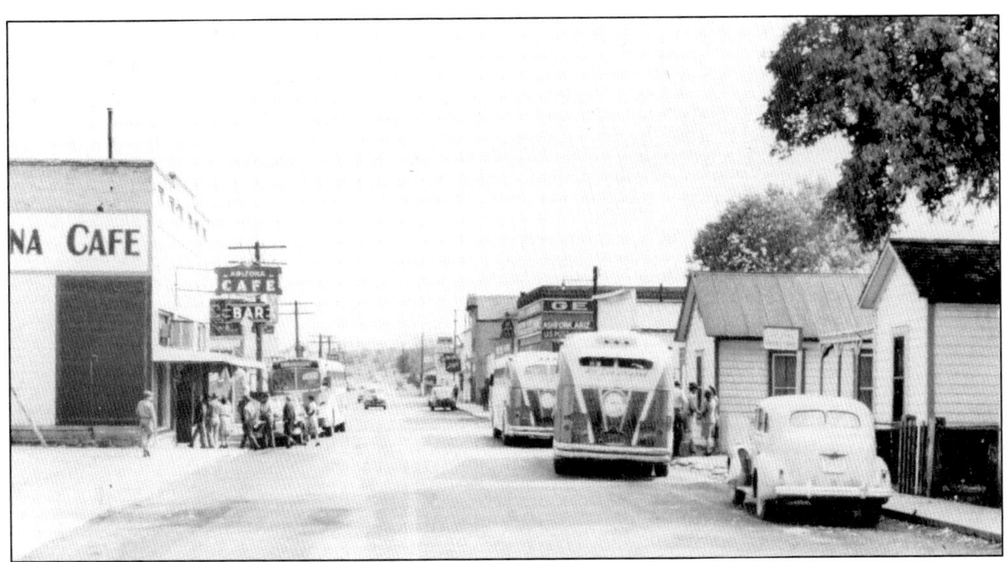

Route 66 opened for automobile traffic in 1926, and Americans took to the highways in increasing numbers. The highway ran parallel to the railroad and passed through Ash Fork on Lewis Avenue, a block south of Railroad Avenue. Route 66 was paved through Ash Fork in 1934, and the highway was completed three years later.

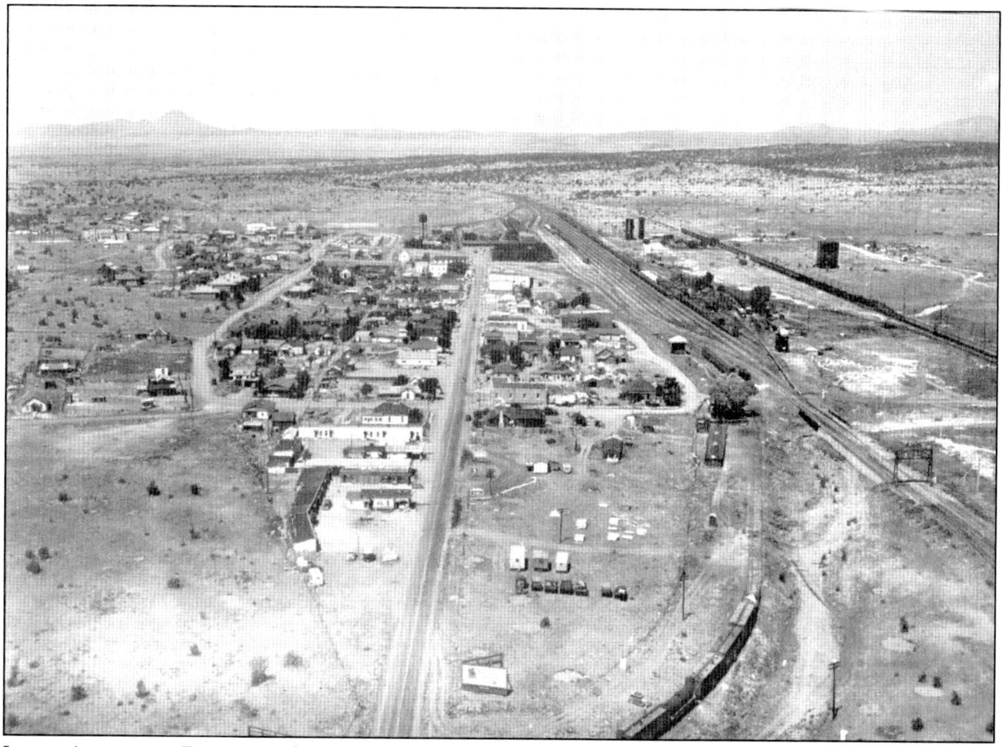

Lewis Avenue, or Route 66, shows much improvement from a few years earlier in this picture from the 1930s. In 1927, the initial two-and-one-half miles of track south of town were switched from the draw east of town to the west side. A year later, a new depot was built west of the Harvey House, and the old depot on the east side was abandoned.

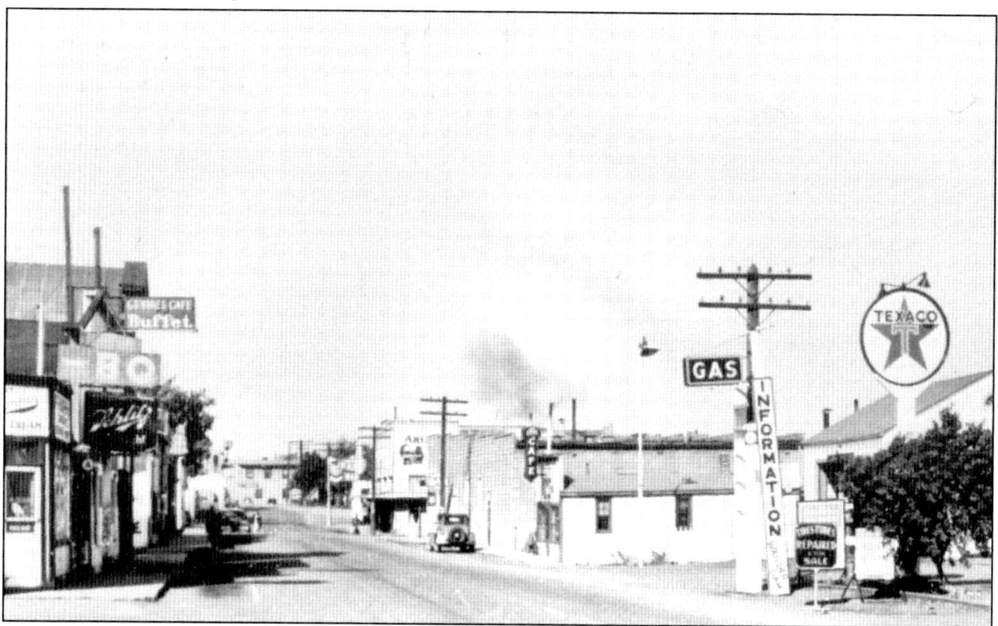

Ash Fork's main street during the 1930s was a popular place for postcard photographers trying to capture the essence of Route 66.

This is Route 66 looking east as it passes through Ash Fork in the 1920s. The highway wouldn't be paved for another decade. On the right is Washington's mercantile store. The tall building behind the car is the old opera house. During the early 1950s, it was Mac's Café. (Courtesy Hume collection.)

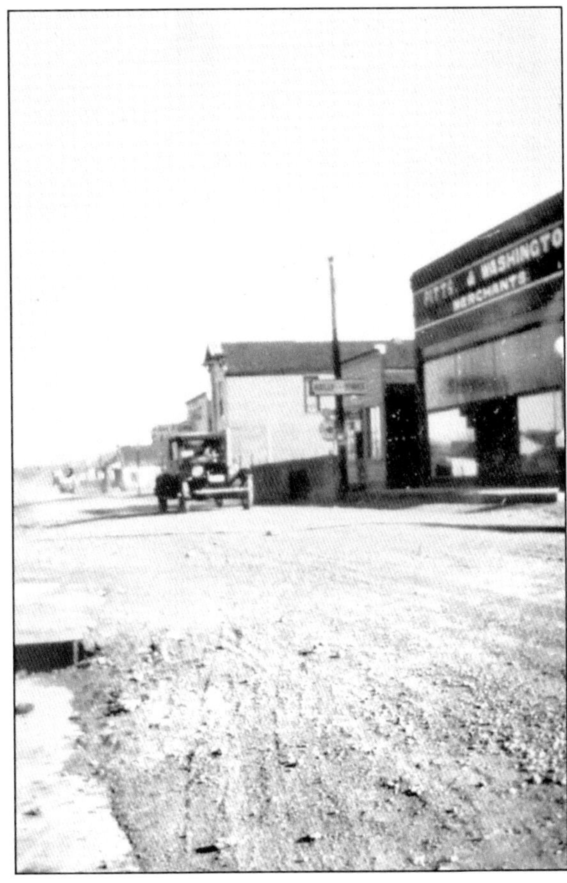

During the Great Depression, dust-bowl refugees made their way from the Midwest looking to find the Promised Land in California along the highway immortalized by John Steinbeck as the Mother Road. Leave it to Oklahoma's Will Rogers to put the mass migration into perspective. "When the Oakies left Oklahoma and moved to California," he reckoned, "it raised the average IQ in both places."

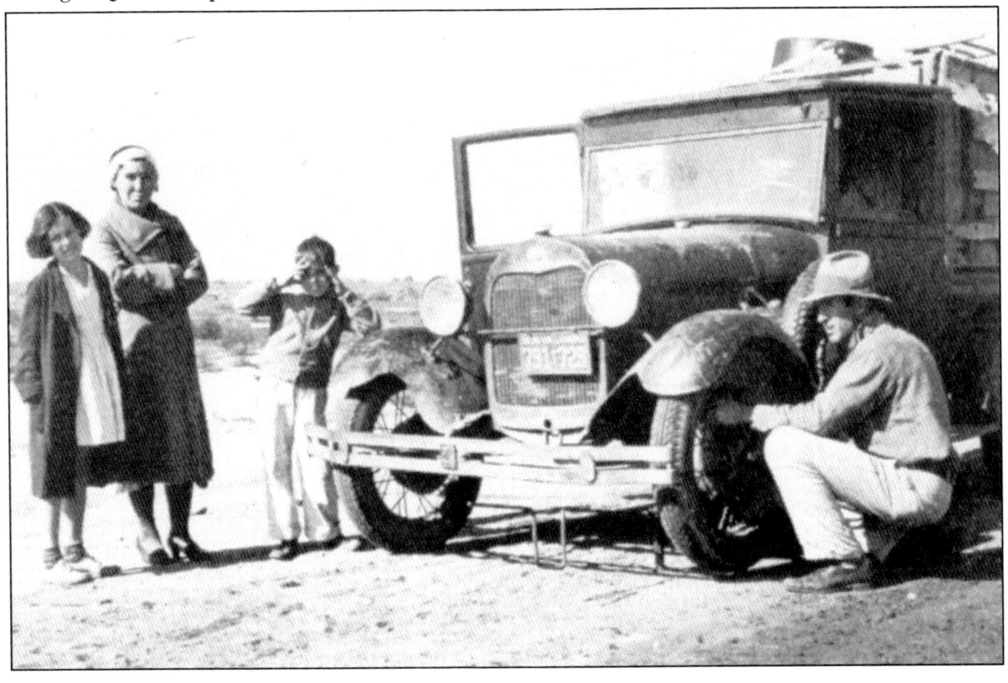

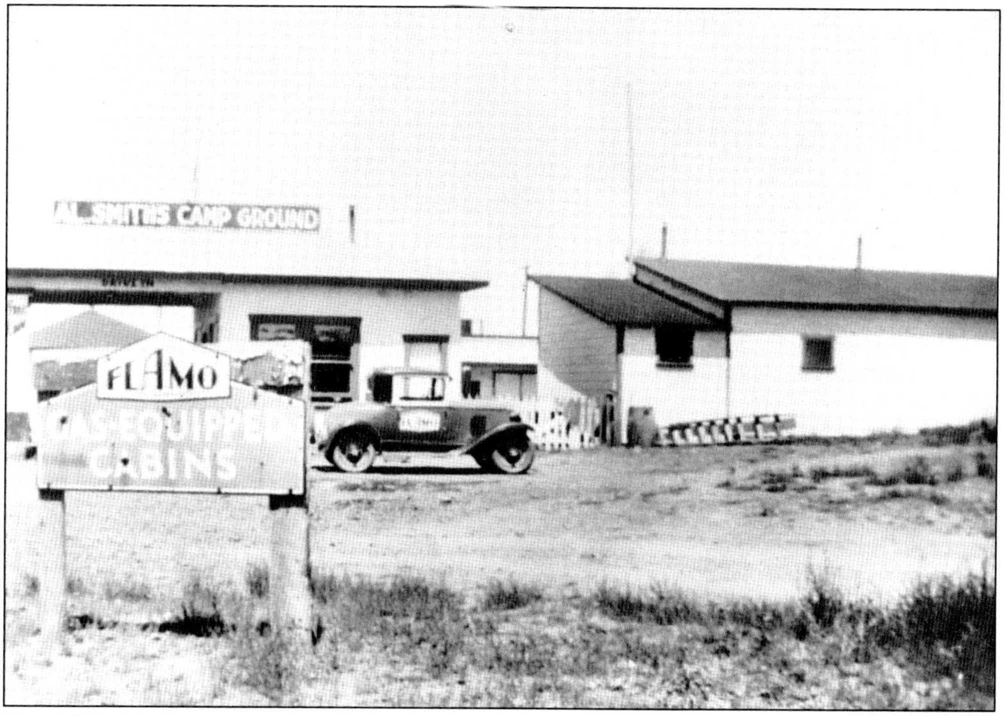

The Al Smith Campground, with the landmark Santa Fe water tower in the background, was built in the 1930s to accommodate tourists on Route 66 and was later acquired by A. C. "Mac" McCoy, who changed the name to McCoy Motel. Mac also ran a small Texaco gas station dispensing Fire Chief gasoline. Coincidentally he was also Ash Fork's fire chief. The McCoy Motel became the Stage Coach Motel in the 1970s and was one of the few to survive the sharp decline in business when the Interstate 40 bypassed the town in 1979. Today it houses Ruby's Eighth Street Deli restaurant.

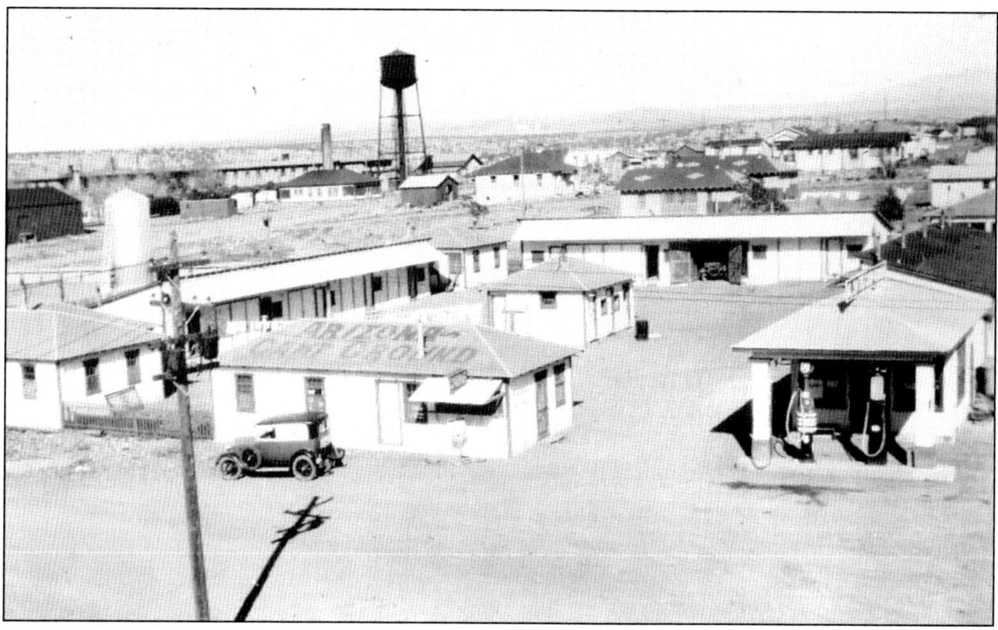

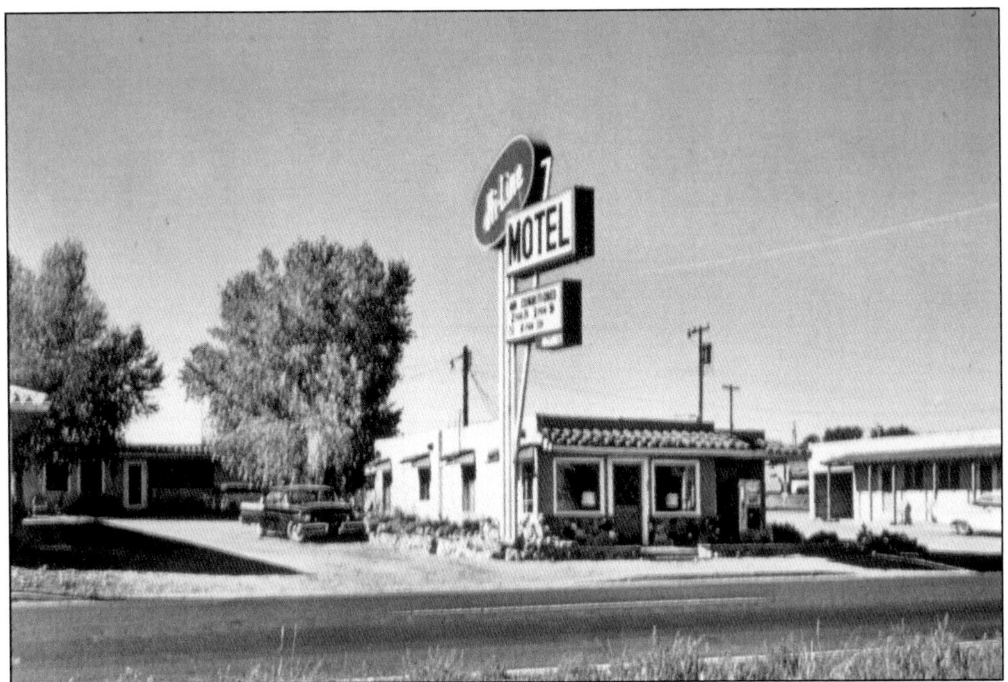

The Hi-Line Motel, on the east end of town, was built around 1936 and was owned by the Alton McAbee family. The Hi-Line is a good example of the standard design for motels during the heyday of motor courts. (Courtesy Hume collection.)

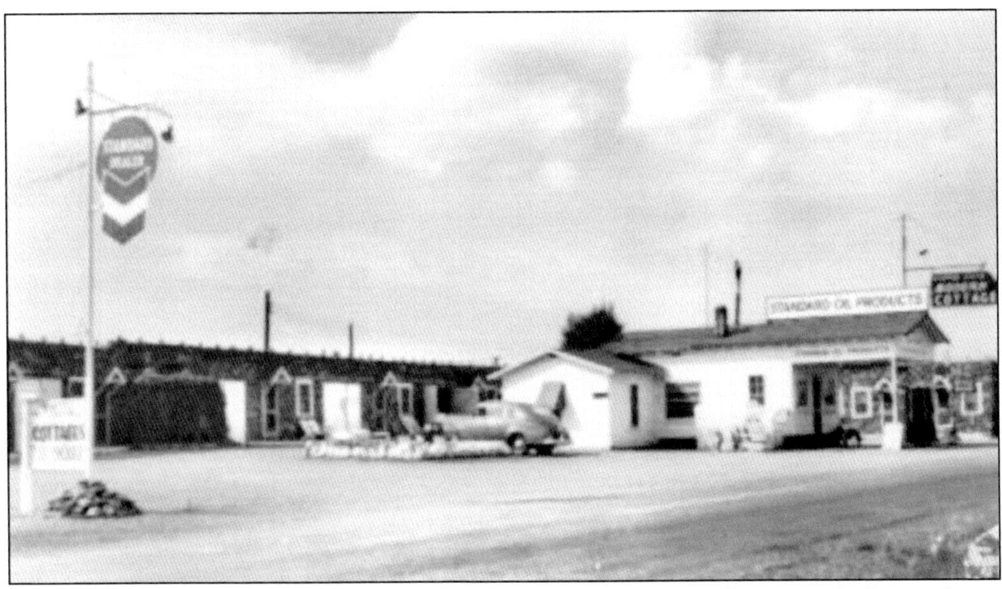

The Copper State Motel, built in 1933, was the first motor court on the east end of town. It was built of river rock and owned by Ezell and Zelma Nelson. From 1933 to 1975, Zelma and Ezell personified the American experience on Route 66; their gas station grew into a motor court, the Copper State, and the Nelsons watched as thousands of Americans traveled the Mother Road in search of something better. (Courtesy Todd Wilkinson.)

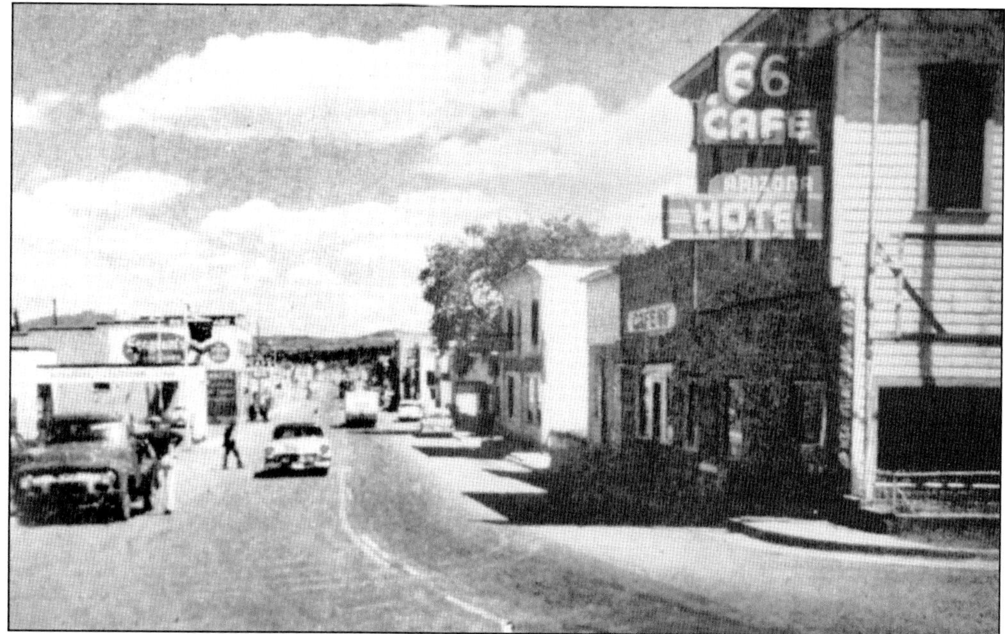

The photograph above is Lewis Avenue during the early 1950s. The photograph below was taken in 1982. The town was bypassed by I-40 in 1979, and traffic had slowed to a trickle. The steep decline began in 1954, when Route 66 became a divided highway through town. Huge construction equipment was brought in to widen Lewis Avenue. The awnings that for years shaded the entrance to the White House and Arizona Hotels were torn down, and the sidewalks through the business district were cut in half. Lewis Avenue was designated to handle westbound traffic. Park Avenue, a residential street, was widened and paved for eastbound traffic. The aesthetic personality of the downtown was destroyed to widen a highway that was destined to abandon the town a couple of decades later.

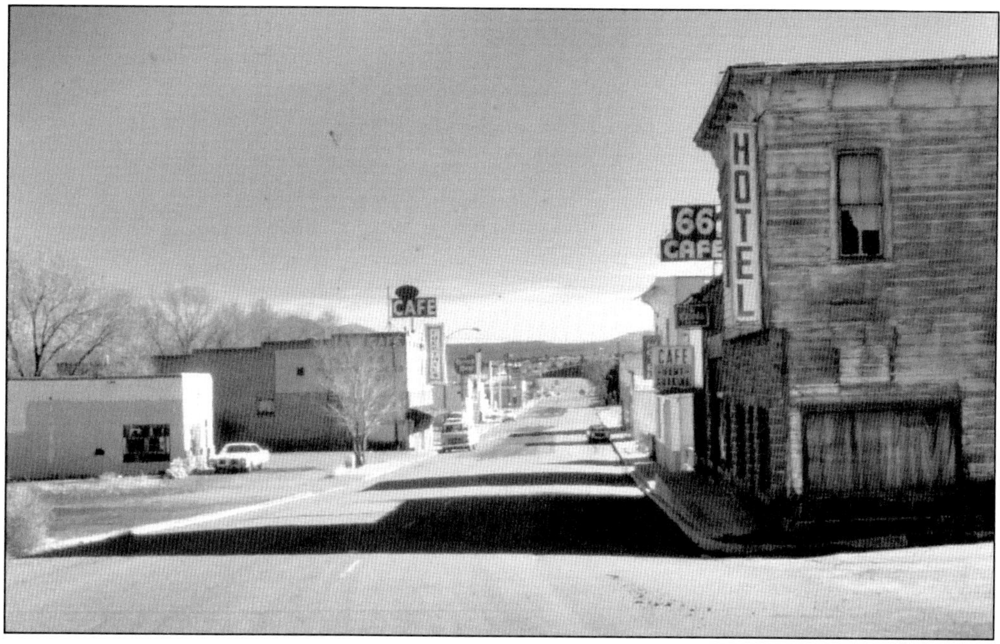

Eight

BOOMTOWN TO BUST
THE 1920S TO THE 1970S

Throughout its history, Ash Fork has known economic ups and downs. With the advent of the horseless carriage, Americans began taking to the open road. Pressure mounted for an ocean-to-ocean highway, and since Ash Fork was located on an ancient east-west corridor, it was a natural for such a highway. In 1916, Congress passed the Bankhead Act, which would pump millions of dollars into the building of national highways. In 1922, the Old Trails National Highway came through the town, passing along Lewis Avenue, and shifted the business district from Railroad Avenue to Lewis. In 1926, the U.S. highway system officially designated it Route 66.

With the coming of the Great Depression, because of Ash Fork's location along a main line highway and railroad, the town was crowded with transients on their way from somewhere to nowhere.

Federal funds for road-improvement projects brought some relief by the mid-1930s. In 1938, Route 66 would be the first transcontinental highway to be completely paved.

With Americans on the move again, motor courts, gas stations, and roadside cafés appeared in the communities.

World War II ended the Depression, but shortages restricted travel and building. Still, there was a great demand for mineral and agricultural products. Troop trains rolled in and out of town day and night, and thousands of soldiers poured off the trains to stretch, with time and money to spend. After the war, even though rail traffic dropped off dramatically, several passenger trains passed through town daily until the mid-1950s.

Postwar traffic increased on Route 66, as gas was plentiful again and Americans were enjoying unprecedented prosperity. While the nation prospered, however, towns along Route 66 like Ash Fork began to fall on hard times. By the early 1960s, the Escalante Hotel was gone, and the railroad had moved its main line. America was building freeways to replace the old highways. Route 66 was fast becoming a relic of the past.

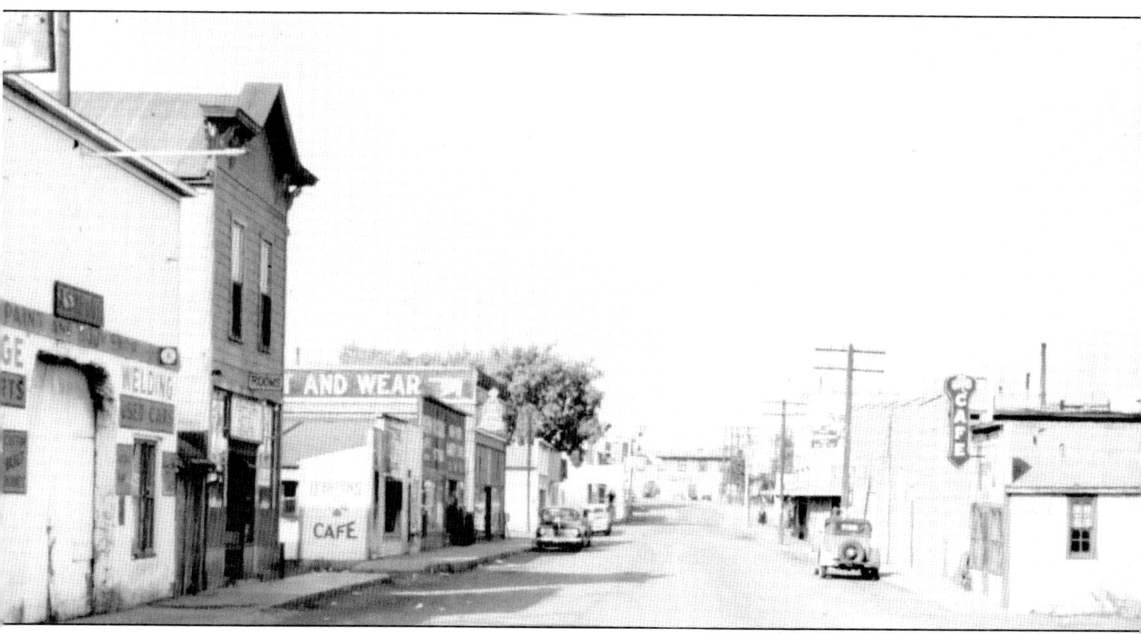

Ash Fork is pictured here in the early 1940s. Route 66 had been paved, but traffic through town was light on what appears to be a Sunday morning in late fall. On the left is a welding shop where Flander's Drug Store would be located later in the decade. The tall, gabled building is Lockett's Opera House and boardinghouse. It would become Mac's Café in the early 1950s. Across the alley is O'Brian's Café. A recent fire had closed the restaurant, and O'Brian's relocated across the street to the Shamrock Café. O'Brian's would become the Do Drop In Café. The barbershop is west of the café, and a variety store finishes off the row of common-wall buildings. The last building on the block is the Big Store. On the right, west of the Shamrock Café, is Joe Gorra's pool hall and bar. It was destroyed by fire in 1946. Further down is the Arizona Café and Bar. The Harvey House is in the center.

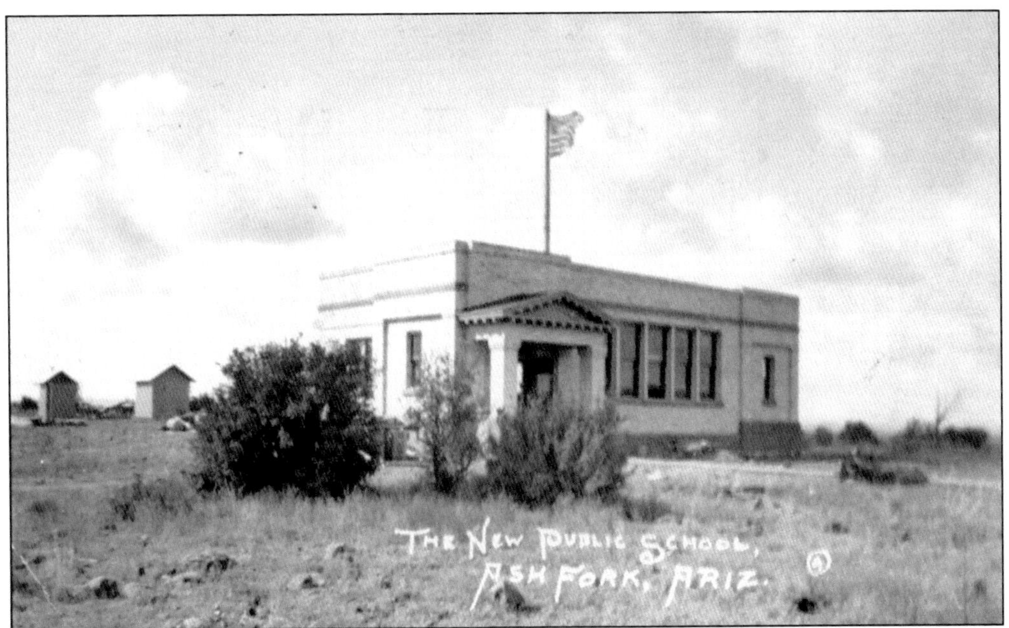

A new school was built in 1915. This one was brick and had a gymnasium, stage, and outdoor basketball and tennis courts. The gym served as a community center for meetings, talent shows, and dances. Up until the opening of the State Theater around 1947 and the Yavapai Theater in 1949, old movies were shown in the gym one night a week. (Courtesy Hume collection.)

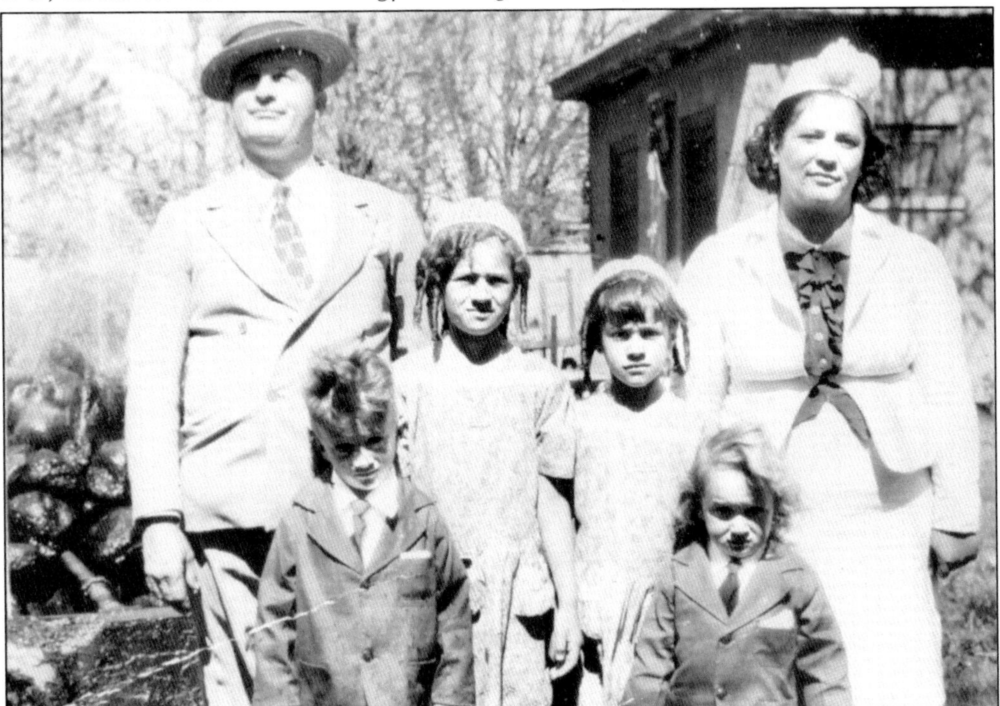

Severo Cruz was a chef at the Escalante for many years. He is pictured here with his family. They are, from left to right, (first row) Jimmy and Henry Cruz; (second row) Mary and Virginia Cruz; (third row) Severo and Ramona Cruz. (Courtesy Hume collection.)

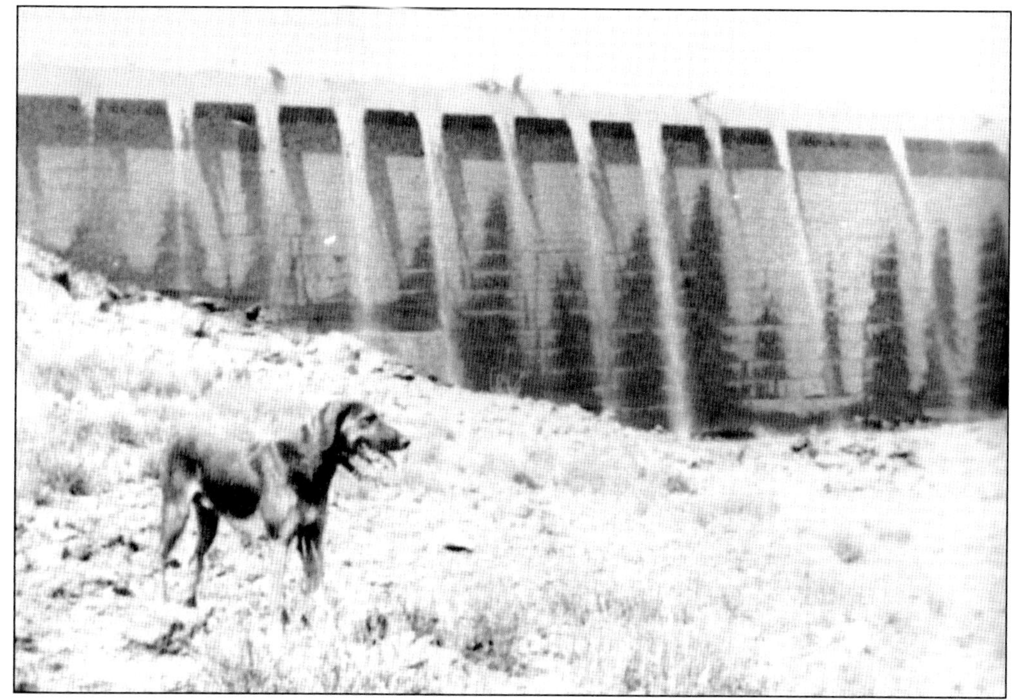

Steel Dam in Johnson Canyon, five miles east of Ash Fork, was completed in March 1898. It was built to catch spring flow and impound water for the Santa Fe's steam locomotives. Water was carried by gravity in a six-inch steel pipe down to Ash Fork. The dam is reputed to be the first of its kind in the country and one of only two in the entire United States. (Courtesy Hume collection.)

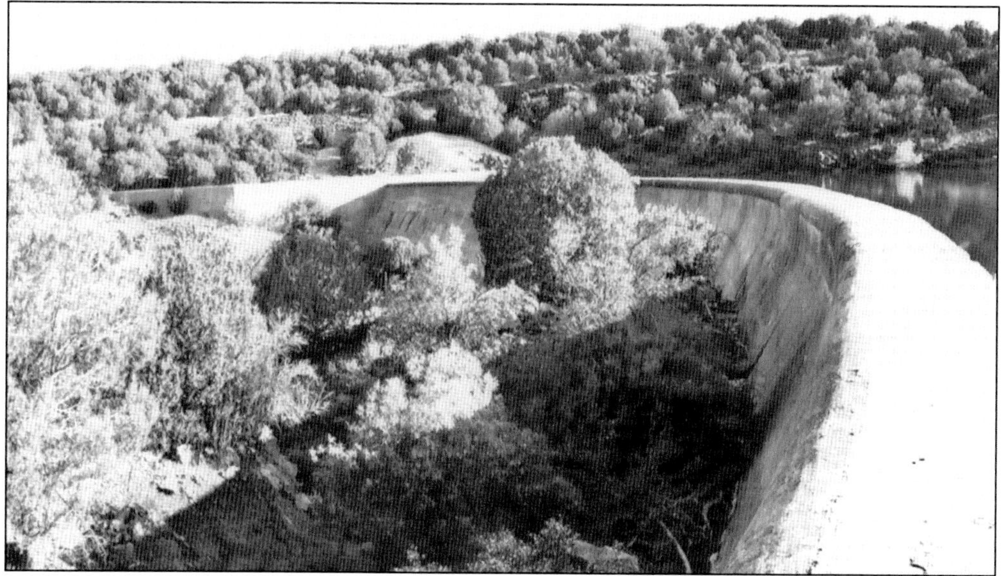

Stone Dam, built in 1911 in Johnson Canyon a short distance above Steel Dam, created a reservoir to hold water for the steam locomotives stopping in Ash Fork, five miles further down the hill. Stone Dam and Steel Dam were connected by a 10-inch water pipe. The dam was gifted to the town by developer and philanthropist John F. Long in 2003. (Courtesy Hume collection.)

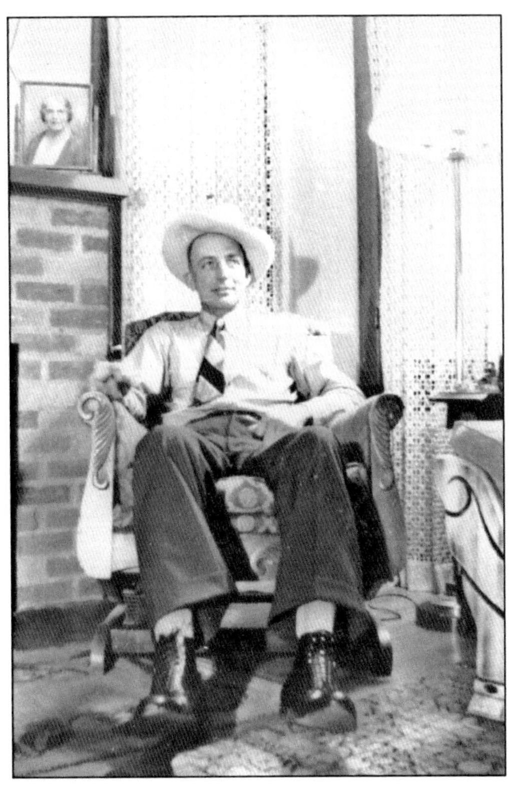

A. C. "Mac" McCoy was born in Oklahoma and came to Ash Fork in 1916 as a machinist for the Santa Fe before becoming a division foreman. He married Polly Greenlaw of Flagstaff and soon went into business for himself. He was also an agent for Standard Oil and then Texaco. Mac and his wife bought the Al Smith Campground and changed the name to the McCoy Motor Court, where they operated a Texaco gas station. He was very active in community affairs and the Highway 66 Association, was a school trustee, and was a player-coach on the Ash Fork baseball team. He was elected to the state legislature in 1952 and died in office at the age of 60 during his first term. (Courtesy Hume collection.)

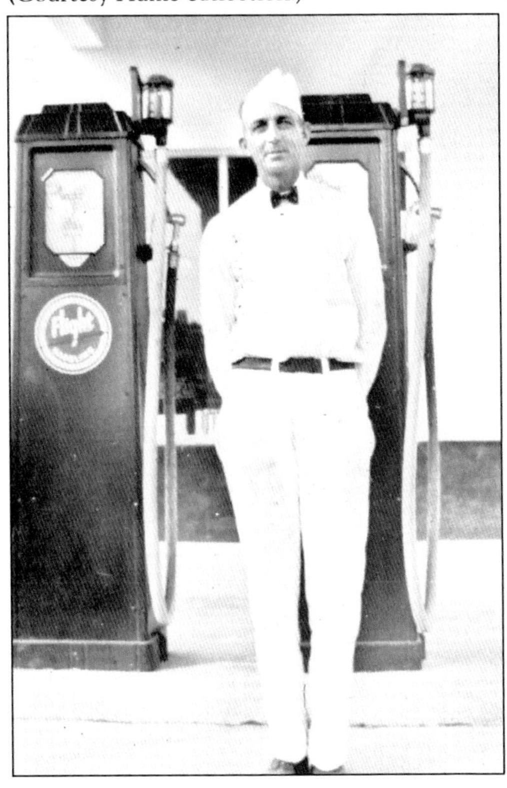

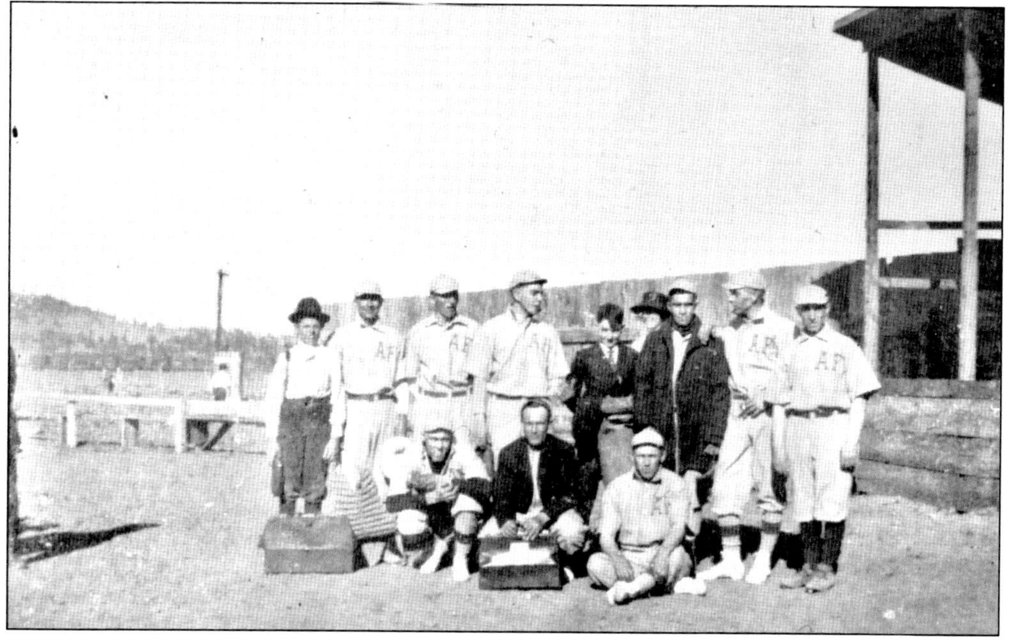

Semiprofessional or "town team" baseball was popular, especially from the 1920s through the 1960s. Local merchants sponsored teams, and a player wore the sponsor's name on the back of his flannel baseball shirt. Ash Fork competed with towns all across Northern Arizona.

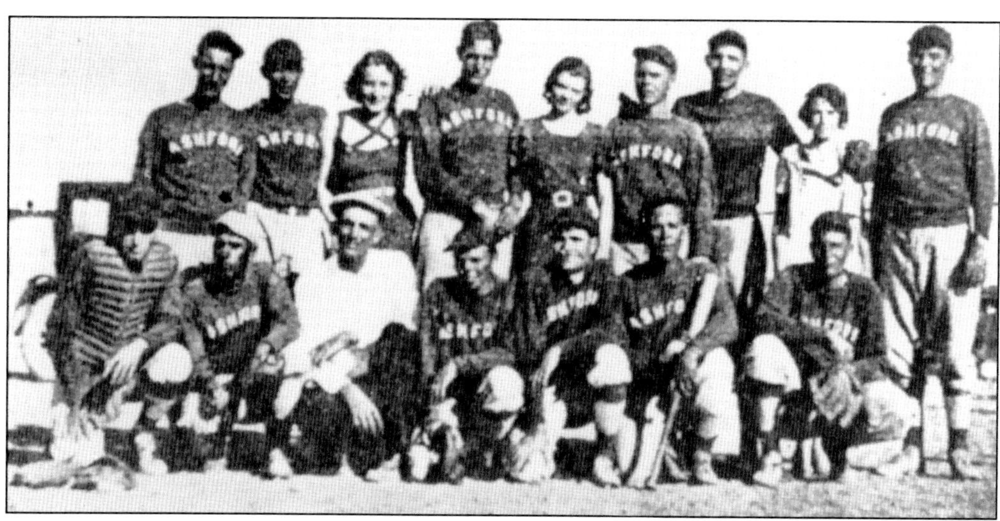

The Ash Fork semiprofessional ball club was the West 66 Baseball League champions several times during the 1930s. Adding a pleasant touch to the team photograph are three pretty women who might have been bat girls.

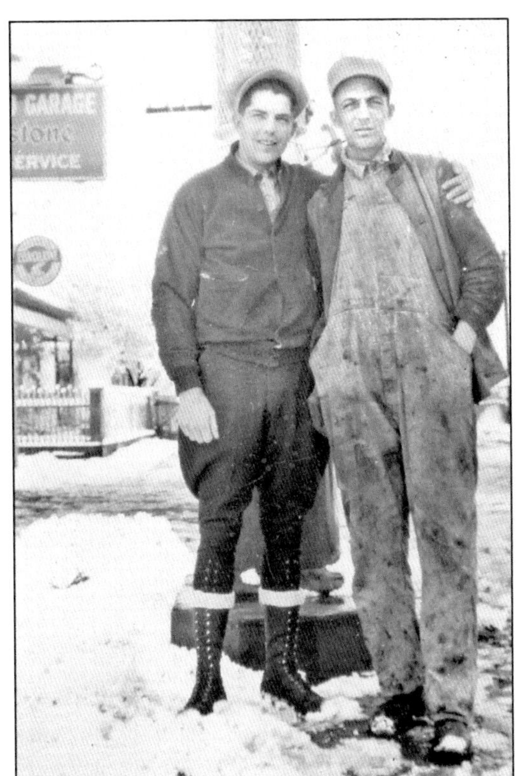

The McCoy boys, Roy and his older brother Mac, were both tall, strapping athletes and great baseball players in the Northern Arizona Baseball League. Both brothers served as coaches and mentors to Ash Fork's youth baseball teams.

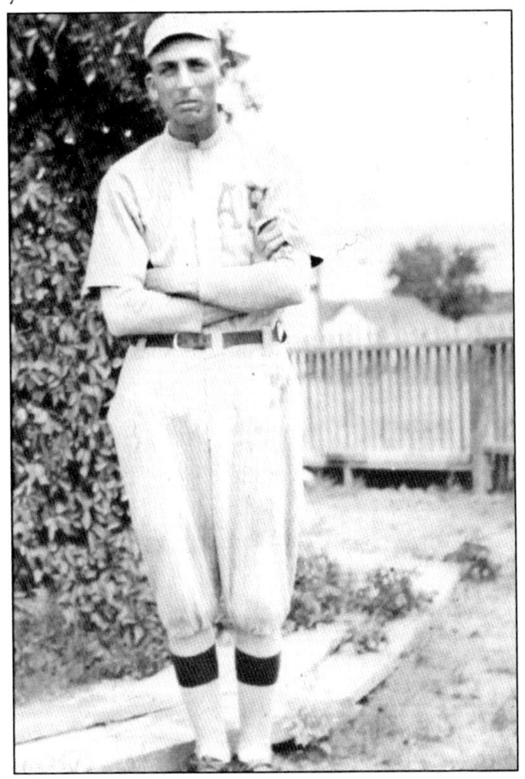

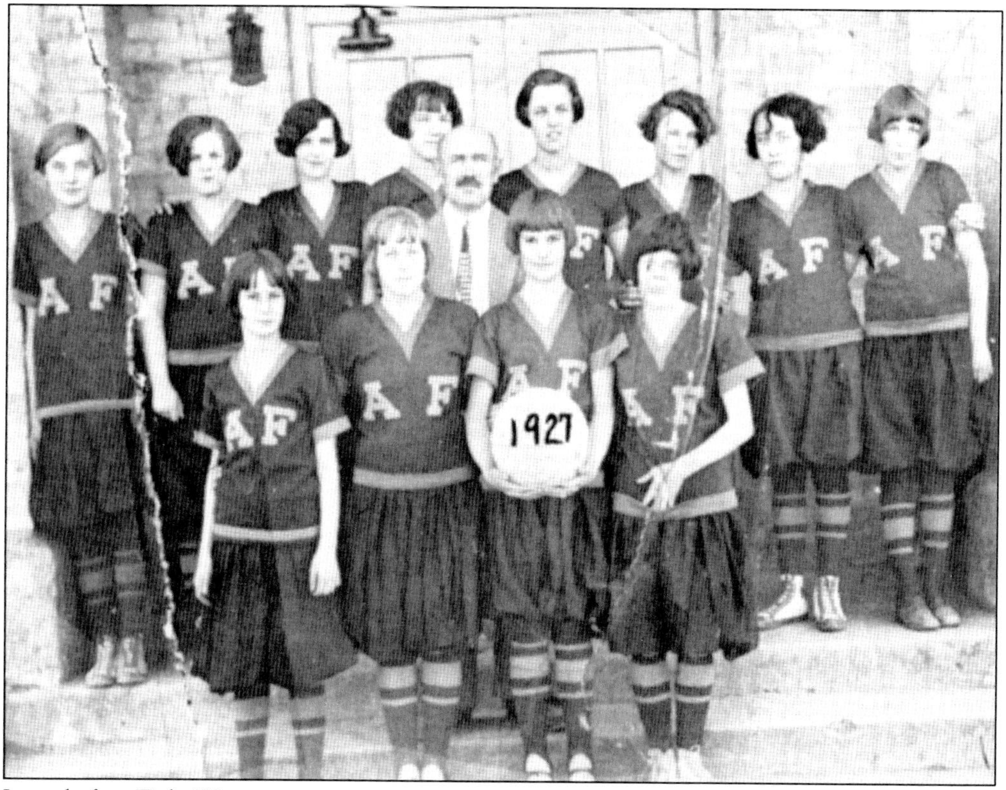

Long before Title IX, young women were competing in interscholastic sports. Pictured is Ash Fork's 1927 girls' basketball team. (Courtesy Hume collection.)

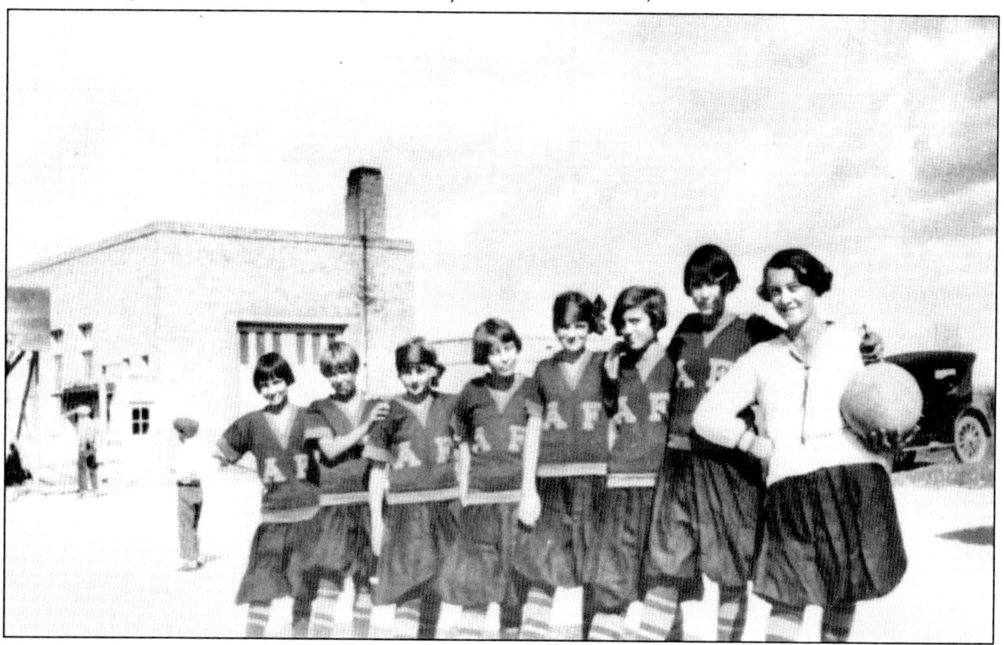

The Lady Spartans of Ash Fork's 1928 basketball team line up adjacent to the school building. (Courtesy Hume collection.)

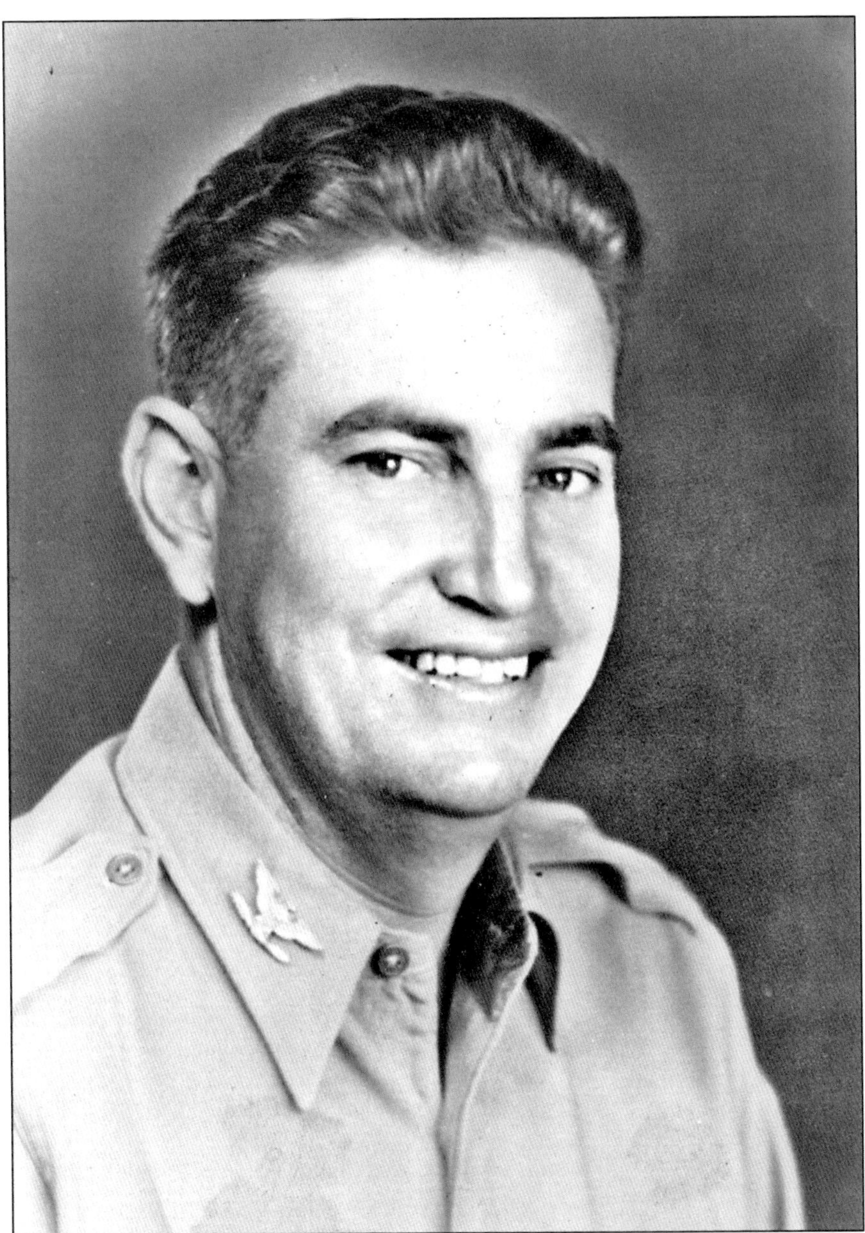

Raymond Schwanbeck was Ash Fork High School's greatest alum. He was one of six in the school's first class in 1929 and went on to star in football and basketball at Arizona State College at Flagstaff. During his senior year, the Lumberjacks (Axmen) beat both the University of Arizona and Arizona State in football and basketball. He joined the army in 1930 while still in college. After graduation he enlisted in the U.S. Army Air Corps and was in the Philippines when Pearl Harbor was attacked in 1941. At the same time, the Japanese bombed Clark Field in the Philippines, and Ray was wounded by bomb fragments. In the South Pacific during World War II, he was considered one of the finest B-17 Flying Fortress pilots in the army. One of the Air Corps' most decorated pilots, he was cited for bravery at Java for sinking an enemy ship. Just before his death in 2001, he was inducted into the Arizona Aviation Hall of Fame. (Courtesy Robert Schwanbeck.)

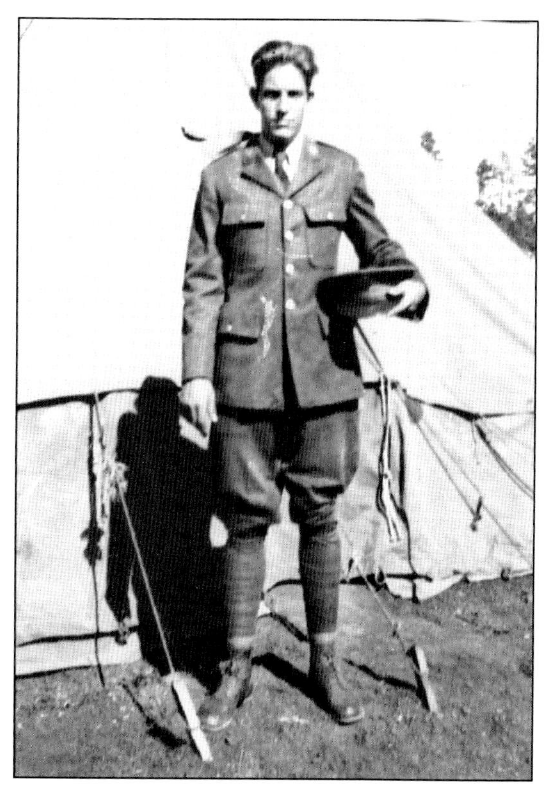

Ray Schwanbeck was a product of what Tom Brokaw called "the Greatest Generation." While attending Arizona State College at Flagstaff (Northern Arizona University), he joined the National Guard. His football coach, the legendary Rudy Lavik, was commander of Company I of the 158th Infantry. The pay was $1.92 for each weekly drill, enough to provide all the spending money he needed in school. In late 1932, he was promoted to sergeant. After graduating from NAU, he applied to the U.S. Army Air Corps and was commissioned a second lieutenant in 1934. He was one of the first pilots to fly the B-10, the first all-metal bomber. He would later become one the first to fly the legendary B-17. In the photograph below, he has landed on a dirt runway west of Ash Fork to visit his little daughter Sue. (Courtesy Jo Schwanbeck.)

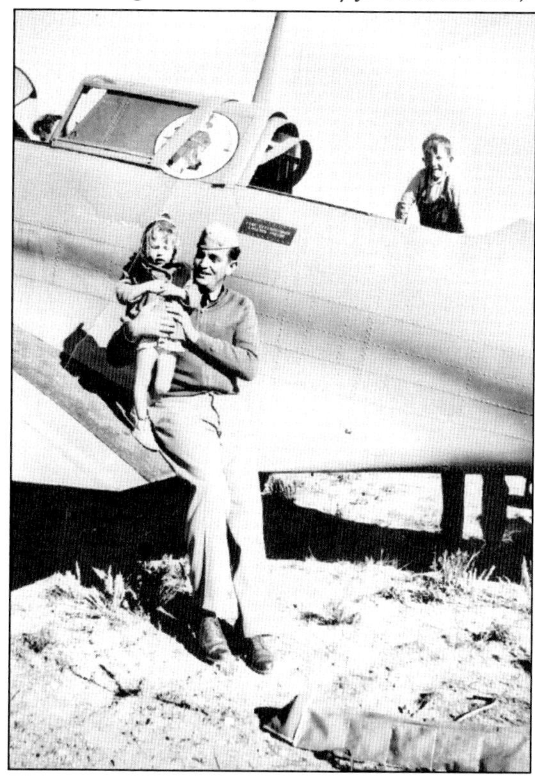

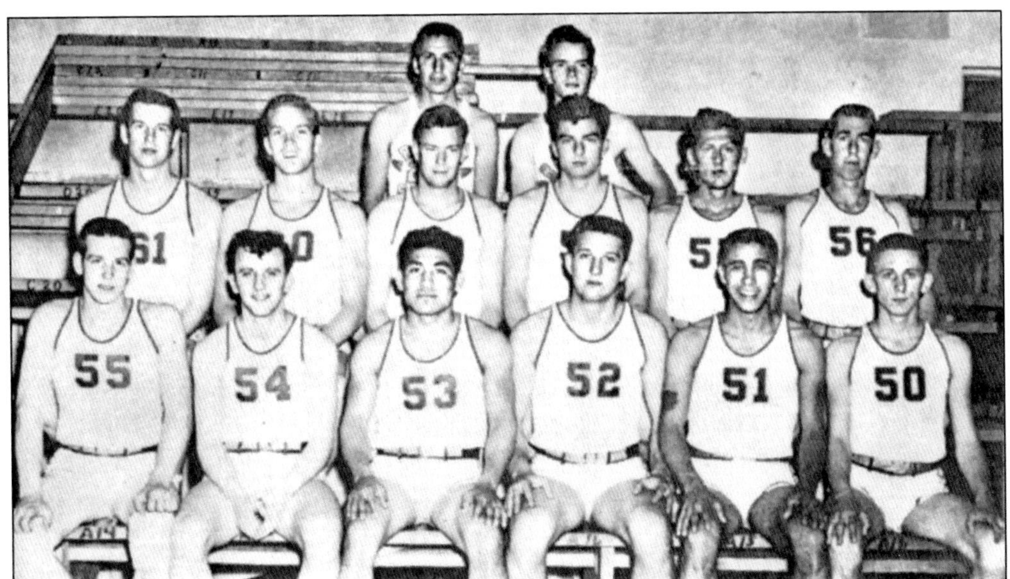

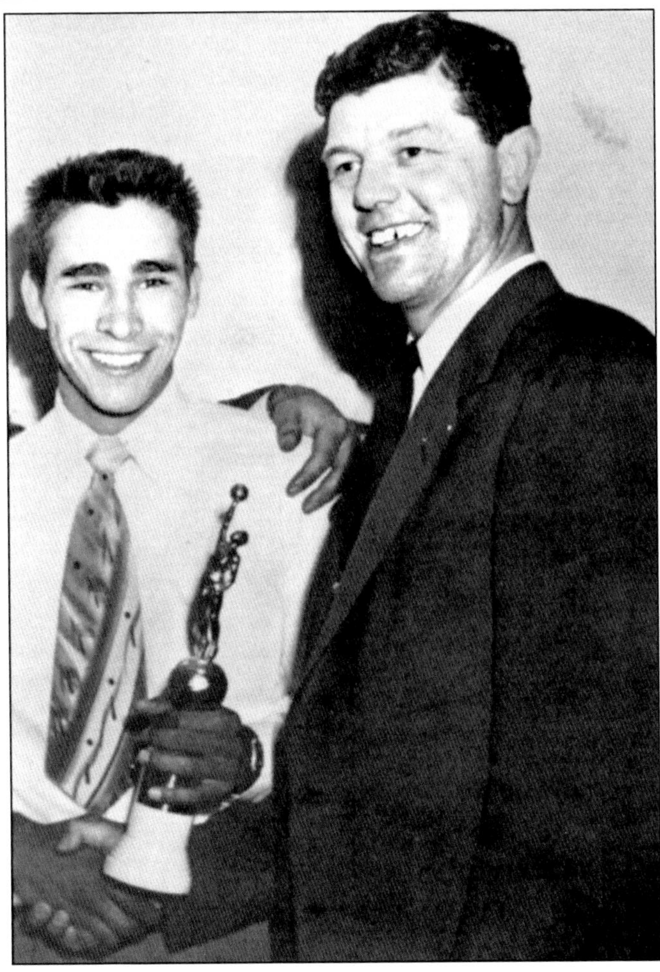

Elmer Garcia was one of the greatest athletes to come out of Ash Fork High School, where he starred in basketball, track, and baseball. After graduation, he was an outstanding basketball player for the Lumberjacks at Arizona State College at Flagstaff (NAU). Elmer is wearing number 51. At right, Joe Rolle presents Elmer with the Joseph Rolle Most Valuable Award for basketball for the 1950–1951 season at NAU. (Courtesy Elmer Garcia.)

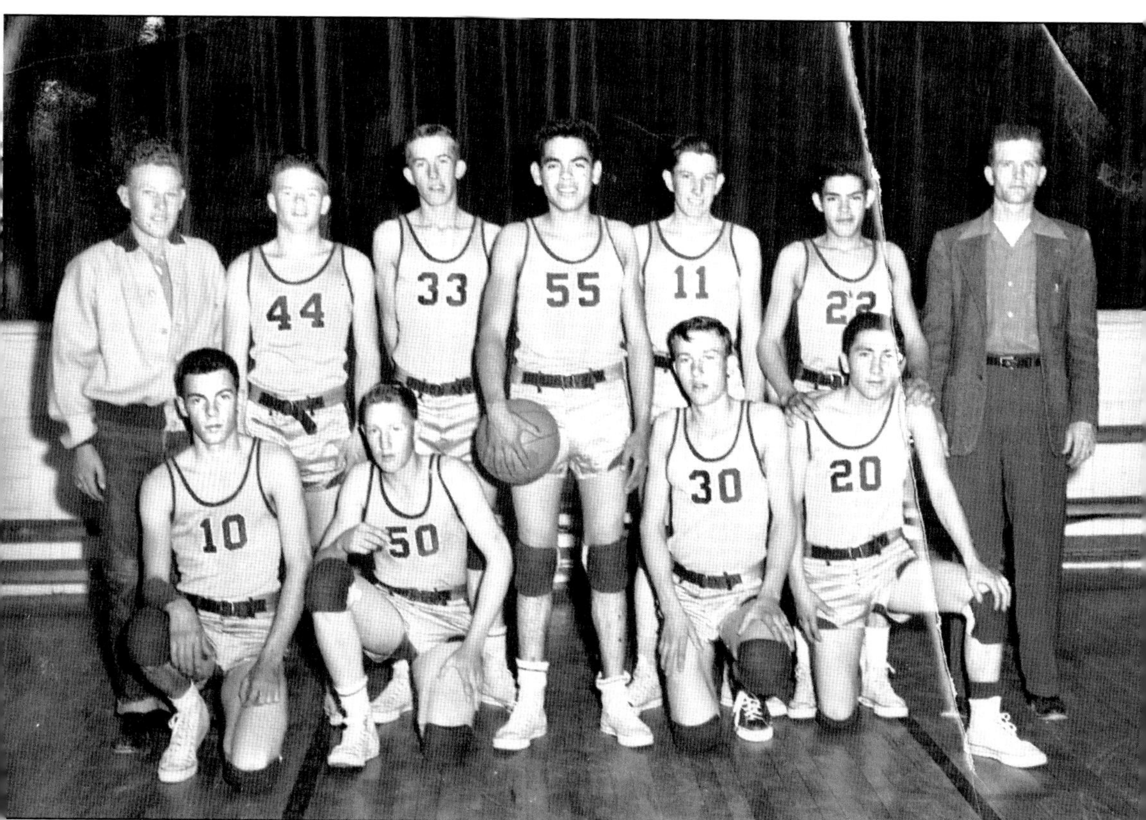

Ash Fork High School's 1950–1951 basketball team was one of the best in the town's history. The Spartans, led by Angel Cervantes, won the Consolation Championship in the Northern Arizona Class B Basketball Tournament at Flagstaff, defeating McNary 57-47. Angel scored 108 points, averaging 27 points a game, and was named the tournament's Most Valuable Player. From left to right are (first row) Clifford Thompson, Jerry Dunbar, Bill Storms, and San Juan Romero; (second row) manager John Reeves, Bob Hume, Les Storms, Angel Cervantes, Bob Schwanbeck, Jimmy Pena, and coach Ken Johnson. (Courtesy Robert Schwanbeck.)

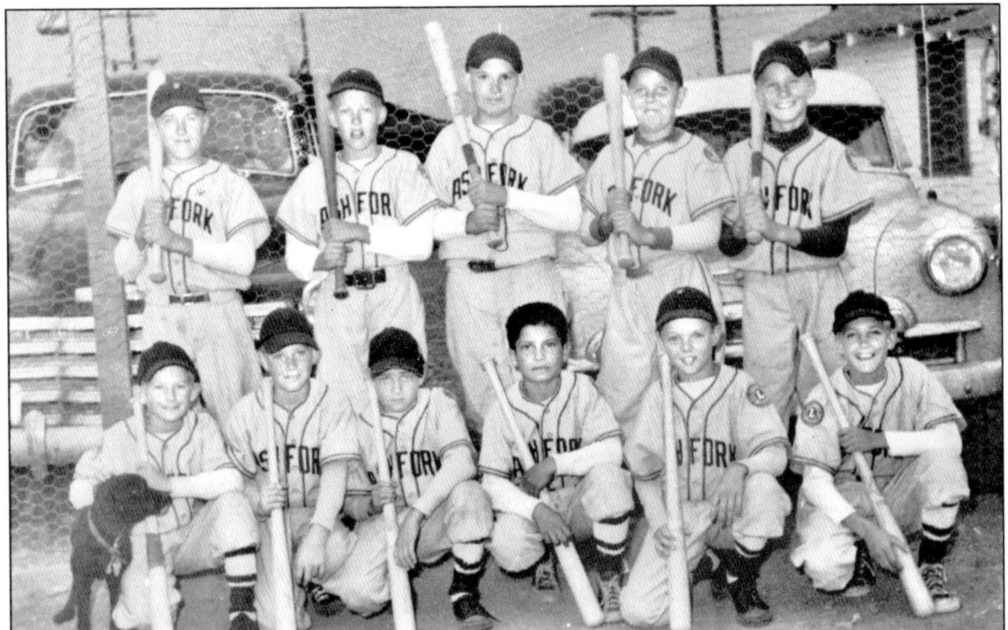

Ash Fork's first little league team, organized in 1951, competed against teams from Seligman and Williams, losing only one game all season. From left to right are (first row) Dan Trimble, Dick Griffith, David Wilbanks, Paul Bivins, Douglas Brown, and Ken Davis; (second row) Bob Starr, Ted Storms, Louis Schwanbeck, Charles Sharp, and Marshall Trimble. Dick Griffith later played for Arizona State University. Absent are Ray McCoy and Bill Herron.

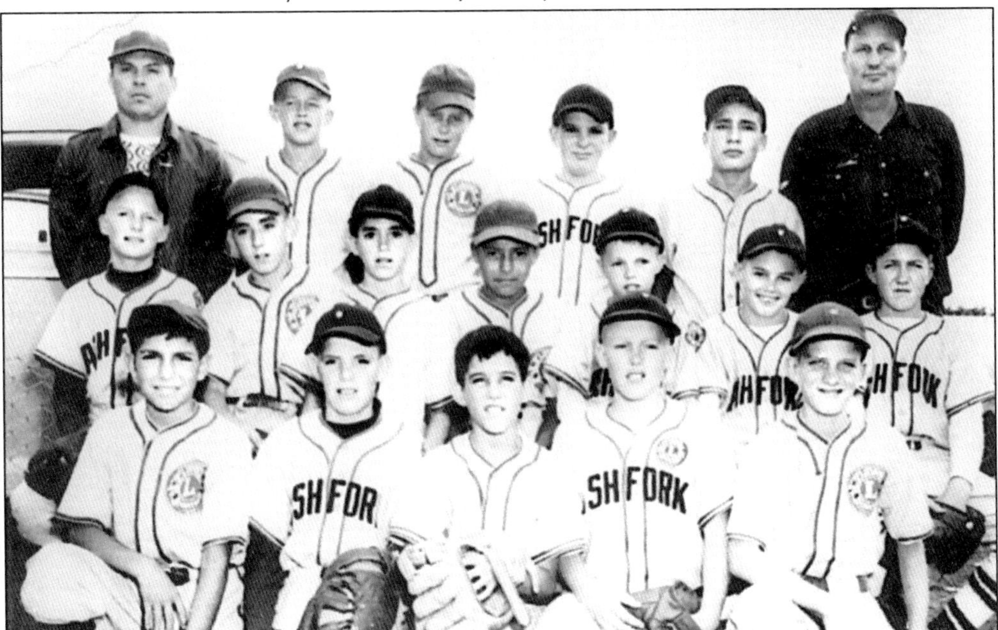

In 1951, Ash Fork, Seligman, and Williams formed an all-star team that was runner-up for the Arizona State Little League State Championship, losing to Prescott 2-0. Ash Fork players inlcluded Louis Schwanbeck, Marshall Trimble, Doug Brown, Bill Herron, Bob Starr, Ray McCoy, and Ted Storms. Herman Schwanbeck, top right, was one of the coaches.

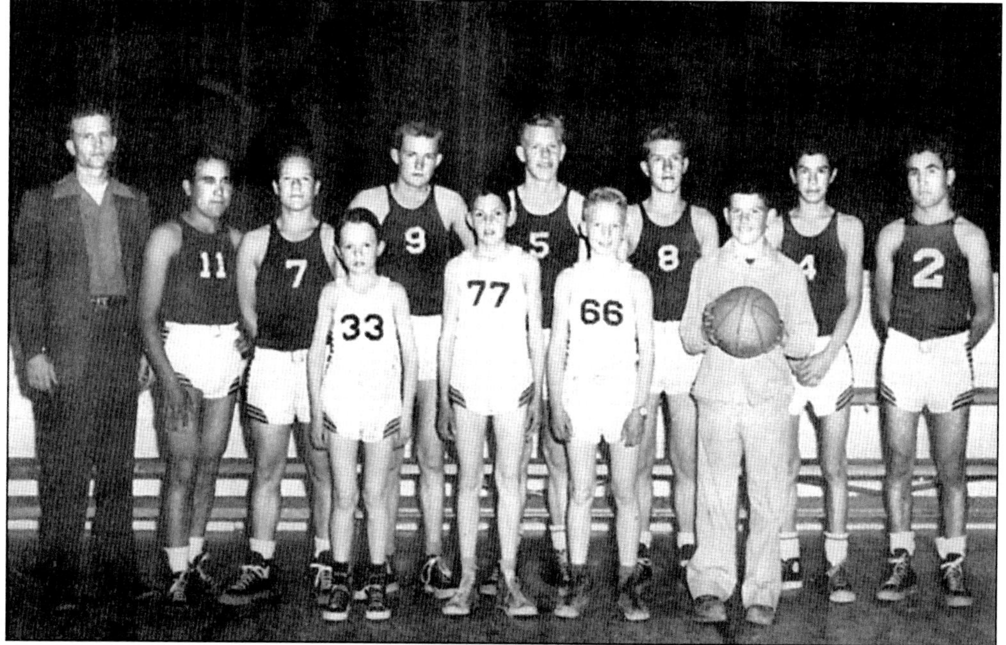

Ash Fork's seventh-, eighth-, and ninth-grade basketball team in 1951 is, from left to right, (first row) Doug Brown, Ray McCoy, Marshall Trimble, and Arlie Anderson; (second row) coach Kenneth Johnson, Vincent Martinez, Roger Williams, Mike Beach, Dan Beigel, Tim Storms, George Garcia, and Ramon Martinez.

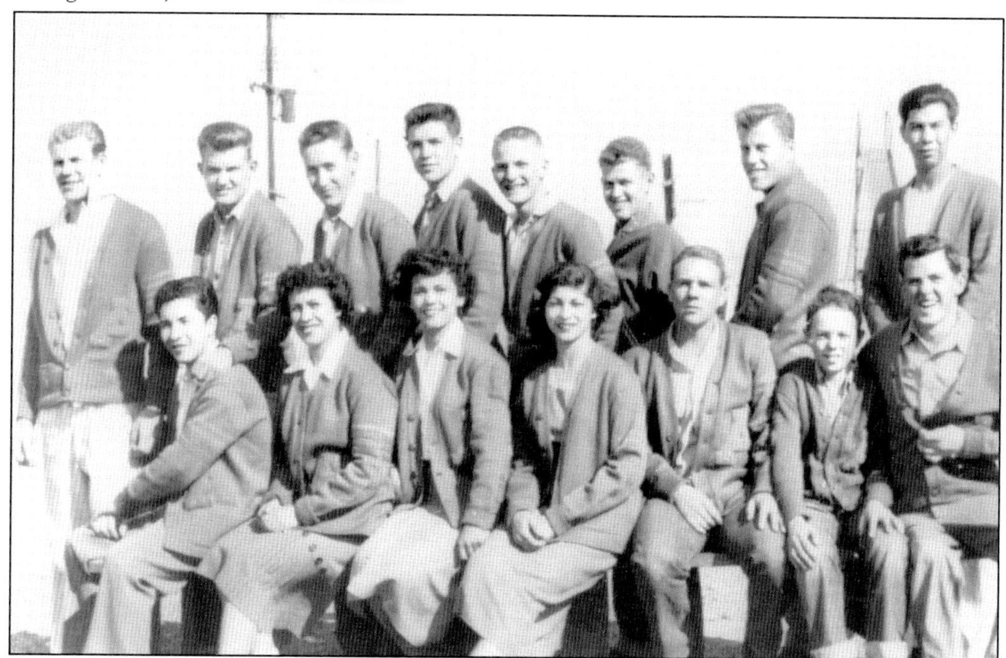

Here are some of the same boys in 1954 as members of the Ash Fork High School Lettermen Club. From left to right are (first row) Willie Sena, Virginia Cruz, Irene Mensi, Barbara Gorra, Roger Williams, Doug Brown, and Arlie Anderson; (second row) Dan Beigel, Mike Beach, Morris Terrell, Don Greer, Marshall Trimble, Eugene Scott, Chuck Rooks, and George Garcia.

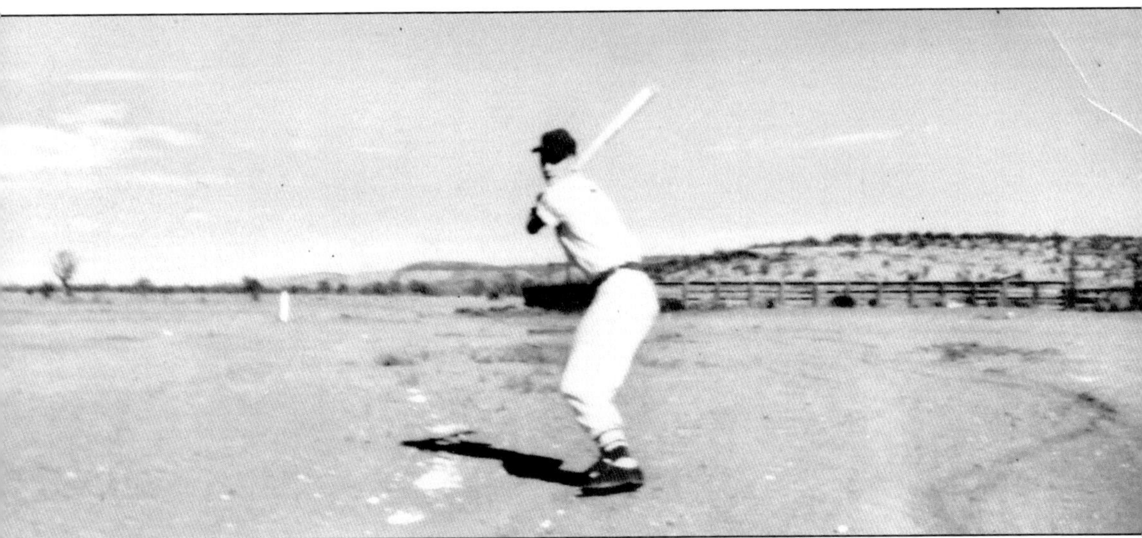

In 1954, Marshall Trimble, age 14, was catcher on the Ash Fork men's team. The high school baseball tournament ended on a Saturday, and the following day, some of the Spartan players changed uniforms to play for the men's team. The teams only played on Sundays, traveling up and down Route 66 from Kingman on the west to Holbrook on the east. The 1954 team played most of its games in the Prescott League. This photograph was taken at the local baseball field next to the stockyards on the north side of the railroad tracks. Russian thistle (tumbleweeds) materialized full-size in the outfield overnight, and ballplayers swore they could stand at their position and watch rocks emerge from the ground right before their eyes. The new baseball field, built in 2007, has a beautiful, smooth infield and artificial grass, a far cry from days of yore. Trimble had aspirations of playing professional baseball, but those plans were thwarted when a scout gave him a tryout and then said solemnly, "Son, there's only one thing keeping you from being a good baseball player and that's your ability."

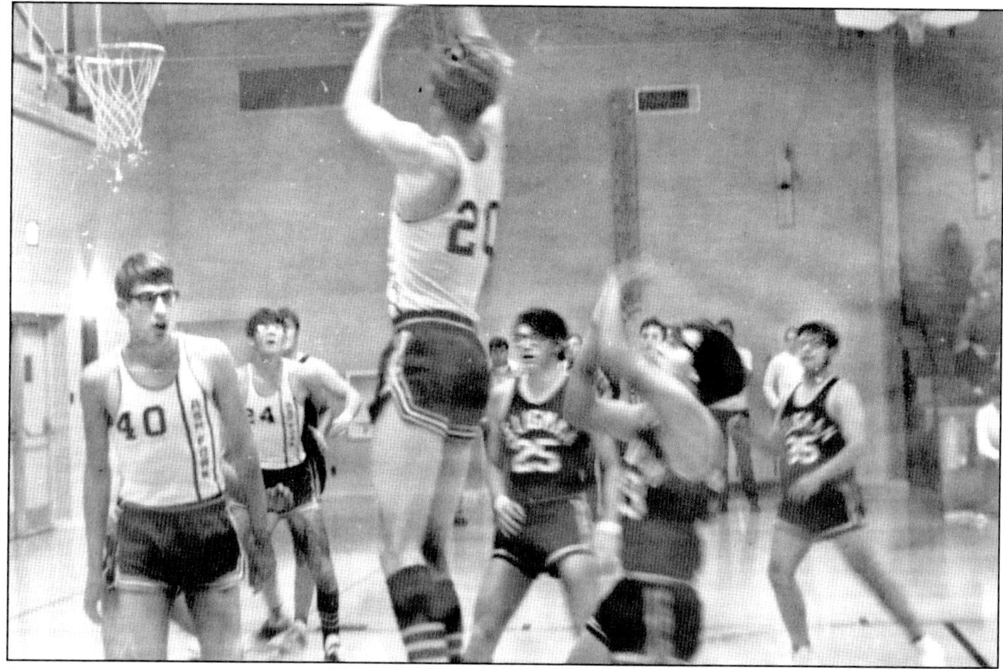

The 1972 Spartans defeated archrival Seligman; Rick Murphy pops a jump shot as Greg Emery (No. 40) and Roy Hume (No. 24) block. (Courtesy Hume collection.)

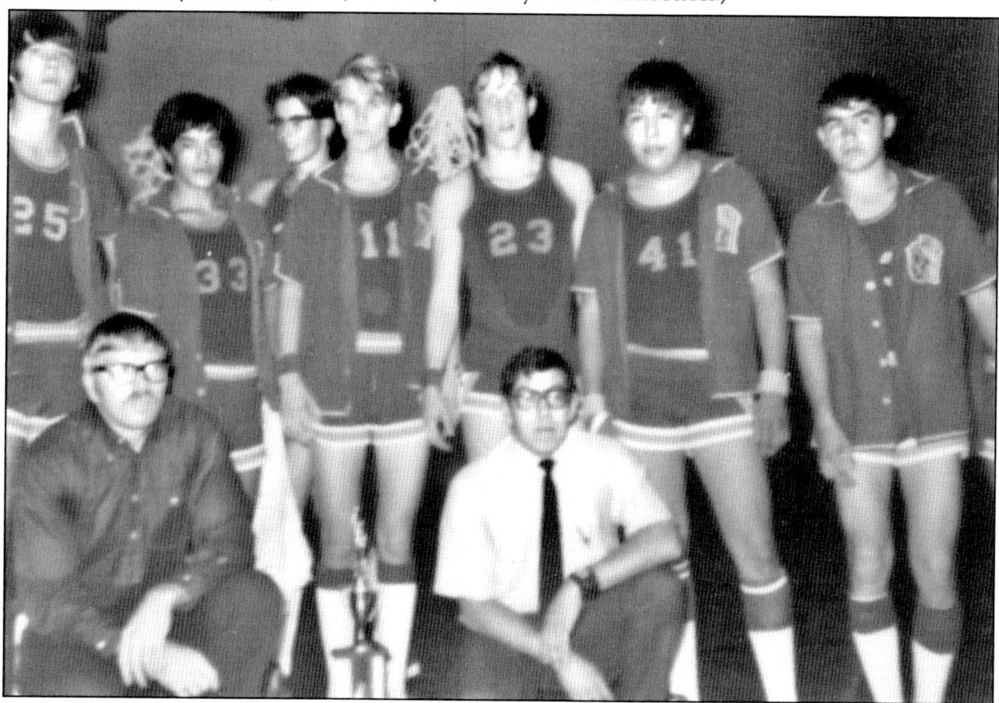

Sometimes the Spartans had to settle for second. In 1972, they lost to McNary in the championship game. From left to right are Roy Hume, David Reyes, Greg Emery, Jerry Martin, Rick Murphy, Alfred Acosta, and George Garcia Jr. The coaches are Tom Matthews and Paul Rodriquez. (Courtesy Hume collection.)

Fred Fernow was born in Ash Fork in 1932. As a youngster, he shined shoes at the Harvey House and delivered ice at the local house of prostitution. He starred in baseball and basketball before graduating from high school and served in the navy during the Korean War. After the war, he came home and owned businesses in the town until 1994. (Courtesy Fred Fernow.)

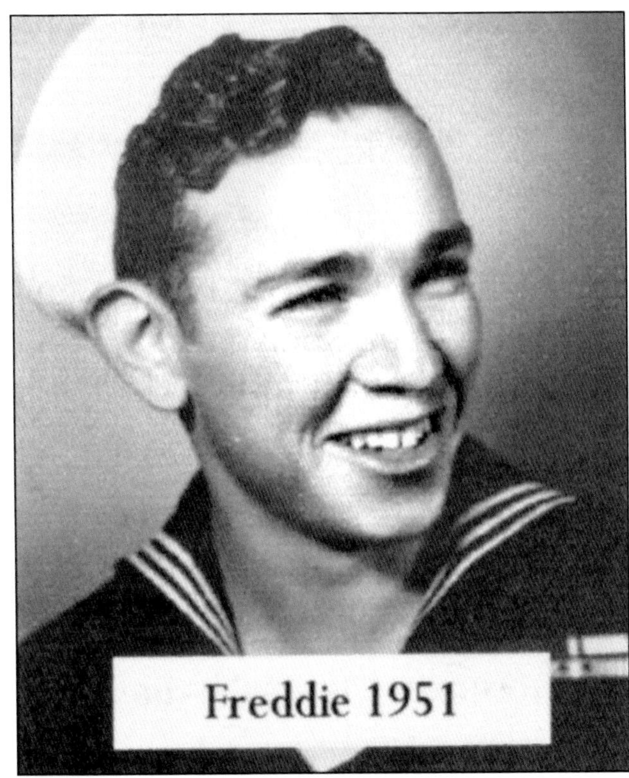

Frank (left) and Nora Gum owned the popular Gummies Buffet. Pictured here in 1955 with bartender Tommie Rose, Frank was known for his community involvement and business acumen. He often entertained his customers with jokes and magic tricks. (Courtesy Terry Cauthen.)

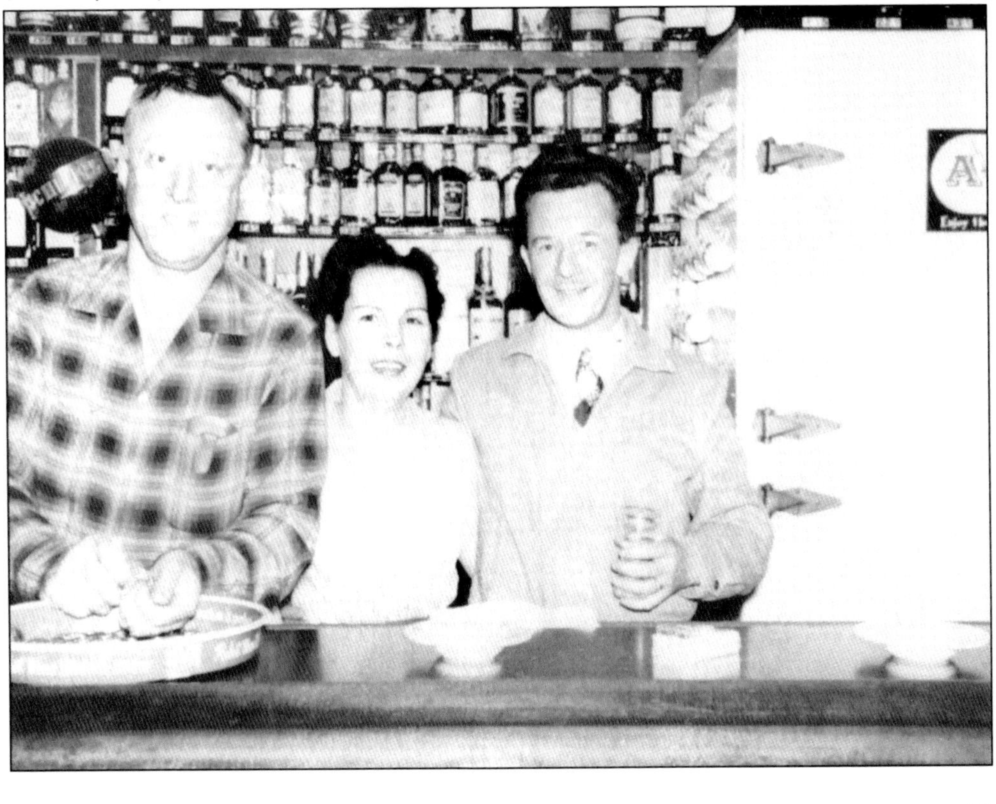

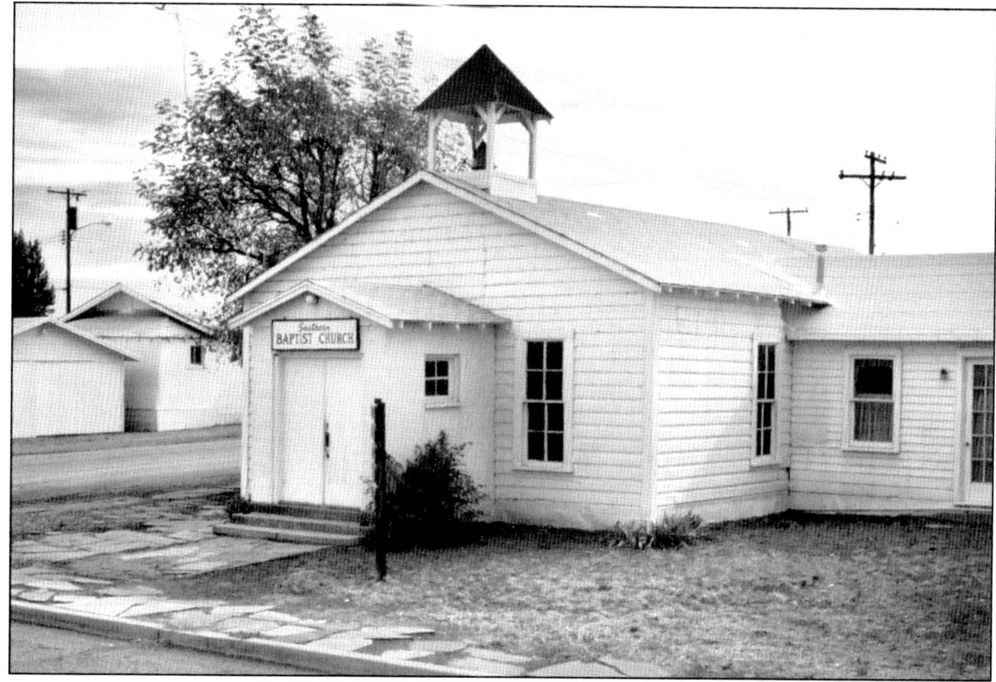

The First Southern Baptist Church has been sitting on the southwest corner of Lewis and First Street for almost 60 years. During the early 1950s, today's Grand Canyon University was located at the Arizona National Guard Armory in Prescott. Each Sunday, students from the college would take turns driving up to Ash Fork to deliver a sermon.

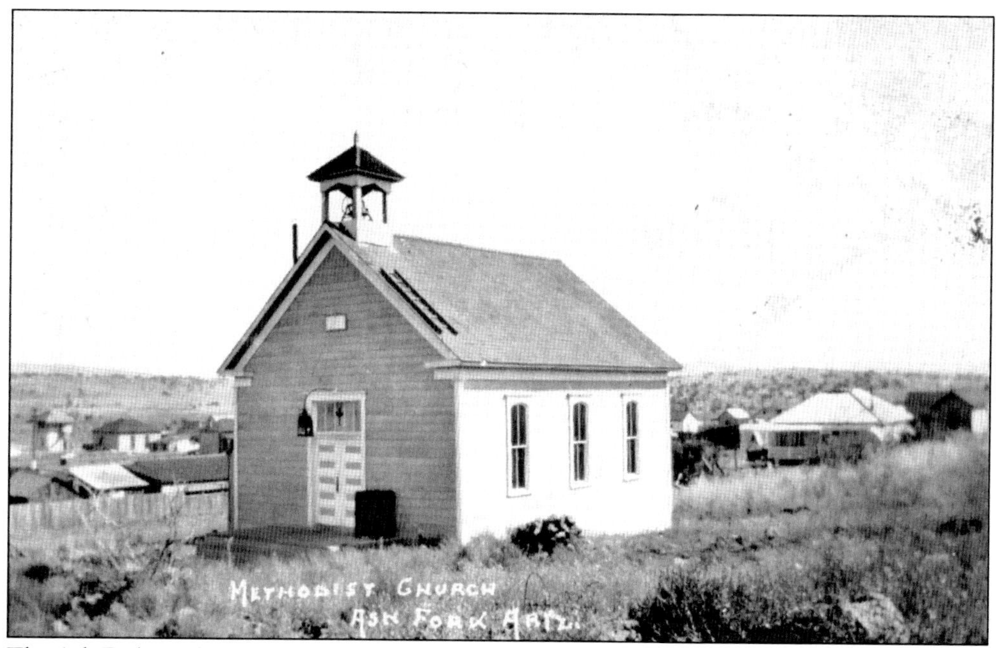

The Ash Fork Methodist Church, the "church on wheels," was originally located on the east side of Third Street between Lewis and Park Avenue. From there it was moved west of the Arizona Hotel facing Lewis Avenue, where the fire hall is today.

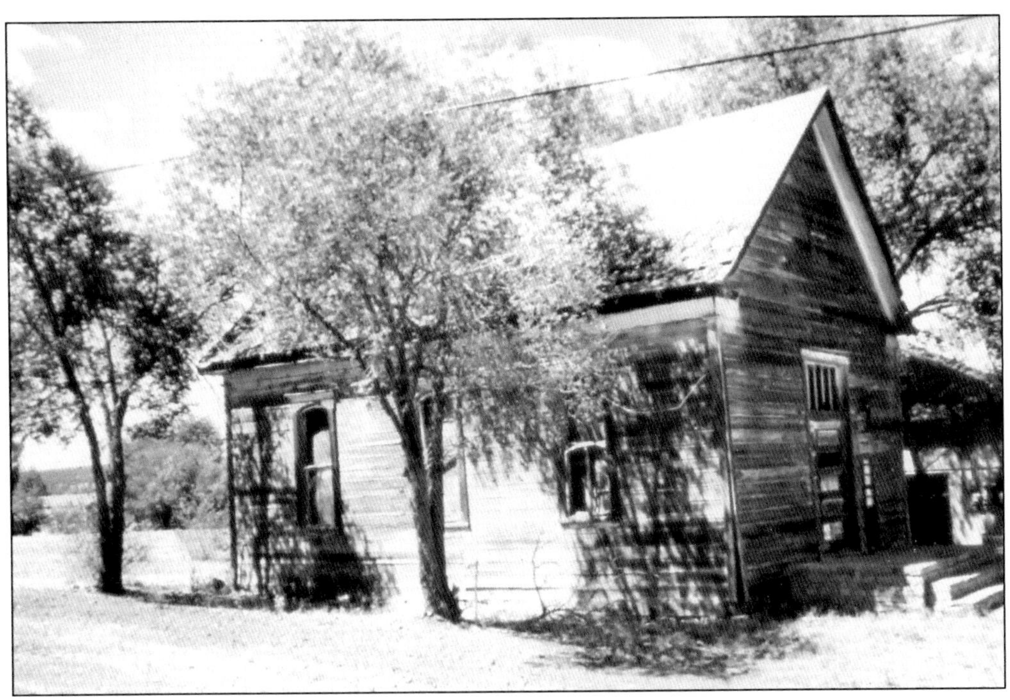

Today the church sits on its final resting place south of the old fire house and sheriff's office. In 1984, there was a fire, and although the damage was not severe, the steeple collapsed. The hole was later repaired, but the familiar steeple and church bell were gone forever. An old adage about the immorality of rough-and-tumble Western communities said a "town had everything except a church and a jail." Ash Fork's citizens placed a church adjacent to a jail as if to keep visitors and journalists from drawing such a conclusion.

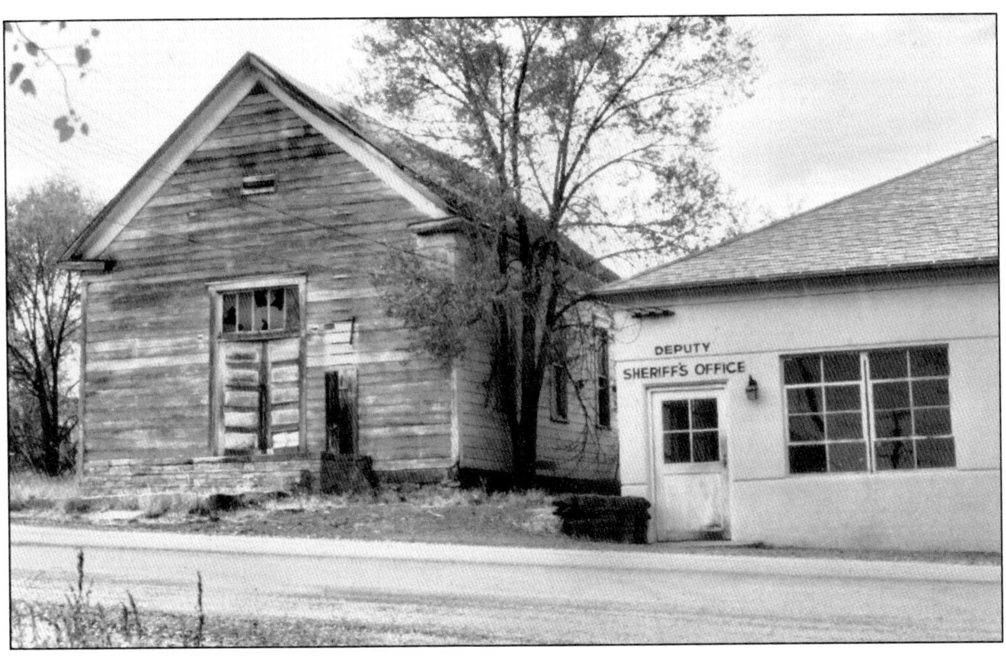

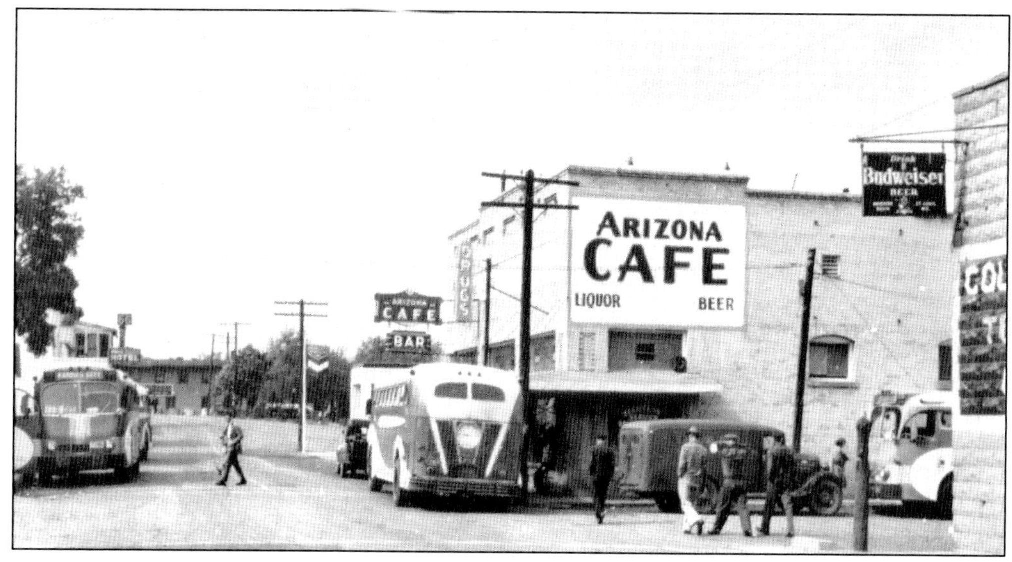

Today the Methodists congregate on the northwest corner of Fourth Street and Lewis Avenue in one of the few original buildings from the town's heyday. During the mid-1920s, it was Winchester "Chet" Dickerson's Northern Arizona Commercial Company. The store was one-stop shopping at its best. One could purchase dry goods, fresh meat, auto parts, fabrics, and produce. A post office was located at the rear of the store. In 1935, it opened as the Arizona Café, owned by Joe Gang. It was well known for the large murals on the walls depicting Arizona scenery. On the east side was the Arizona Bar. A conscientious parishioner took some white paint and attempted to cover up "Bar" on the outside wall.

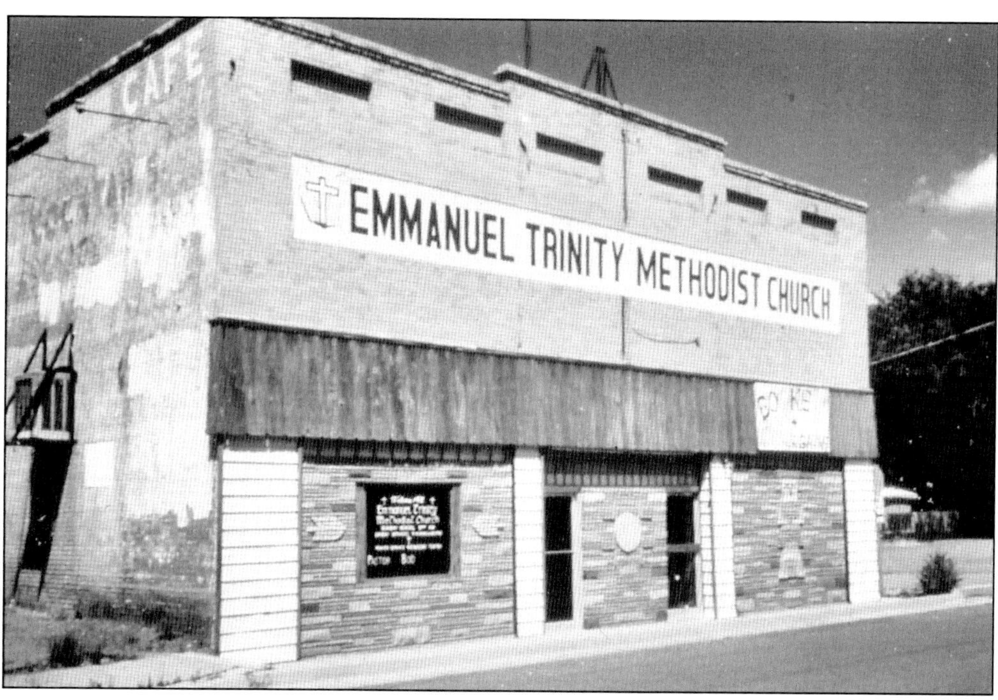

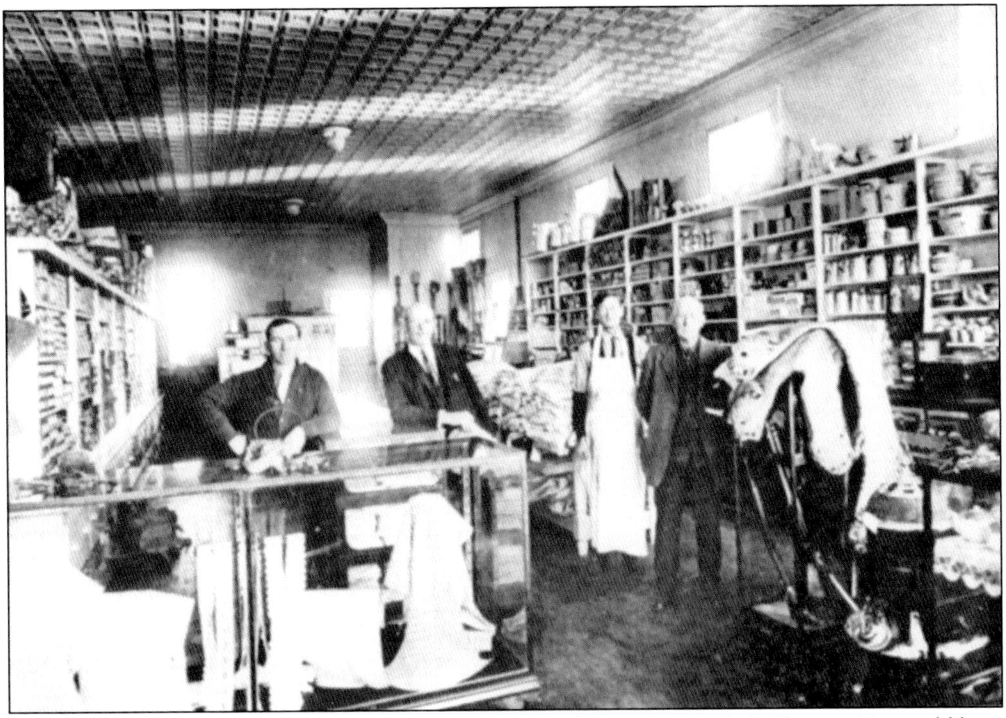

Dickerson's general store is seen here in the 1920s. Behind the counter is Jack Slamon. He would later own his own variety store, where he also presided as justice of the peace for the community.

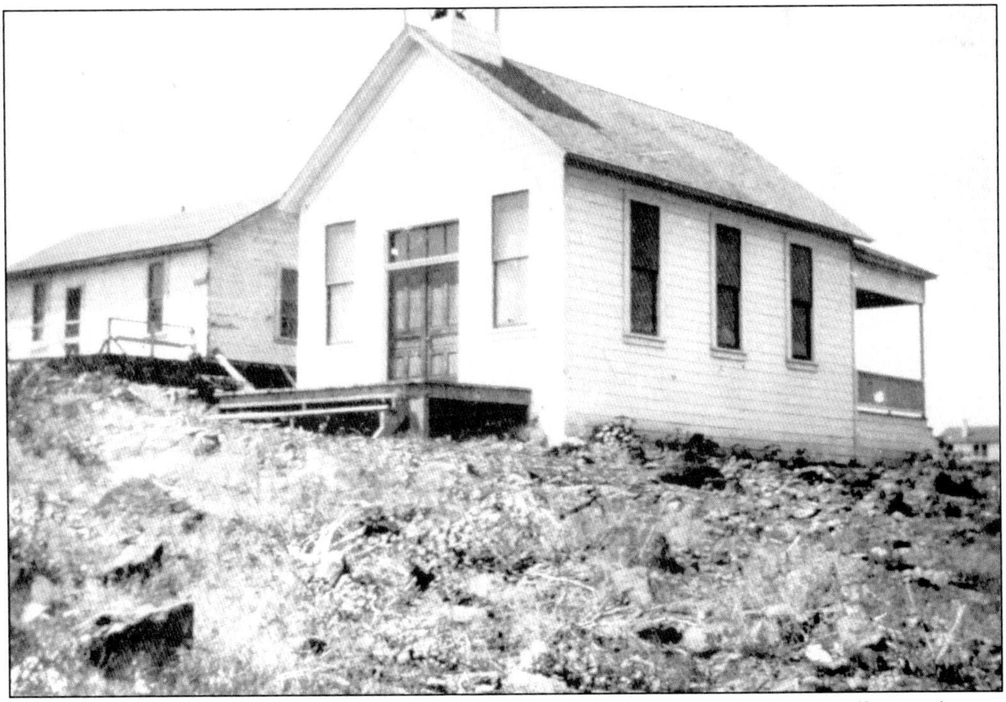

St. Ann's, built in 1905, was the Catholic parish for 50 years. (Courtesy Hume collection.)

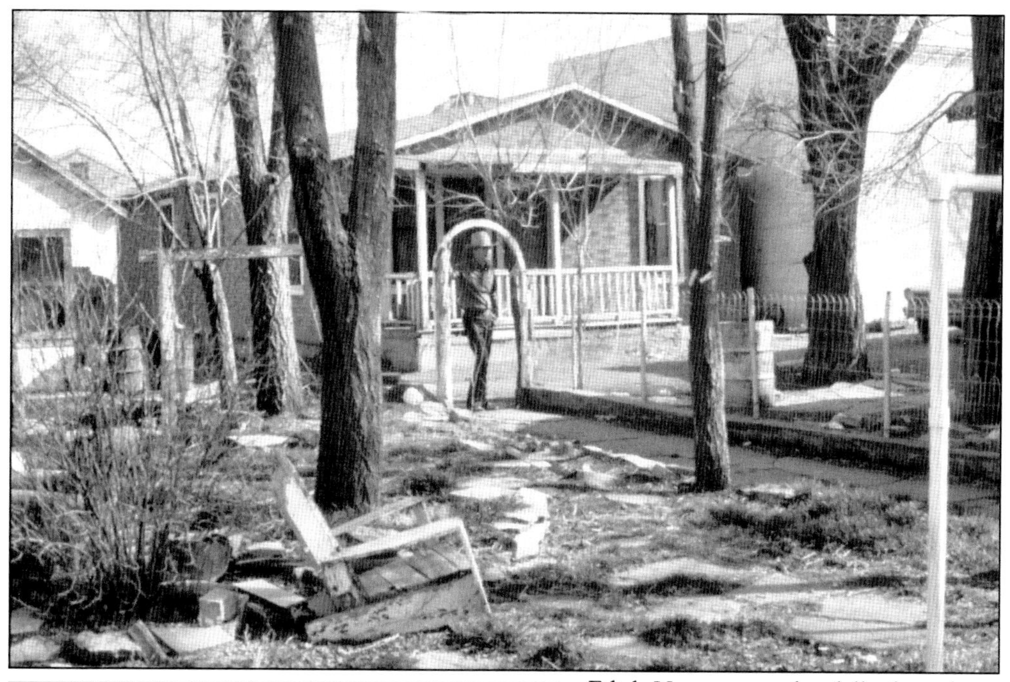

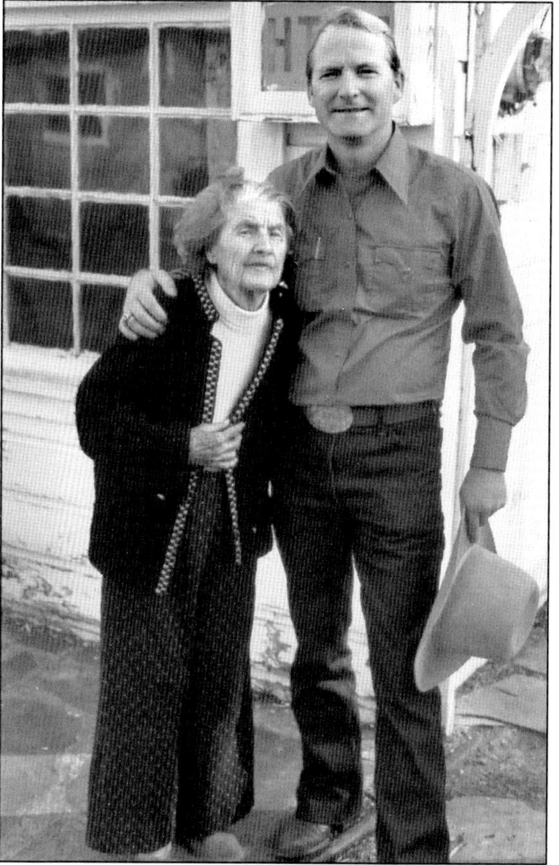

Edith Hauser ran a bordello down by the railroad tracks. During World War II, business boomed, with the troop trains stopping regularly in Ash Fork to let the soldiers stretch their legs. She was well known for her generosity. On more than one occasion, she paid a poor youngster's tuition to attend the college at Flagstaff. The author delivered newspapers to her establishment in the early 1950s and 40 years later stopped to pay his respects to an old friend.

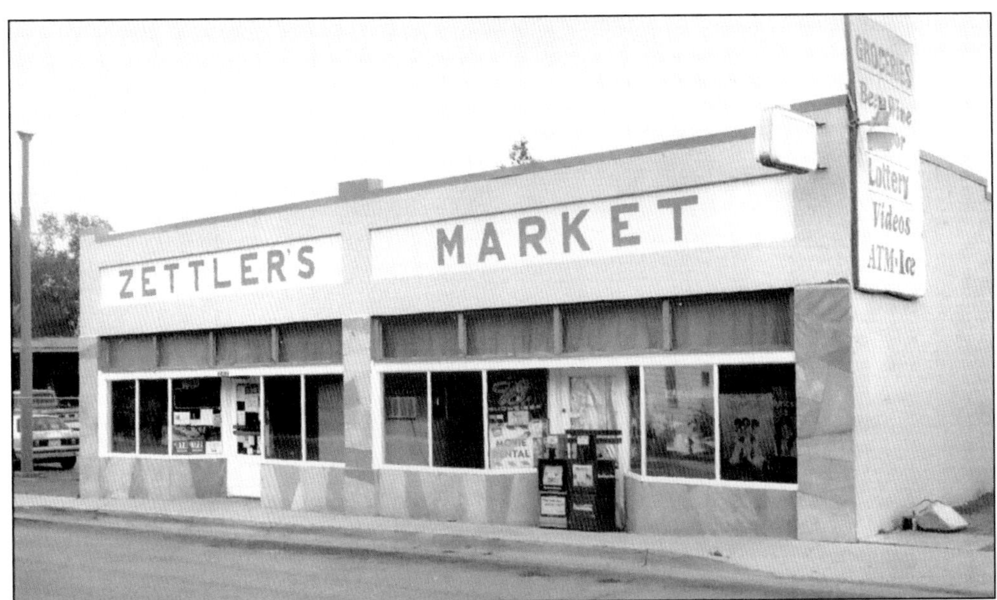

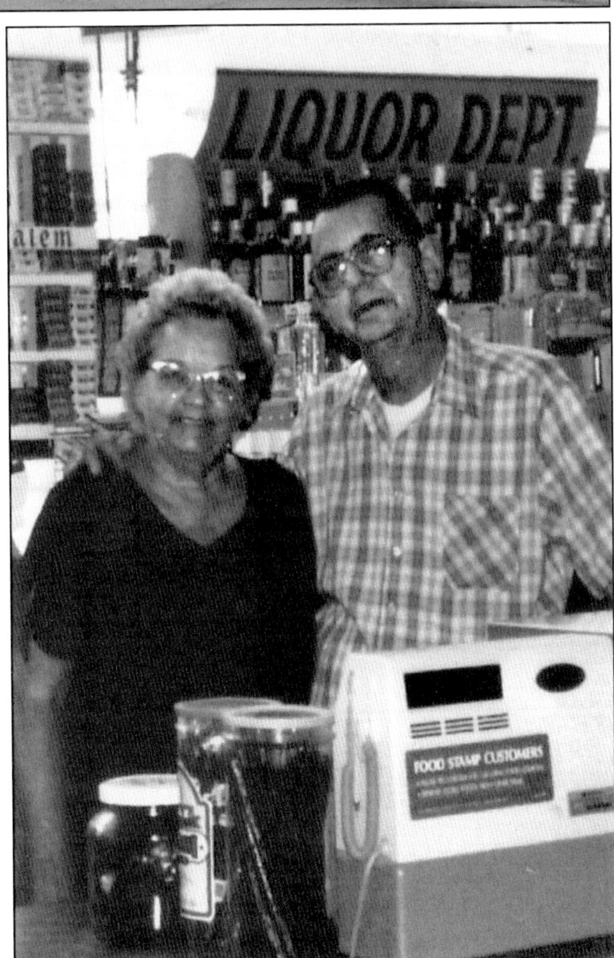

Zettler's Market is one of the oldest surviving businesses in Ash Fork. Homer and Marie Zettler and their family arrived in 1930 and opened a bakery. A difficult family situation required Vernon, their oldest son, to quit school and go to work to help support the family. In October 1941, Vern married Marge Halverson. Just three months later Pearl Harbor was attacked, and America was at war. Vern went off to war, and when he came home he and Marge bought the family bakery and turned it into Zettler's Market. While others businesses closed or moved closer to the freeway, Zettler's managed to survive the hard times. For a while, Zettler's Market was the only store in town. When Vern and Marge retired in 1983, they sold the business; however, the new owners kept the Zettler's Market name. (Courtesy Monica James.)

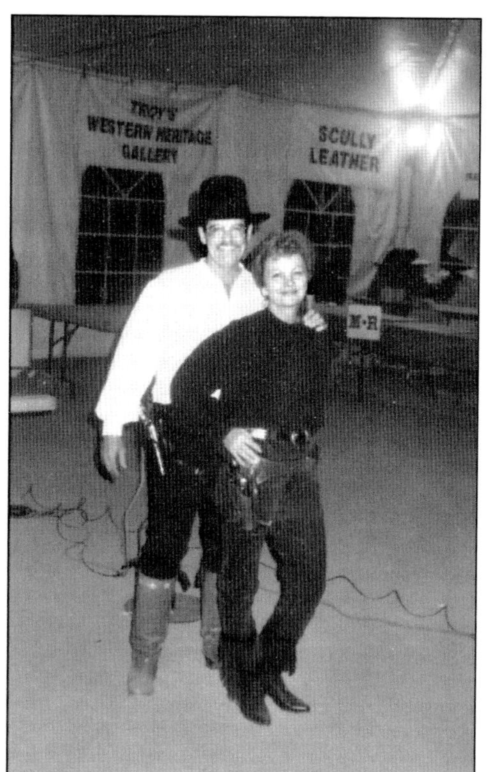

Bob James and Monica Zettler grew up in Ash Fork, married, and took up careers as professional fast-draw shooters. Members of the World's Fast Draw Association, between them they hold championship titles in Arizona, Canada, California, and Colorado, as well as the Worlds and Internationals. Today Bob is recognized as one of the nation's top authorities on Colt single-action revolvers. (Courtesy Bob and Monica James.)

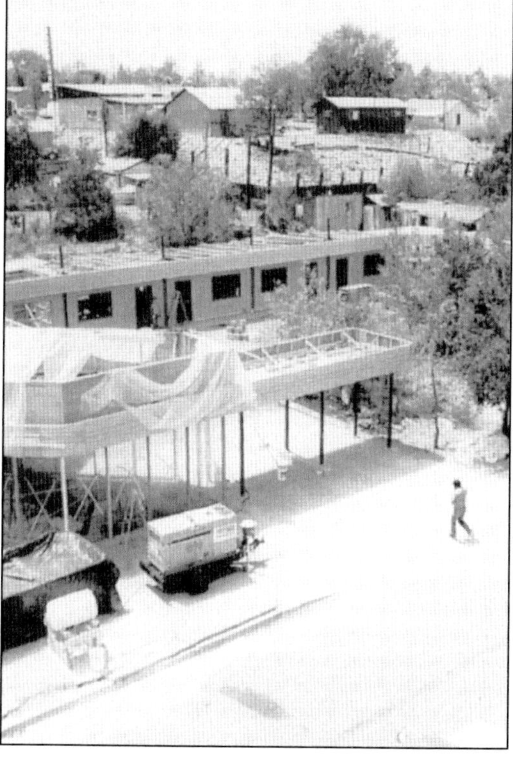

In 1991, Ash Fork attracted the attention of a Hollywood studio. A movie-set motel—some say the nicest motel for miles around—was erected on the site of the old business district to film *Universal Soldier*, starring Jean-Claude Van Damme. As soon as the set was completed, the town's nicest motel was blown to smithereens in an action scene. (Courtesy Hume collection.)

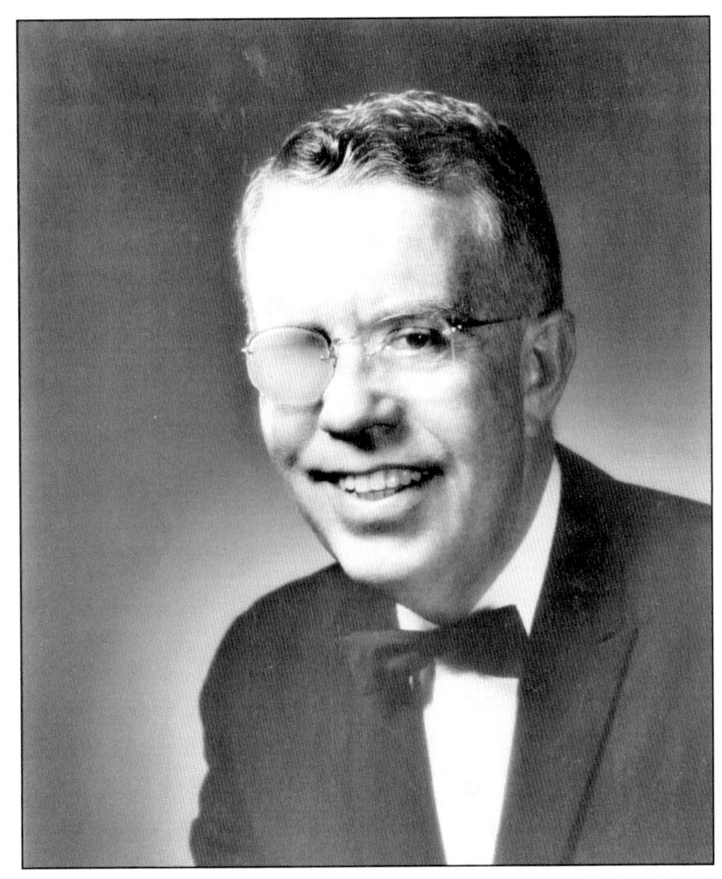

As a child, radio personality, Phoenix mayor, and governor of Arizona Jack Williams called Ash Fork home. The governor's father was employed by the Santa Fe in Ash Fork. His unabashed love for Arizona was well known, but he was not a native. To his everlasting disappointment, when his mother was about to give birth, she was taken by rail to the Santa Fe hospital in Los Angeles, thus depriving Jack of native-Arizona status. He once told the author, "Marshall, I might have been born in California, but I was conceived in Ash Fork!" Below, a 1982 Barry Goldwater campaign poster graces a telephone pole near an abandoned home on Park Avenue.

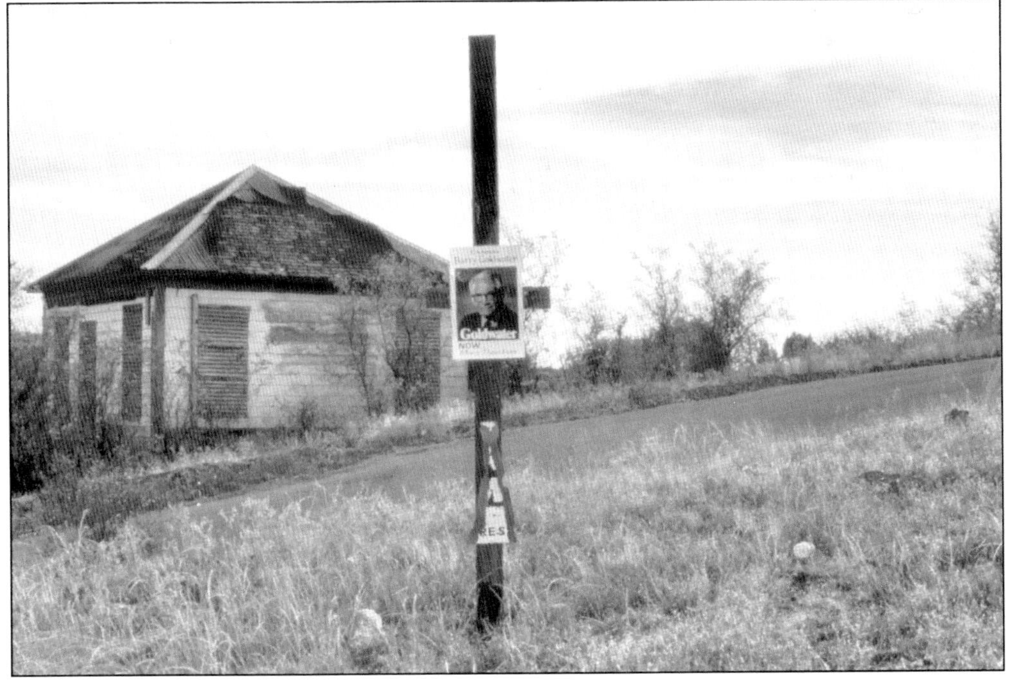

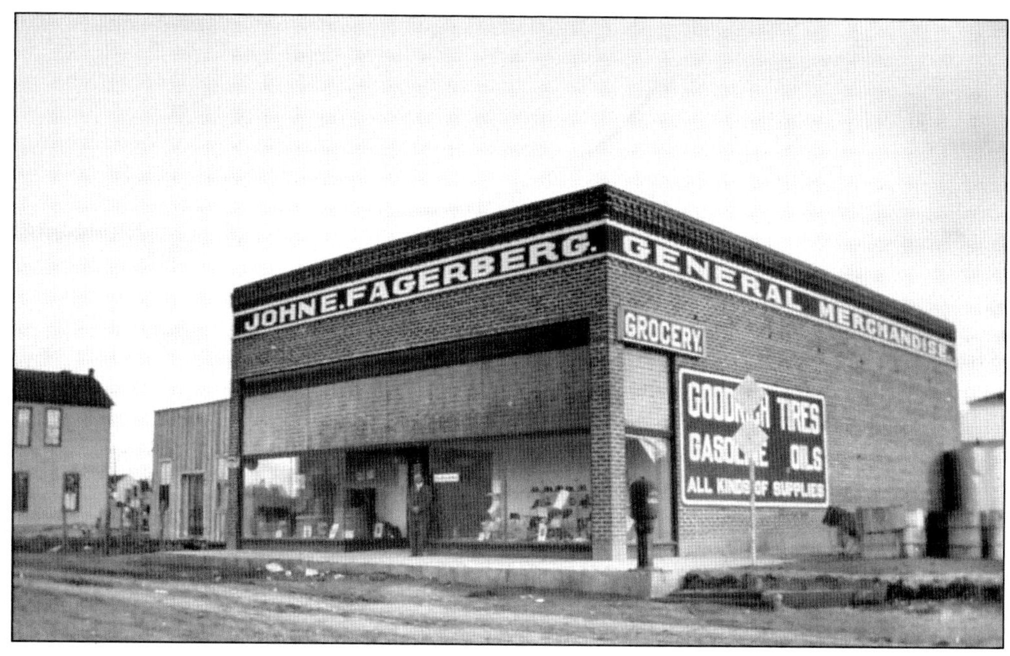

For many years, the big red brick building on Fourth Street and Lewis Avenue was Ash Fork's "Wal-Mart." It changed names several times over the years, but to most locals, it was simply "the Big Store." During the 1970s—when hard times came—like most of the other businesses, it was closed and boarded up.

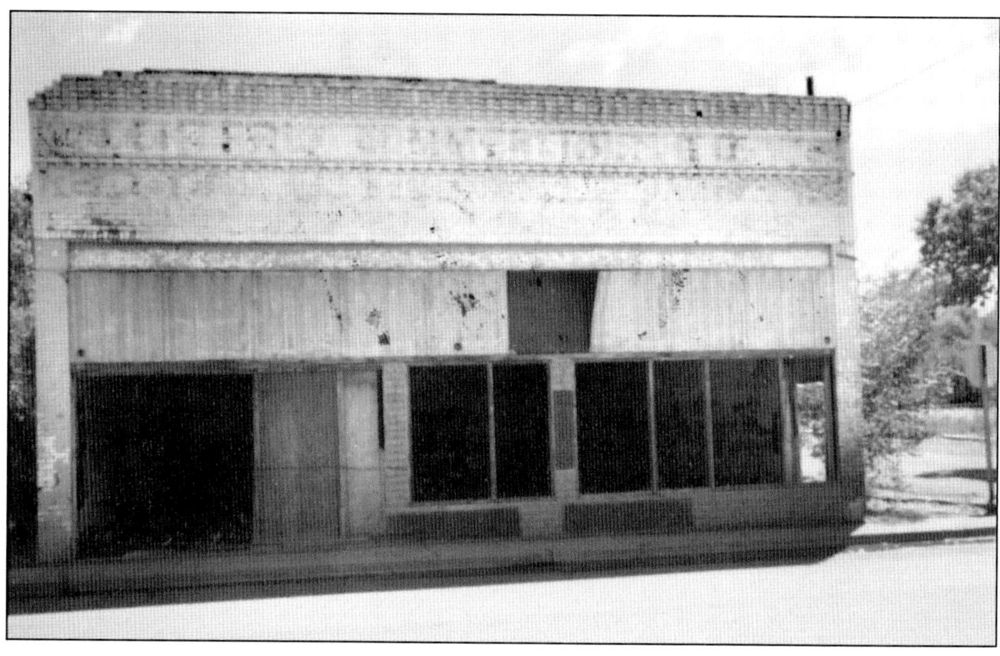

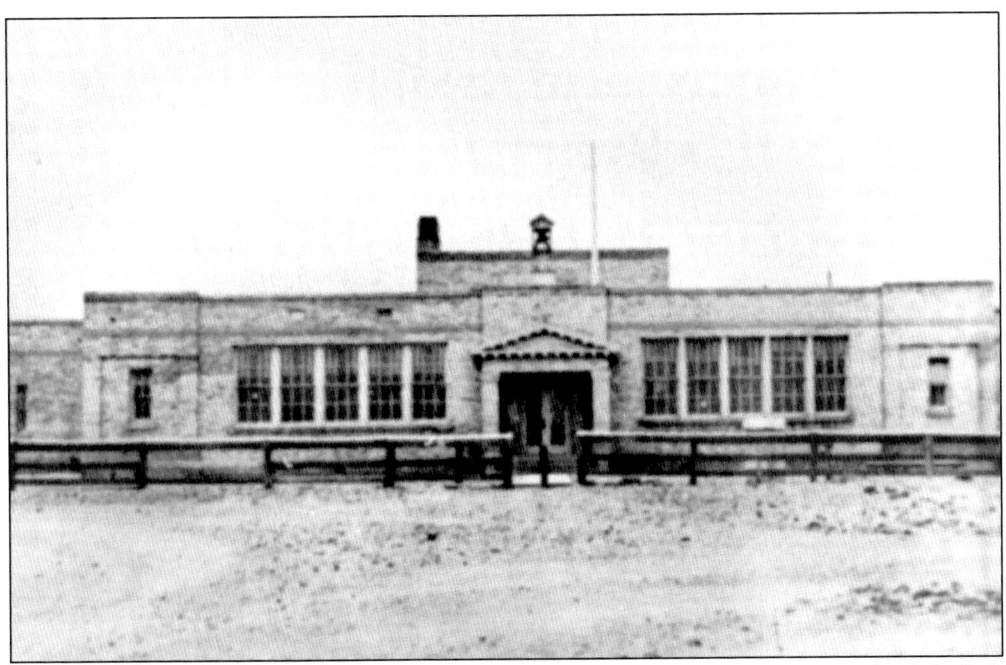

The photograph above is the old school that had so many wonderful memories for Ash Fork youngsters from the late 1920s to the late 1950s. High school classes met on the right of the entrance, and elementary classes met on the left side. In the center was a library and study hall. When the prospects loomed bright for a new cement plant to be located in Ash Fork for the building of Glen Canyon Dam, a new school was built for the anticipated increase in the number of students. The new high school opened in 1959. Unfortunately the new cement plant located in Clarkdale instead. During the 1990s, the old school was demolished, and another important piece of Ash Fork history was lost. (Courtesy Hume collection.)

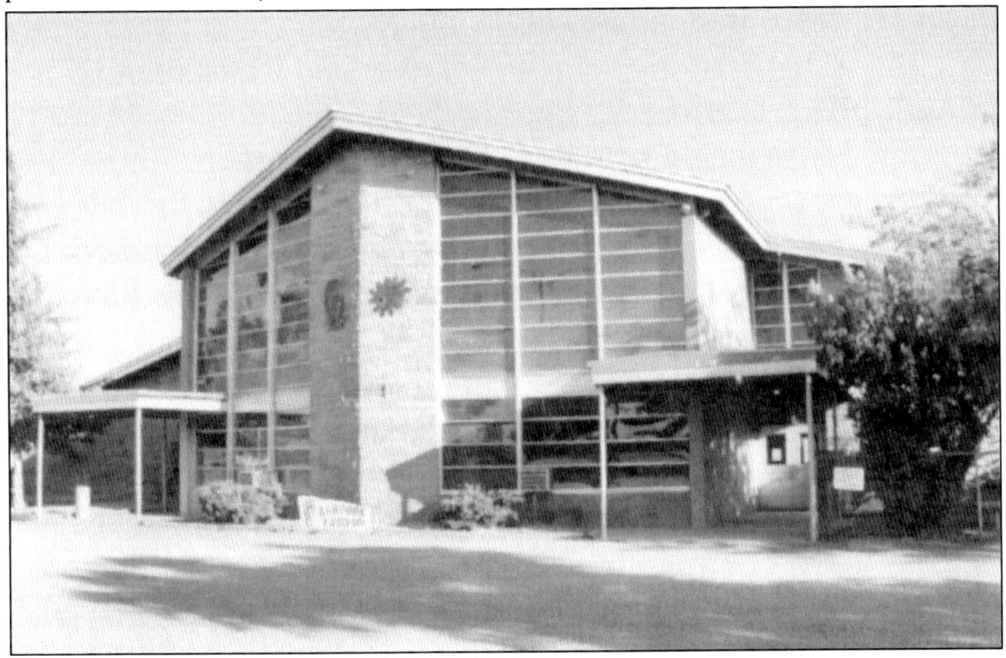

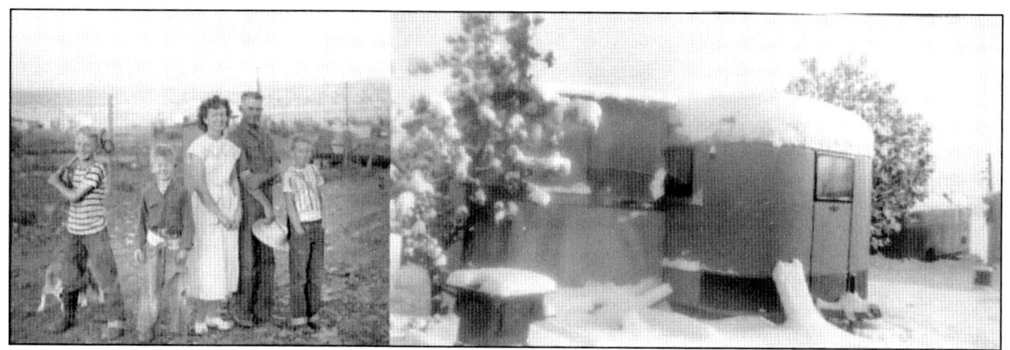

The only time the Trimble family got together for a family portrait was in 1948. From left to right are Marshall, Danny, Juanita, Ira "Happy," and Charlie. The Trimbles lived in a small trailer with no running water or plumbing. "We were so poor we had to steal trash from our neighbors so we'd have something to put out on garbage collection day."

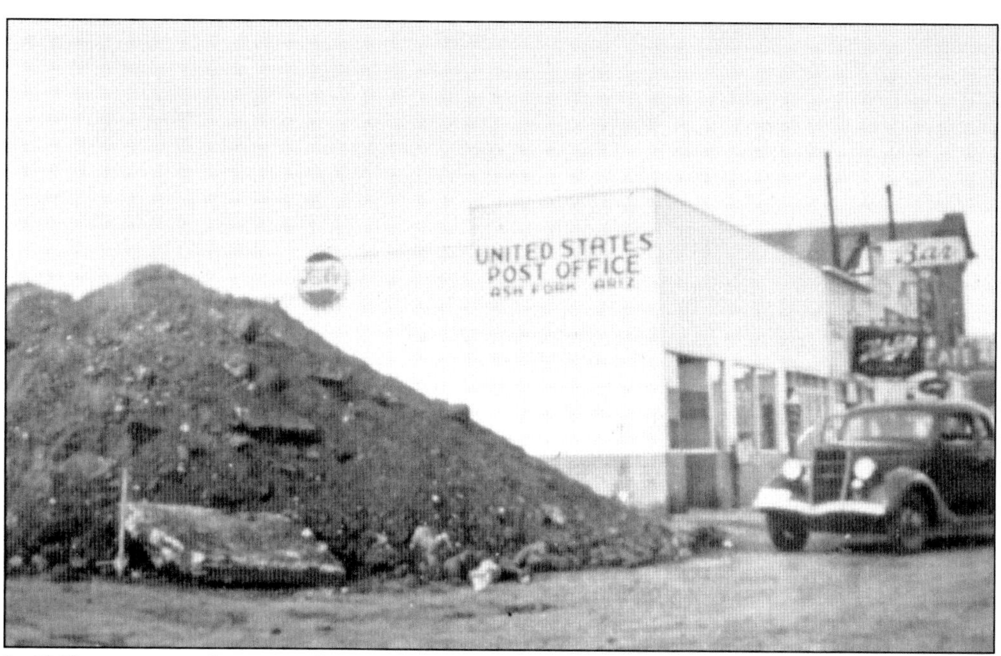

In 1948, excavation began on the new movie theater east of the post office. The Yavapai Theater opened a year later. Admission was 14¢ for children under 12 and 55¢ for adults. Movies were shown four nights a week.

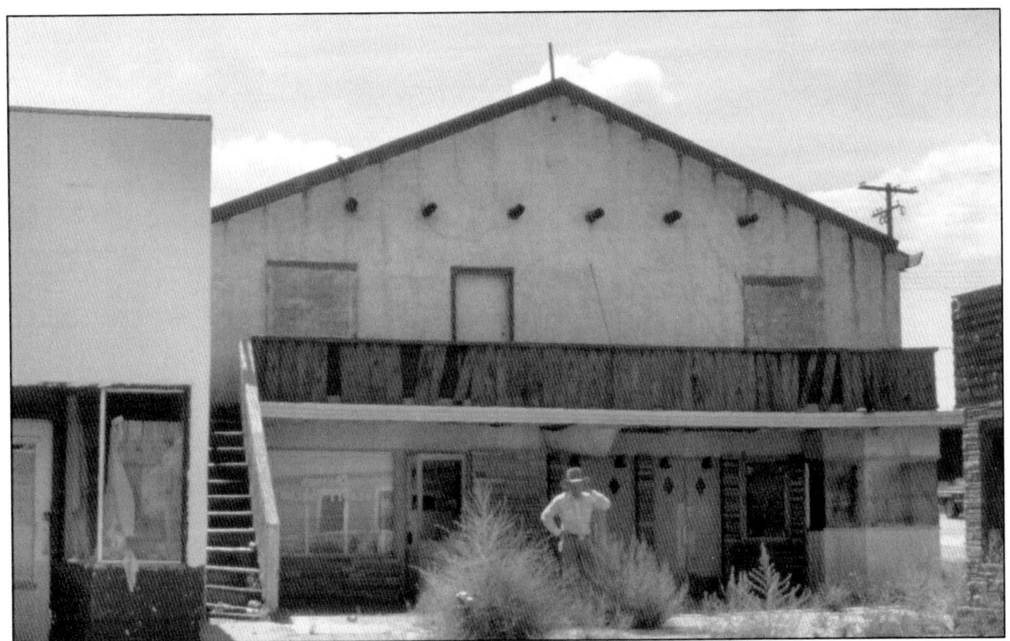

The author attended opening night in 1949 at the Yavapai Theater for its premier picture, *The Big Steal*, starring Robert Mitchum. Like a scene out of Larry McMurtry's *The Last Picture Show*, the Yavapai Theater closed its doors in 1960 as the town went into decline.

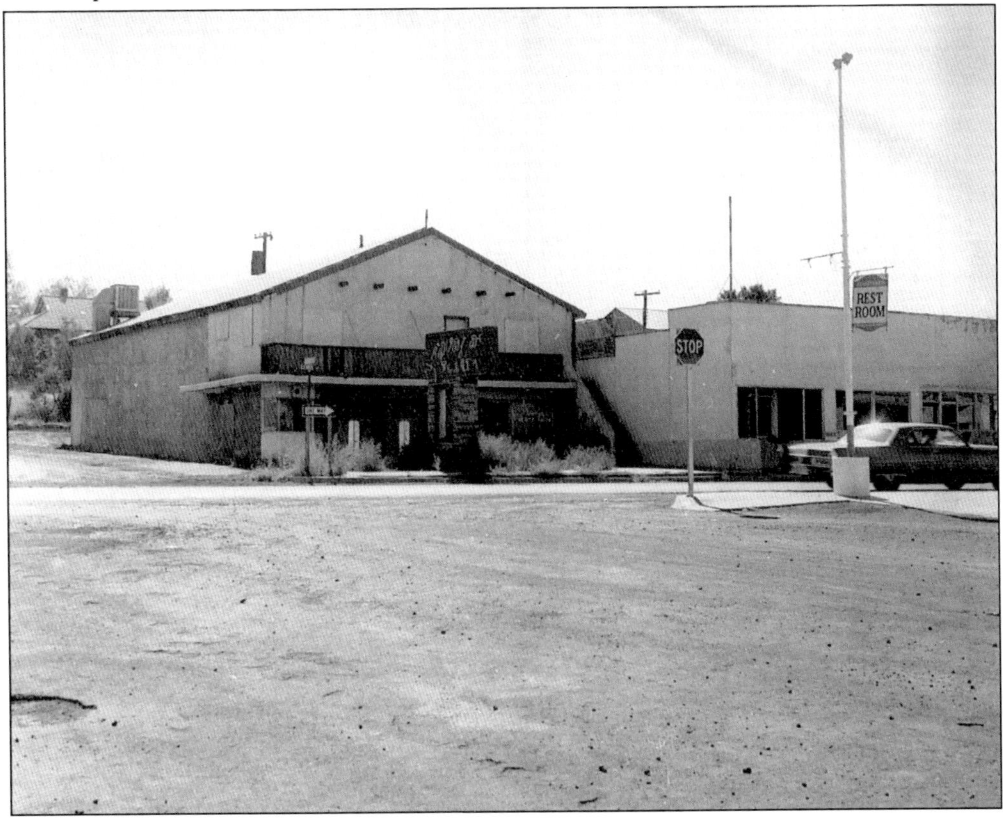

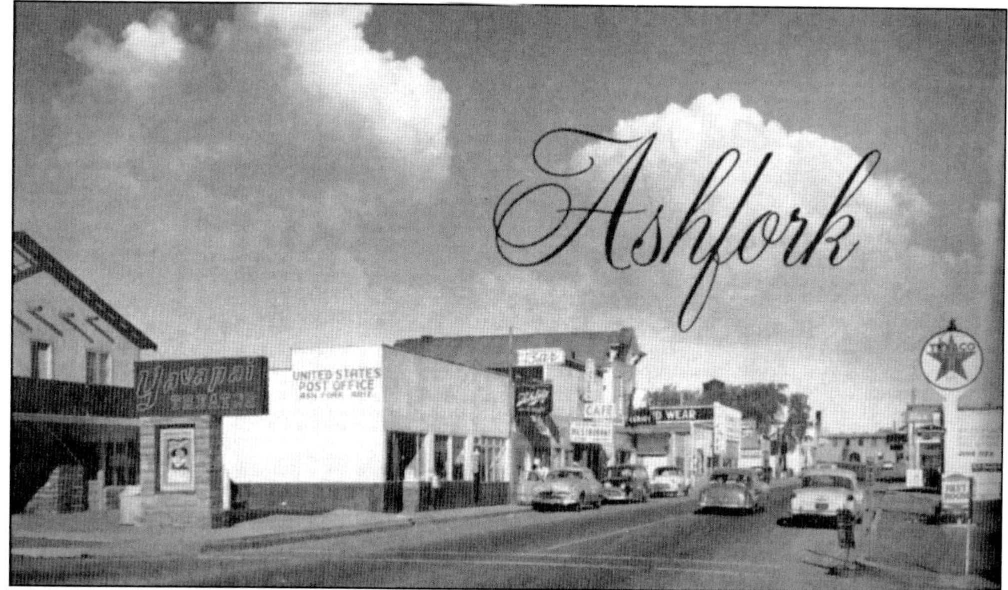

This photograph appeared in a 1956 issue of *Arizona Highways Magazine*. On the left is the Yavapai Theater. It burned, along with most of the rest of the business district, in the big fire of November 20, 1977. (Courtesy Hume collection.)

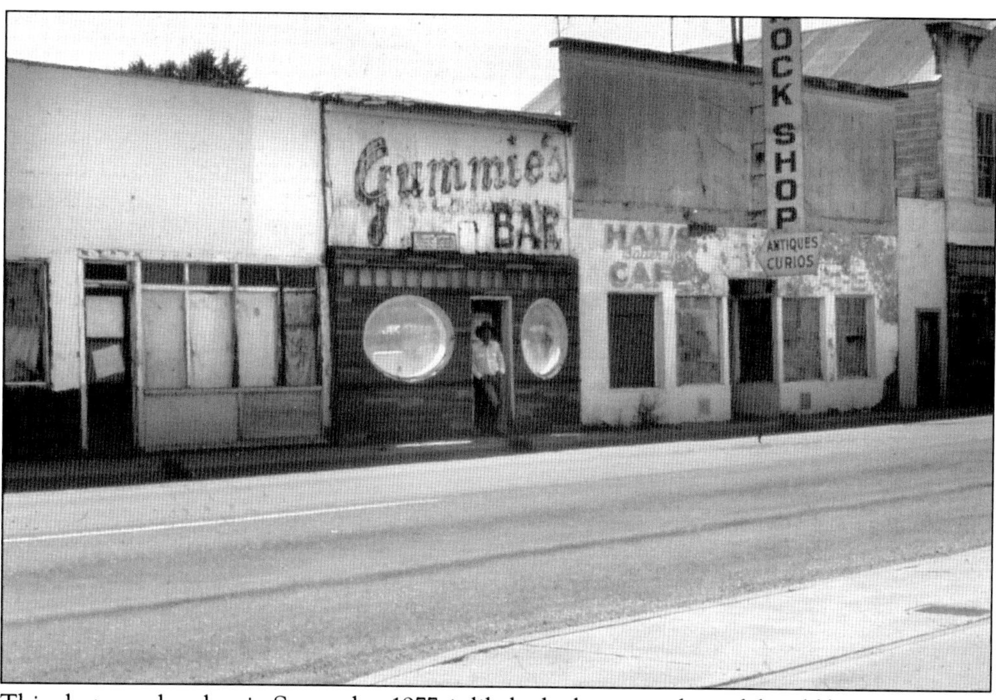

This photograph, taken in September 1977, is likely the last one taken of the old business district prior to the big fire two months later. The author stands in the doorway of Frank and Nora Gum's popular saloon, where he shined boots and shoes during Ash Fork's heyday.

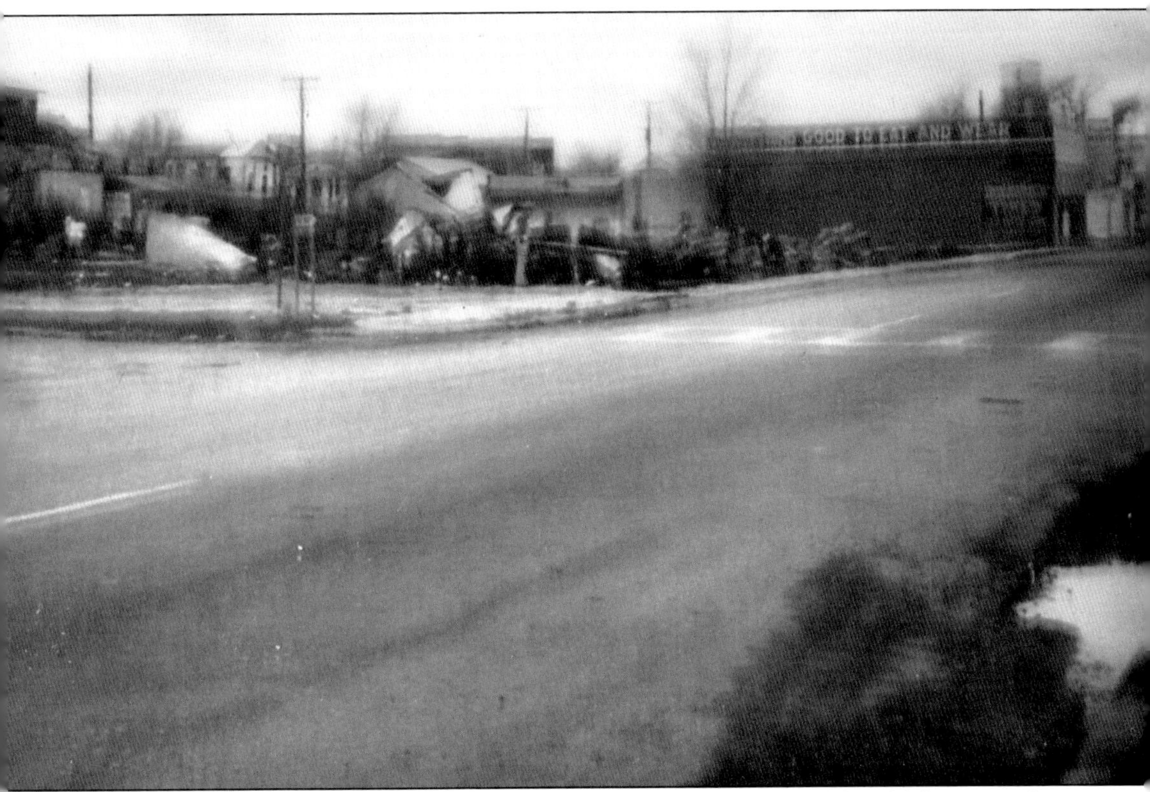

On the cold morning of November 20, 1977, a fire broke out on the roof of the old drugstore. A family had taken up residence in the back of the store and unwittingly ran a stovepipe up through the wooden roof. The hot pipe ignited the roof, and the fire quickly got out of control and spread through the old buildings of the business district. Truckers on Route 66 alerted neighboring communities by CB radios that Ash Fork was going up in flames. There was fear of a gas explosion. Volunteer firemen and citizens rushed out in force but quickly determined it was too late to save the buildings, and they turned their attention towards keeping it from spreading to the homes. They fought the fire furiously for nearly 12 hours before bringing it under control. Destroyed by fire were the Yavapai Theater, post office, two barbershops, Gummies Buffet, drugstore, opera house, Do Drop In Café, and the H&J Café. The only building that didn't burn was the brick-and-mortar Big Store on the corner. (Courtesy Hume collection.)

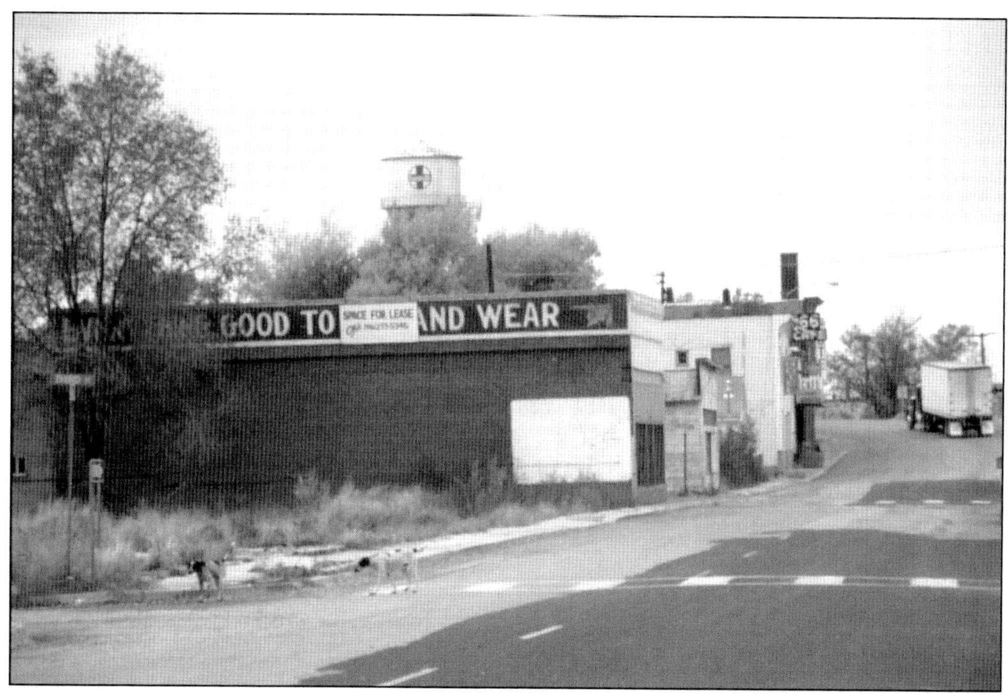

Over the next few years, the old business district was slowly reclaimed by nature. On the southwest corner of Fourth Street and Lewis Avenue was Judge Slamon's Western Variety Store. Judge Slamon usually held court at the candy counter, and even though he was affectionately referred to as the "Roy Bean of Route 66," the judge had a good reputation for dispensing justice fair and square.

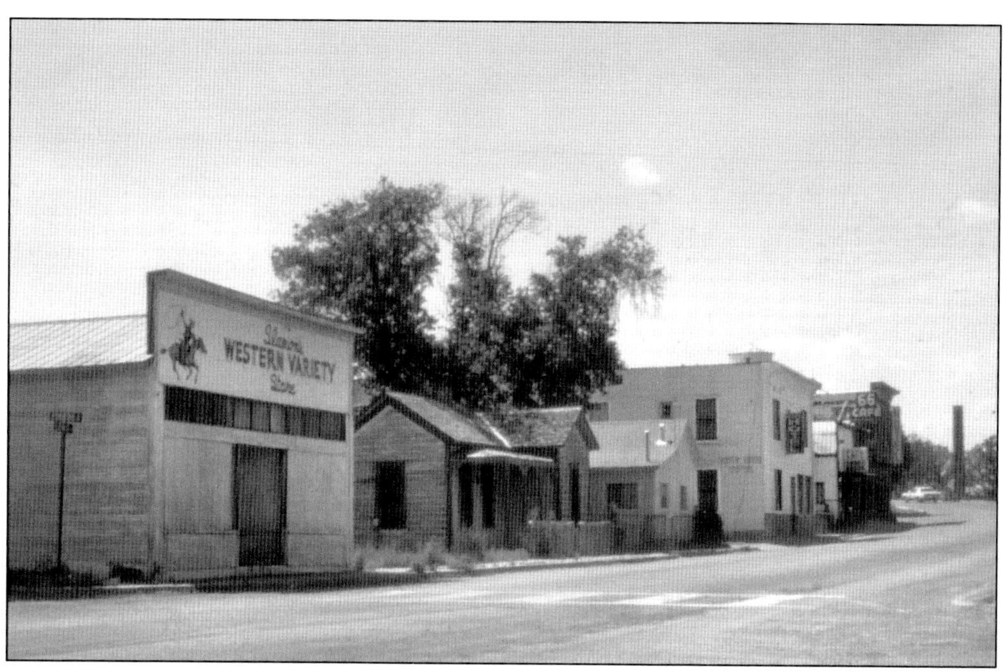

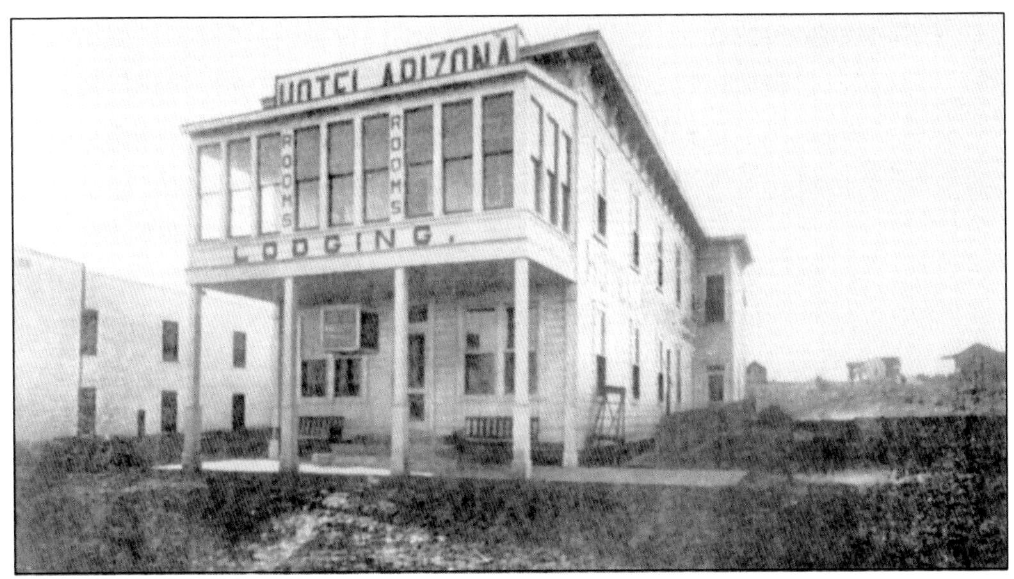

The historic old Hotel Arizona is pictured above in the early 1900s. The photograph below, taken during the 1920s, shows the downtown looking east. This photograph is similar to the one on page 67. The gas pumps are still in front of the Hotel Arizona, but the Arizona Café and Bar has become the 66 Café. The general store on the left is now the Arizona Café and Bar and there is a Standard gas station on the left. Tragic fires in the 1970s and 1980s would destroy nearly every business along the south side of Lewis Avenue.

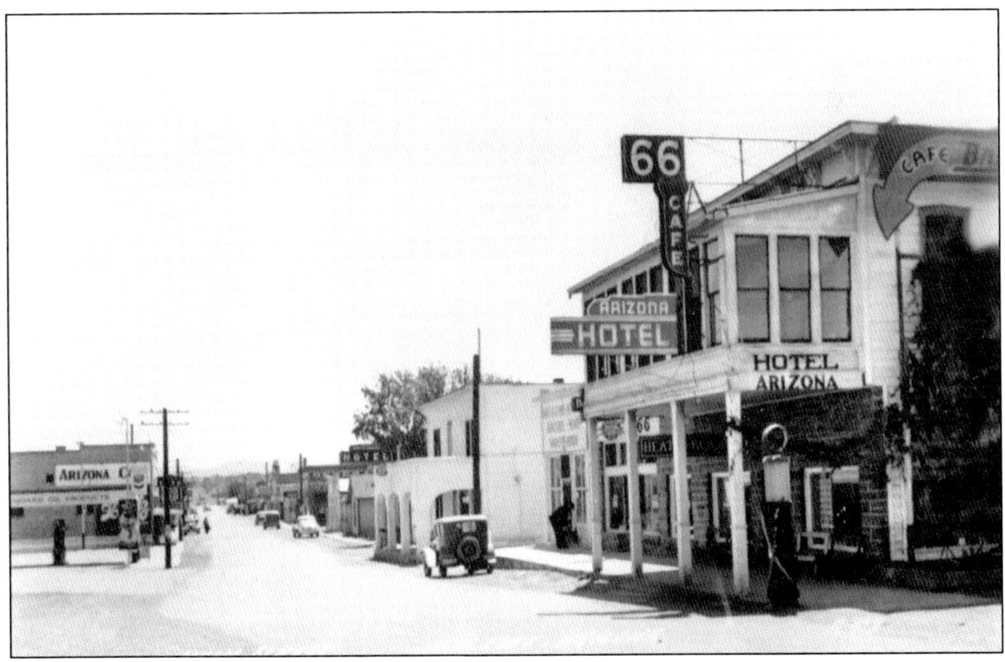

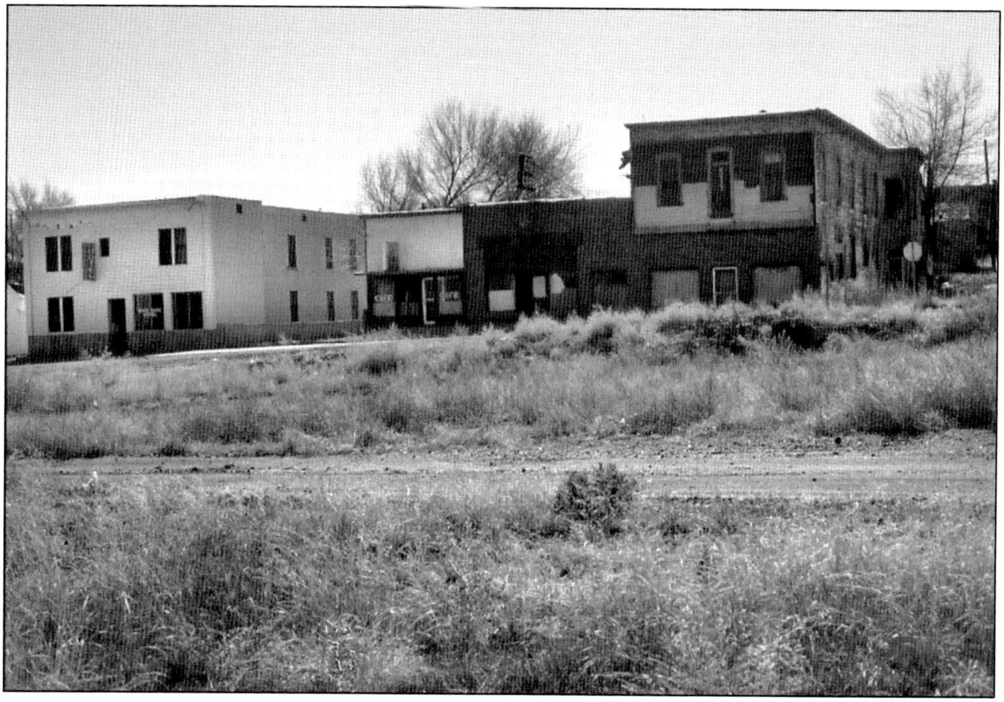

The White House Hotel, 66 Café, and Arizona Hotel were the last vestiges of the once-prosperous businesses along the south side of Lewis Avenue.

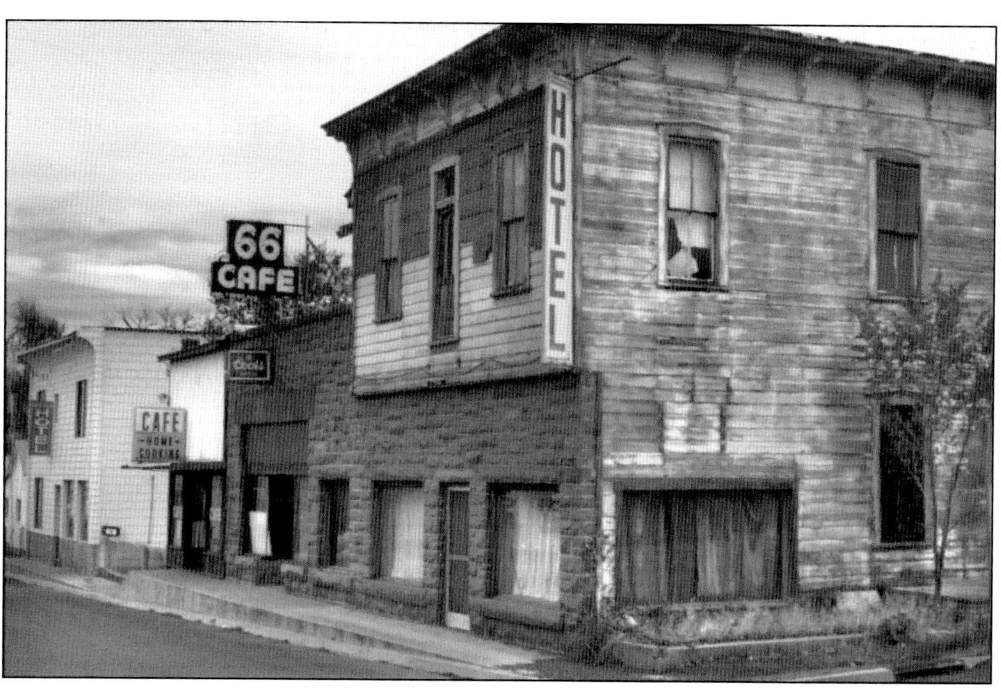

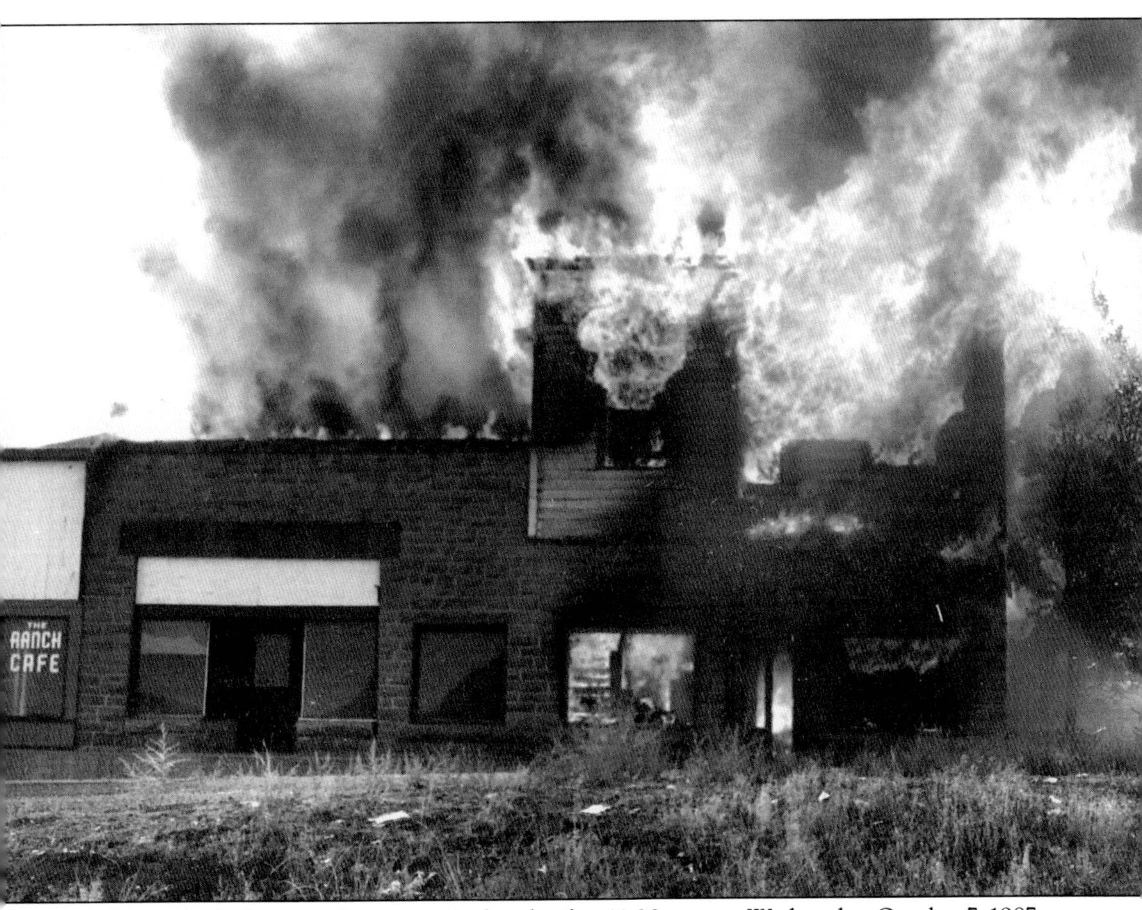

Tragedy struck the business district again shortly after 11:00 a.m. on Wednesday, October 7, 1987, when flames began shooting out of a vacant building. The historic old Hotel Arizona, along with the 66 Café, went up in flames. Ash Fork's volunteer firemen, along with firemen from Seligman and Williams, quickly responded and fought the fire for three hours before the buildings succumbed to the hot flames. Alma Pouquette's White House Hotel, another popular abode for railroaders and visitors, managed to escape the flames thanks to heroic efforts by the volunteer firemen. A westbound truck driver told the Seligman firemen as they rushed to help that it looked like the whole town had gone up in flames. A day later, it was still burning because of flammable tar and tar paper stored in the basement. It was believed to be arson, and a hitchhiker was arrested soon afterwards. All that remained of the two-block row of historic buildings on the south side of Lewis Avenue was the White House Hotel. Over the years, fire has destroyed most of Ash Fork's historic landmarks. (Courtesy Bob Bassett.)

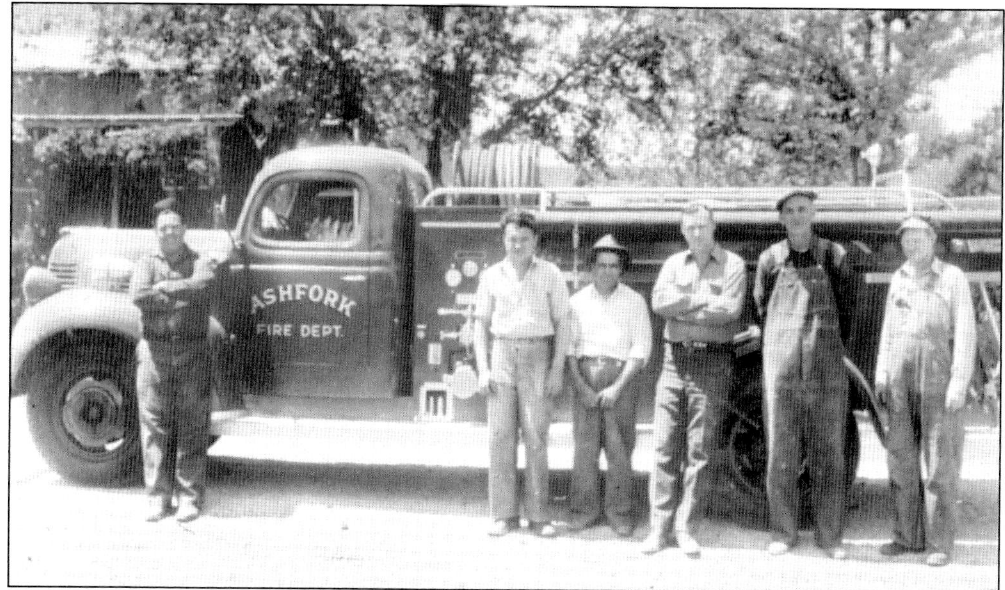

The 1885 fire destroyed the business district because there was no water to fight it. The fire department was organized in 1941, and the first station was built in 1946. A new truck was purchased in 1970. Another new truck was purchased and a new, larger building was completed in 2000. The fire alarm could be heard for a mile. The volunteer firemen sponsored an annual picnic and an annual "Fireman's Ball" fund-raiser in the high school gym. (Courtesy Hume collection.)

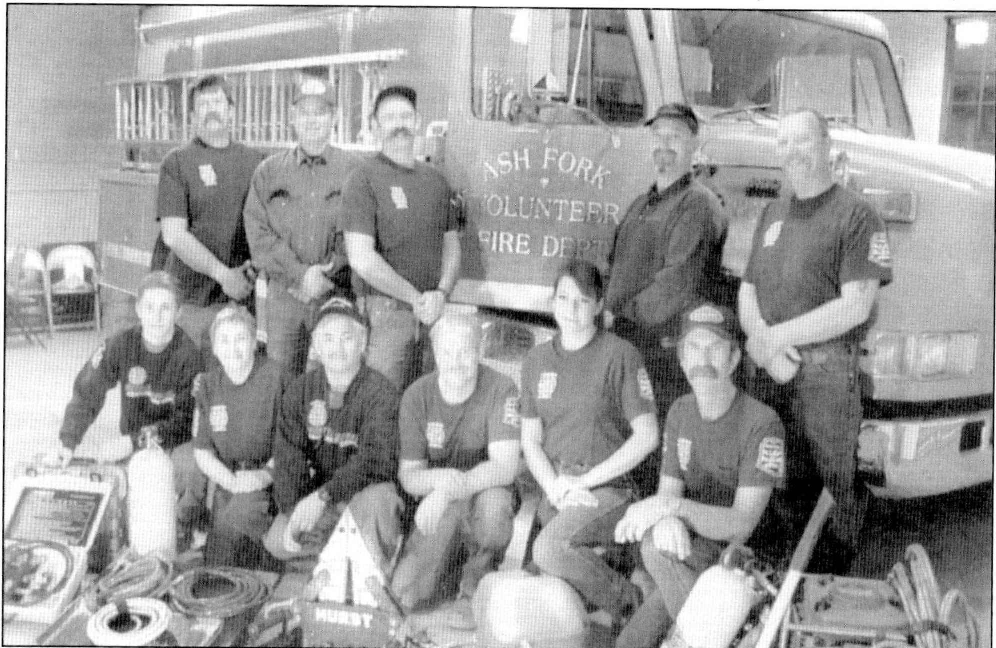

Ash Fork's volunteer firemen are as up-to-date as any large-city fire department. They are well trained and certified. They face many of the same occupational hazards as urban fire fighters. Pictured are (first row) Ronnie Muenks, Pat Whitted, Mario Moctezuma, Robert Mikulic, Lori Bach, and John Musel; (second row) Roy Hume, Ron Muenks, Lewis Hume, Bill Mathews, and Wil Popp. (Courtesy Hume collection.)

Nine

Rock Doodlers
The Flagstone Capital of the World

The Coconino flagstone in the hills around Ash Fork is one of the finest stones for building purposes, as well as walks, patios, fireplaces, and a myriad of other uses. Due to its composition, brilliant and varied colors, and fine cleavage, Coconino sandstone has found a world market. Experts say that because of its lasting beauty, there's no finer flagstone in the world.

Flagstone sheets are split by wedging, graded, and stacked on flatbed trucks from the quarries to cutting yards in town. At the cutting yard, the stone is sorted, graded, sized, and cut to dimension. The palleted stone is stored in yards and then loaded on trucks for shipment.

Most of the stone is sold in slabs as it comes from the quarry. Other stone is cut to dimension with saws. Precision cutting is done with diamond-bladed circular saws.

Although most of the stonecutters today are Mexican immigrants, the cutters from an earlier era were known as "rock doodlers." They were a colorful, hardworking, hard-drinking breed that could raise a ruckus on payday. Rock doodling was a different kind of mining than that of the hardrock miners of places like Jerome, Globe, and Bisbee, where metals like copper, gold, and silver were taken from deep underground mines. Flagstone was quarried from areas near the surface.

The flagstone business was quite small until the post–World War II building boom began. Currently there are a half-dozen stone yards in and around Ash Fork, and the flagstone industry has taken the place of the railroad as the town's leading industry.

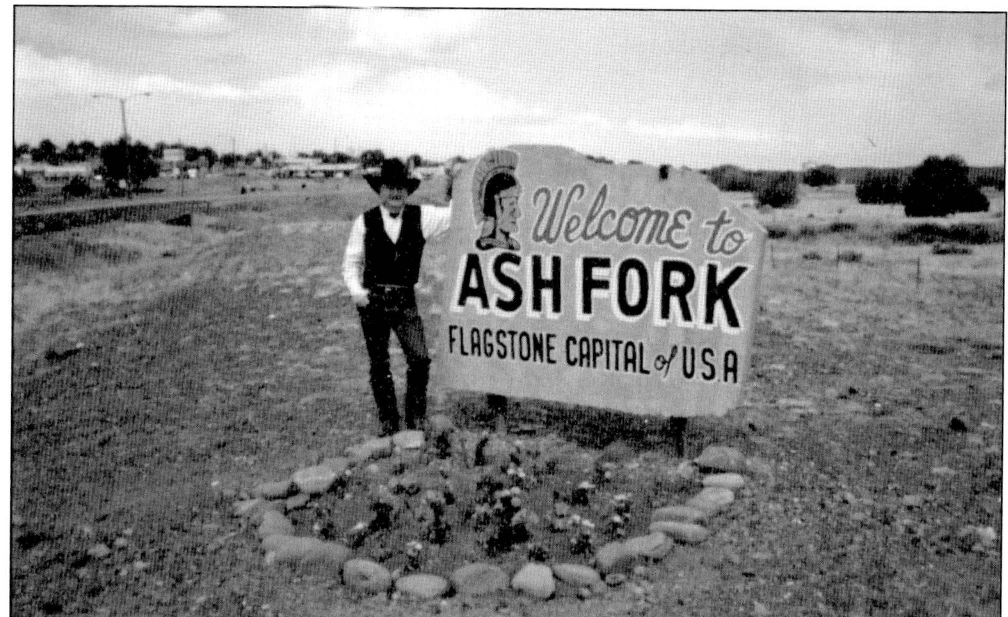

The durable and colorful Coconino sandstone found around Ash Fork is shipped all over the world. Ash Fork can rightfully be called the "Flagstone Capital of the World." Such celebrities as country star George Strait and actor Tom Selleck have homes built with Ash Fork flagstone; the Dallas Cowboys football stadium also features the pinkish sedimentary stone.

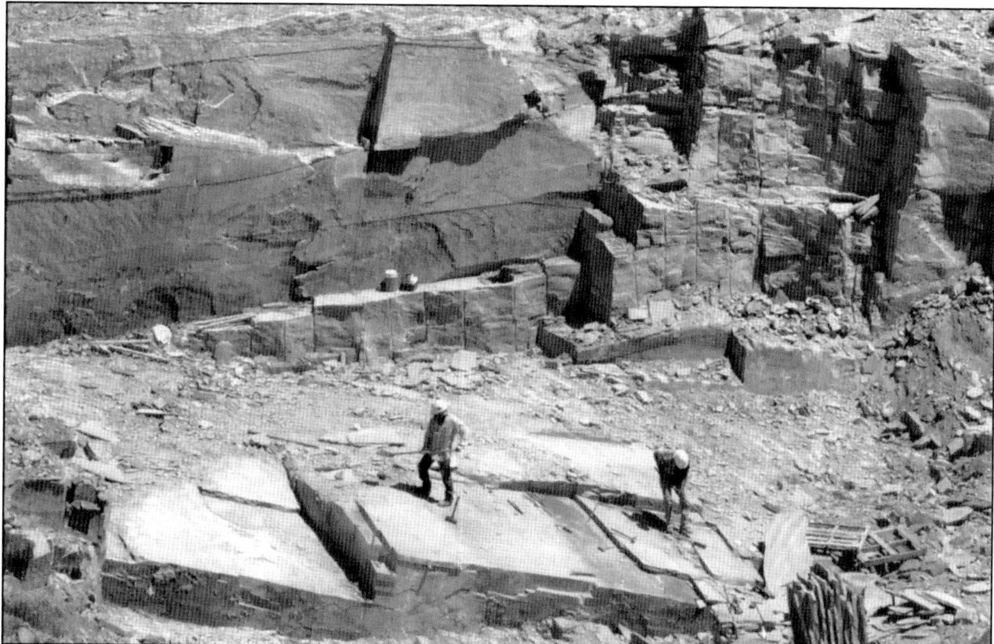

The Coconino sandstone, found in the hills and lowlands surrounding the town, has many uses as a building material. Flagstone is one of the finest stones for building veneers. Other uses range from patios, walks, and fireplaces to buildings, homes, and monuments. Due to its composition, color, durability, and fine cleavage, Coconino sandstone has found a worldwide market. (Courtesy Hume collection.)

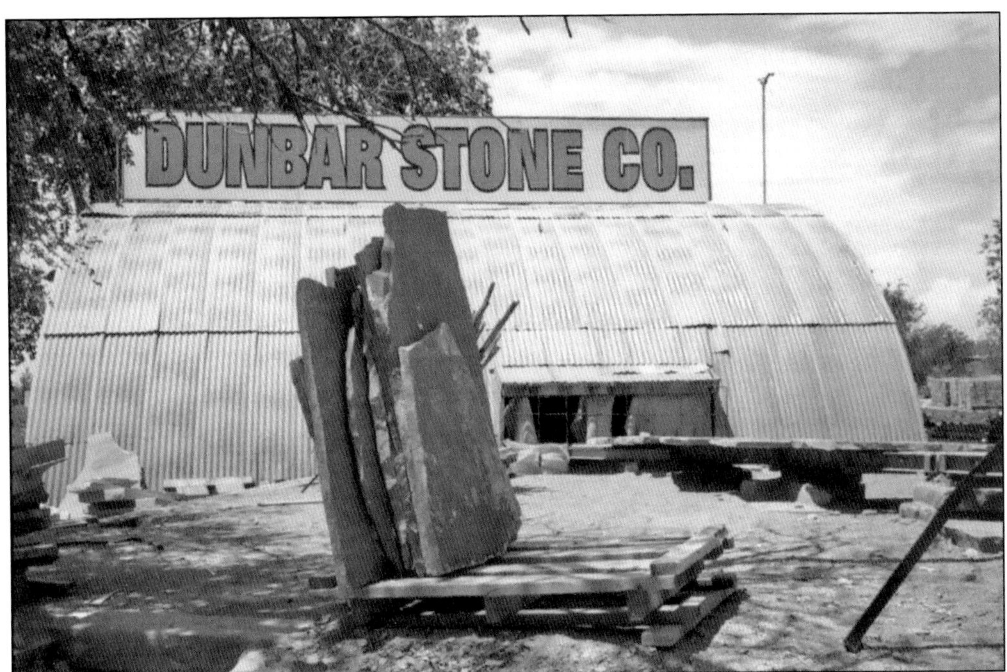

Bob Dunbar established Dunbar Stone Company in 1946. His family continues to run the business. Dunbar Stone has generously donated stone for the monuments and other civic projects in the town. The stone industry also benefited from the railroad to ship flagstone all over the country during the 1950s, shipping hundreds of carloads of flagstone in the course of a season. Out in the quarries, there were about 100 private or independent companies digging rock out of the ground and sending it into town to be processed. It was estimated the flagstone industry brought nearly $350,000 a year into Ash Fork.

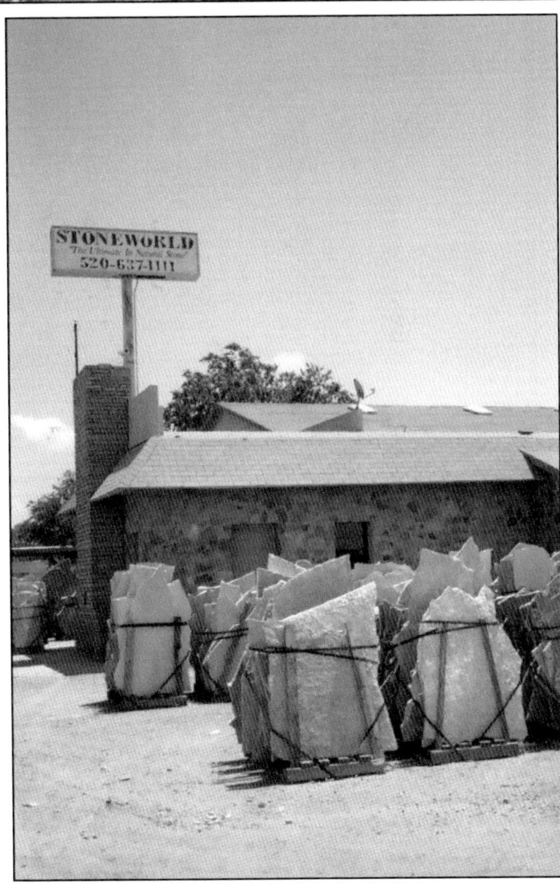

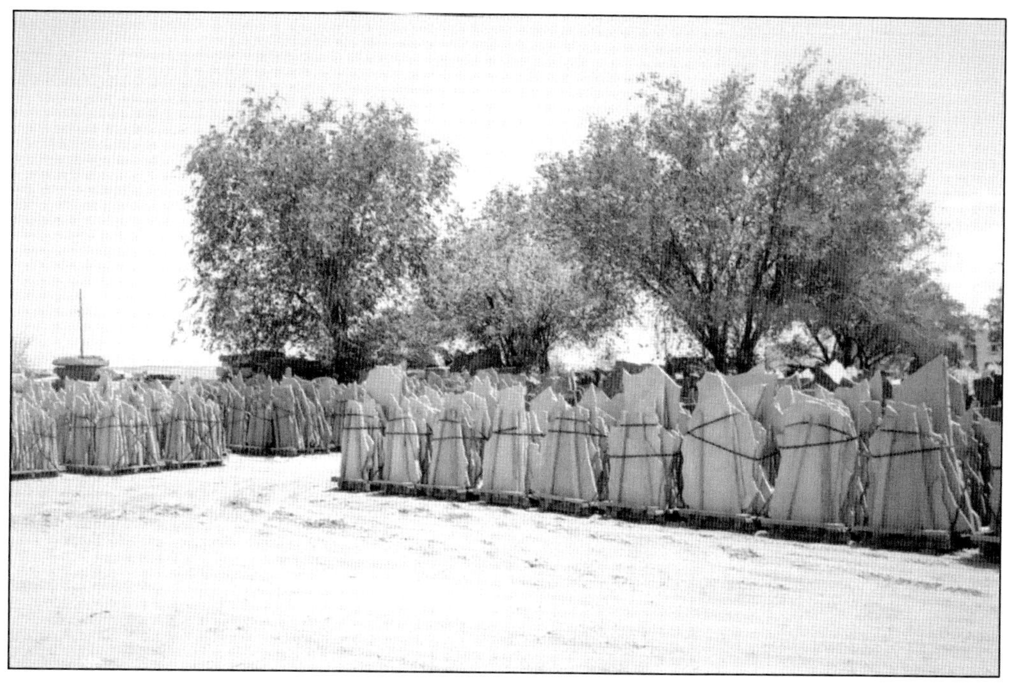

Above, flagstone slabs are stacked and ready to ship. Below, flagstone cut to specific shapes is loaded on pallets and ready to be loaded on trucks.

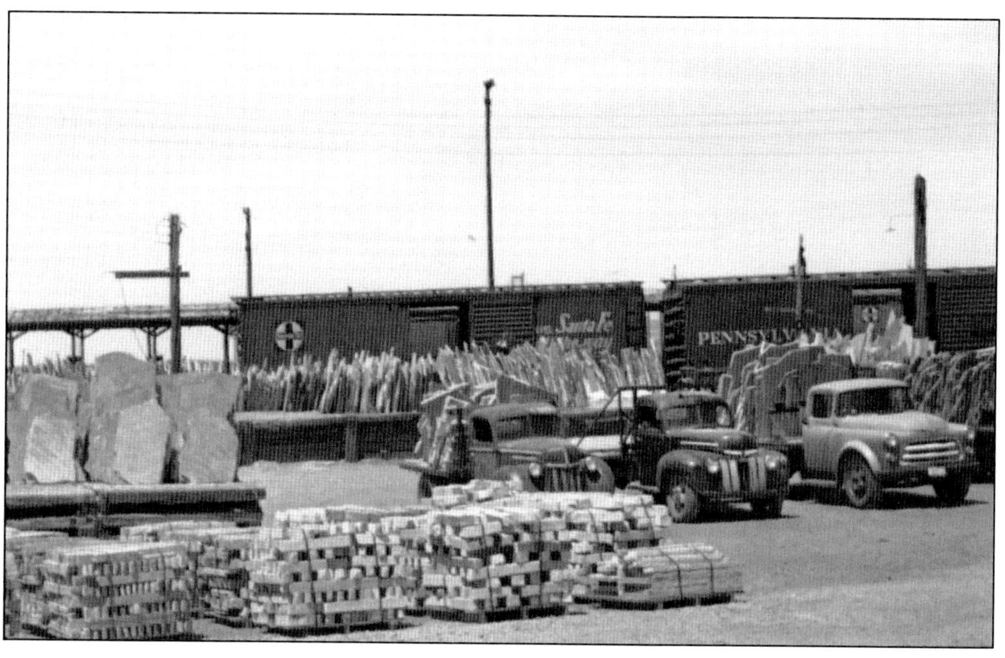

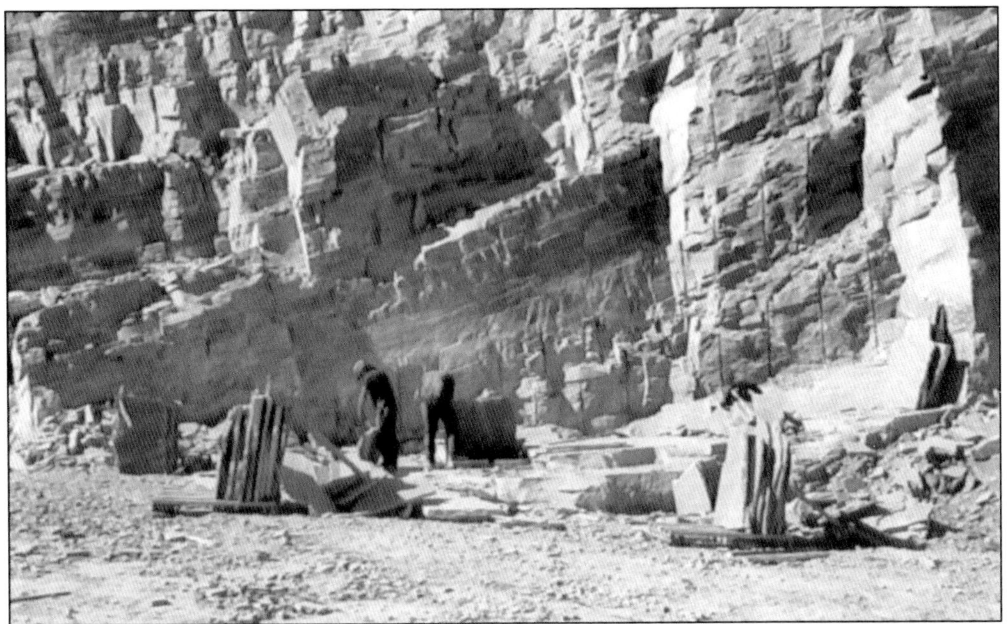

The men who quarry the flagstone in the hills around Ash Fork have always been affectionately referred to as rock doodlers. The old breed of rock doodlers was a rough-and-tumble bunch that worked hard and played harder. They lived in camps at the quarries in those days, and when payday came around, Saturday nights at the local bars were apt to become quite "Western." (Courtesy Drake Stone.)

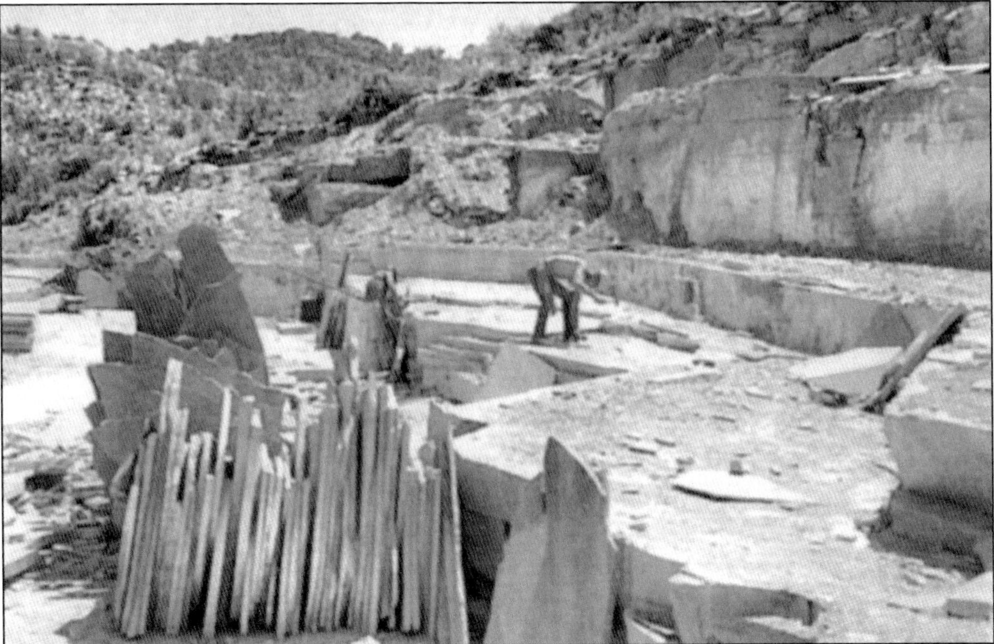

A rock doodler chisels out flagstone during the 1940s. The technique of quarrying the stone has changed little in more than 60 years. Today the flagstone industry in the Ash Fork-Paulden-Drake areas creates some 300 jobs and generates nearly $10 million in earnings annually. (Courtesy Drake Stone.)

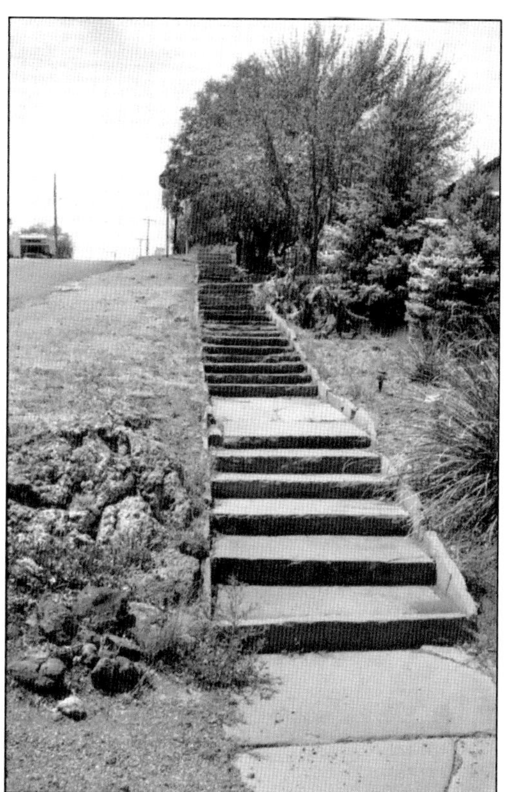

During the Great Depression, WPA workers put in distinctive flagstone sidewalks. There's no mortar holding the stone in place, and the sidewalks have weathered more than 70 years of use.

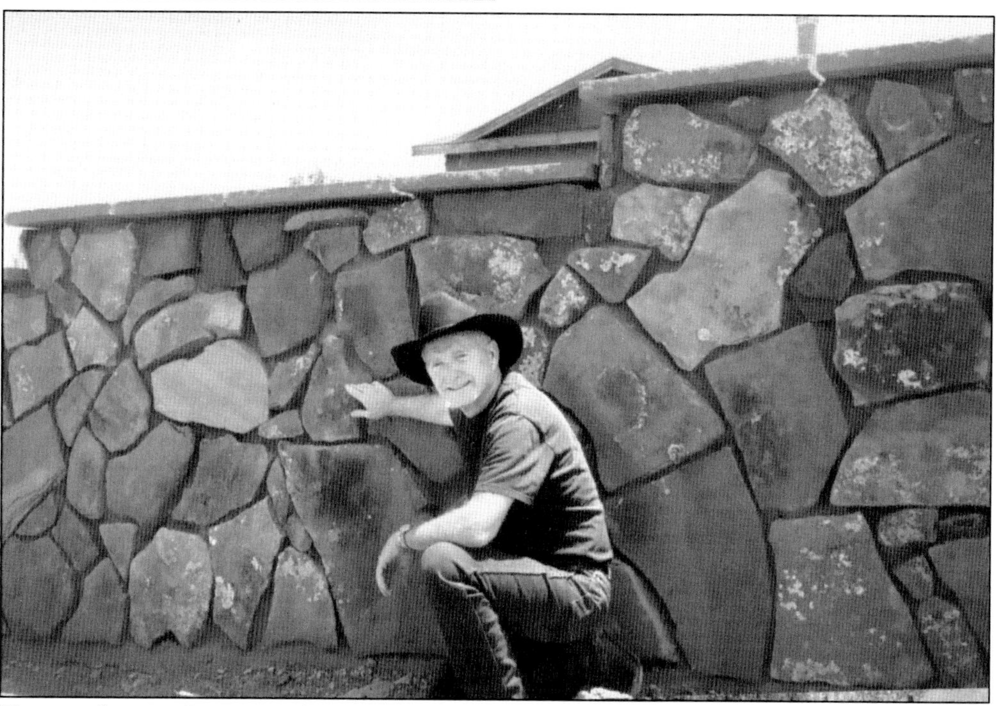

Flagstone has a wide variety of uses. Here is an example of how to put a facade on walls. (Courtesy of Vanessa Logas.)

Ten

A Town Too Tough to Die

Ash Fork Today

The long-anticipated I-40 bypass finally came in 1979. Overnight, the rush of traffic by cars, busses, and 18-wheelers stopped. By this time, many of the shops, store, and restaurants in the business district were closed. A few intrepid business people relocated to the freeway access roads and have become very successful.

The highway maintenance camp was established at Ash Fork in 1922 because it was a junction point on the National Old Trail and Grand Canyon–Nogales Highways. Of primary importance was Ash Fork's location at the junction of two major highways, Route 66 and U.S. 89, which provided east-west and north-south links to the federal highway system. For many years, it was the only highway maintenance facility in Northern Arizona. With the completion of the interstate through Ash Fork in 1979, the maintenance camp was closed. The old building was donated to the town and converted to a tourist center and historical museum in 1998. In 1998, Ash Fork historian Fayrene Hume requested that the Arizona Department of Transportation building be placed on the National Register of Historic Places. It came on March 4, 1999, and is the only building on the register in Ash Fork to date.

Since the nearest hospital facilities were 50 miles away at Flagstaff or Prescott, the Ash Fork Development Association was able to secure grant monies for a health center that opened in 1999. The new public library opened in 2004.

Ash Fork is like an old boxer who keeps getting knocked down but refuses to quit and keeps getting up again to fight another round. The glorious days of passenger trains rolling into town and automobiles cruising Route 66 are gone but not easily forgotten.

Cowboy artist Charlie Russell could have been talking about Ash Fork and her residents, past and present, when he said, "The Old West is dead; you may lose a sweetheart but you'll never forget her."

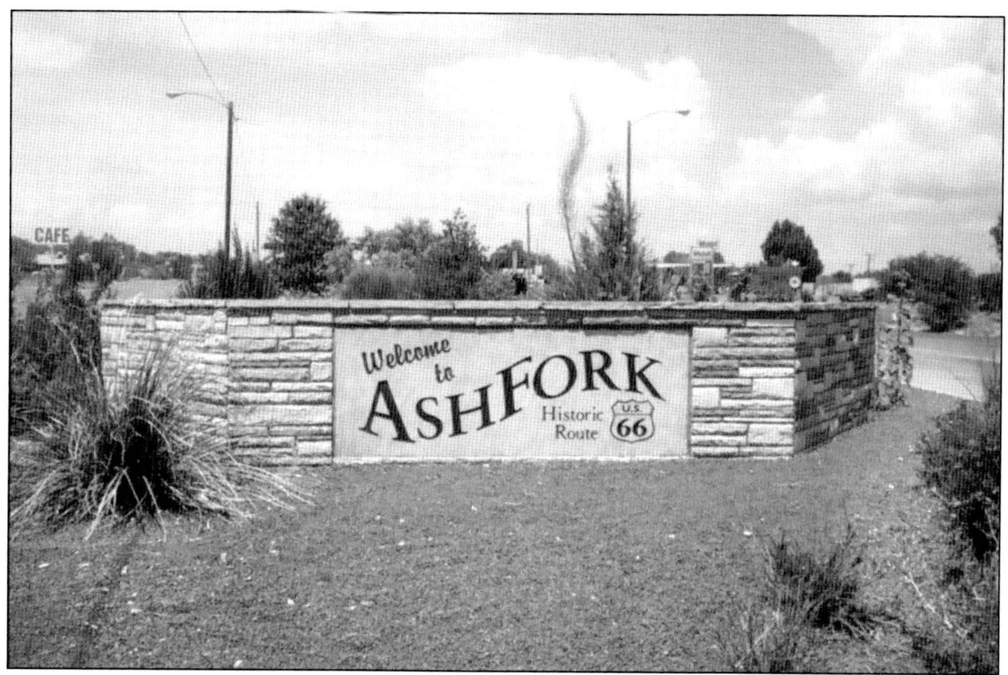

Ash Fork has a long tradition of extending a warm welcome to visitors, tourists, and former residents who often take a sentimental journey back to the old hometown. The trademark flagstone graces the new "Welcome to Ash Fork" signs at both ends of town and the front of the new elementary and high school, which opened in 2007.

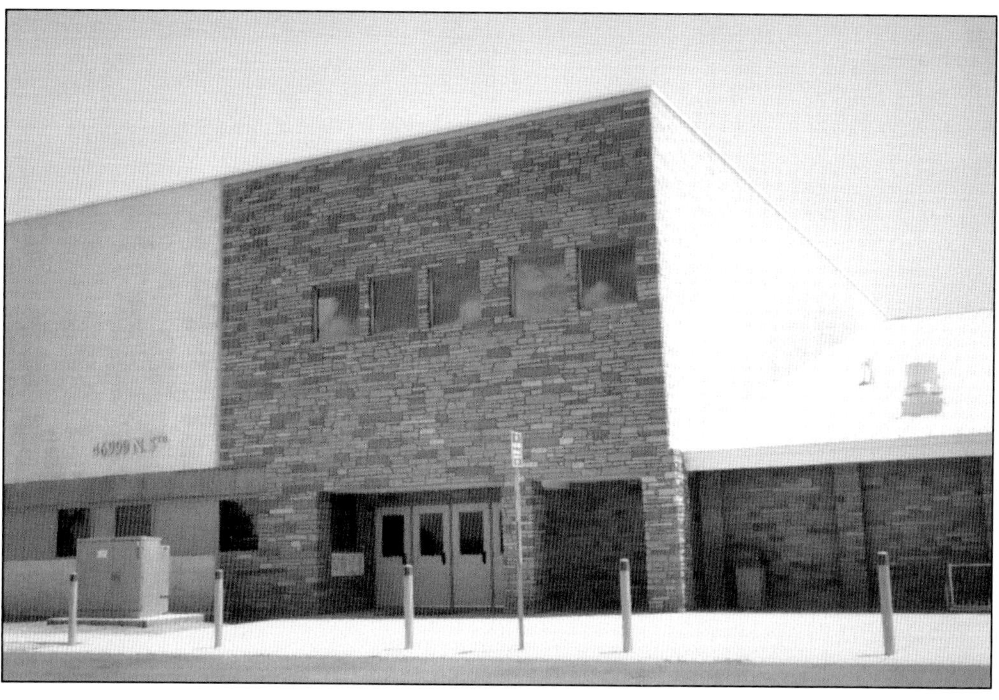

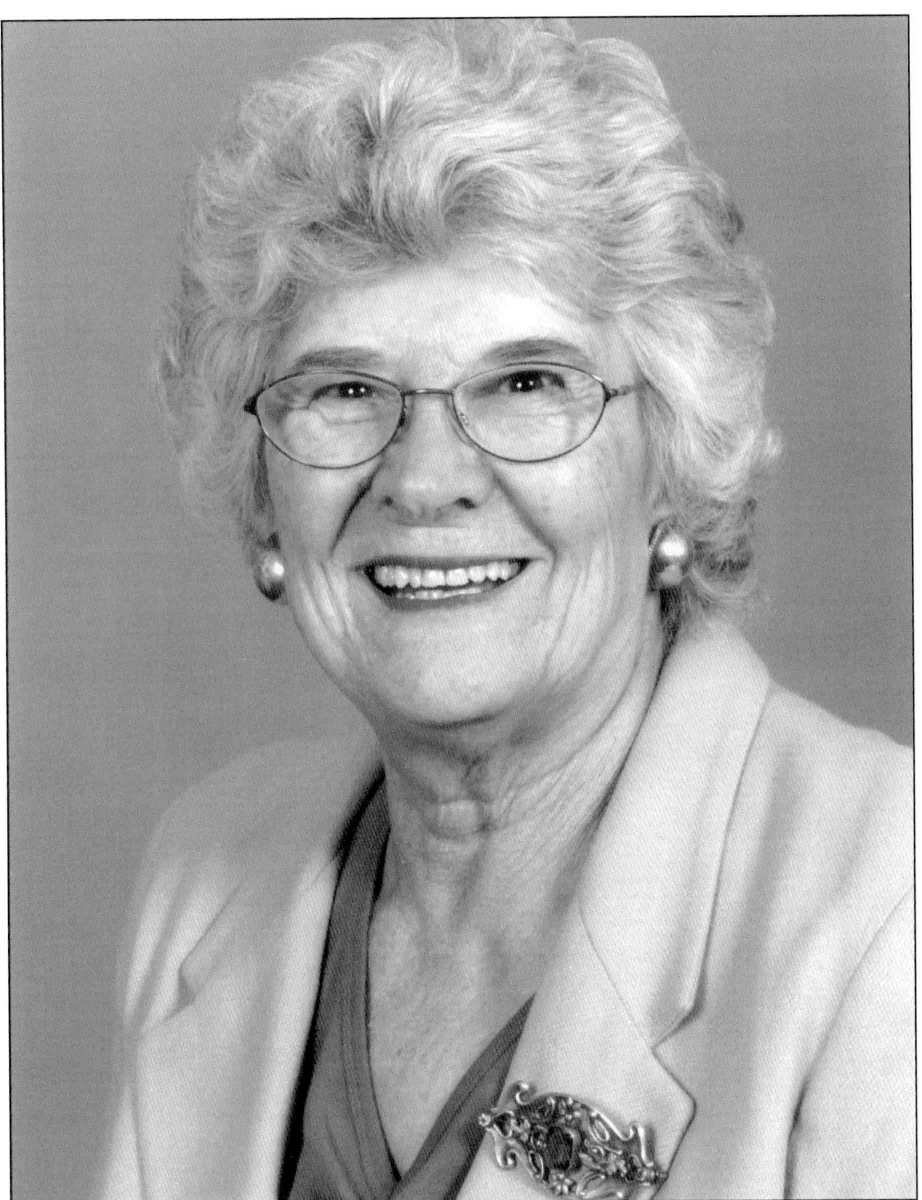

No one has done more to preserve the history of Ash Fork over the past 50 years than Fayrene Martin Hume. She is a very modest woman and has worked countless hours on community projects. Her work as a volunteer is legend. Fayrene moved with her family to Ash Fork as a youngster in 1950. Three years later, she married Ash Fork native Lewis Hume. Fayrene trained herself in grant writing and raised $880,000 in grants and loans to drill a second well at Ash Fork. During the 1982 reunion, she wrote a history of Ash Fork as the town prepared to celebrate its centennial. She was head of the committee collecting oral histories and photographs from former residents scattered throughout the country. In 2004, she was honored with the prestigious Arizona Culturekeeper's Award for nearly a half-century of working to preserve the history and culture of Arizona. Two years later, she was presented the Sharlot Hall Award, given annually to a living Arizona woman. The award recognizes valuable contributions to the understanding and awareness of Arizona and its history. (Courtesy Hume collection.)

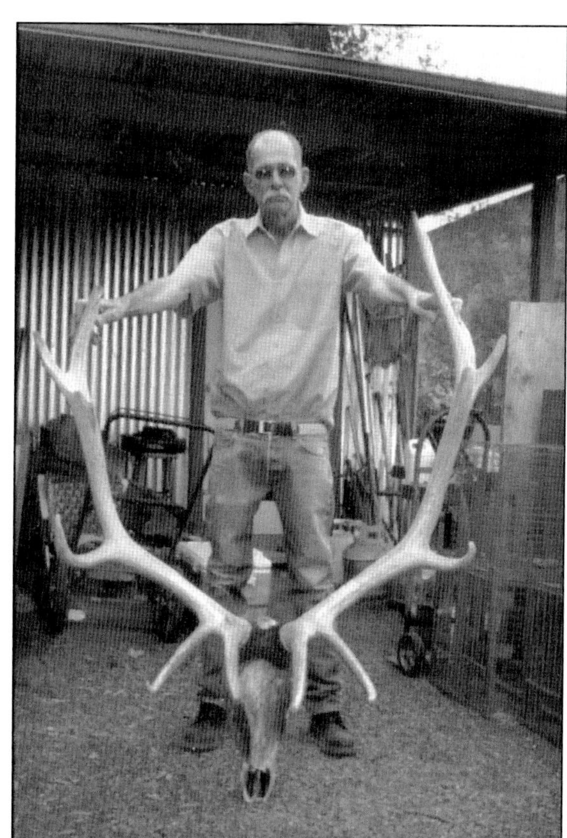

Lewis Hume Sr.—grandson of T. C. Lewis, the town's "First Citizen"—is a third-generation native of Ash Fork. Lewis, an avid hunter, poses with the antlers of a prize elk he bagged. Lewis Hume Jr. and his daughter, Kayla, are fourth- and fifth-generation Ash Fork natives. (Courtesy Hume collection.)

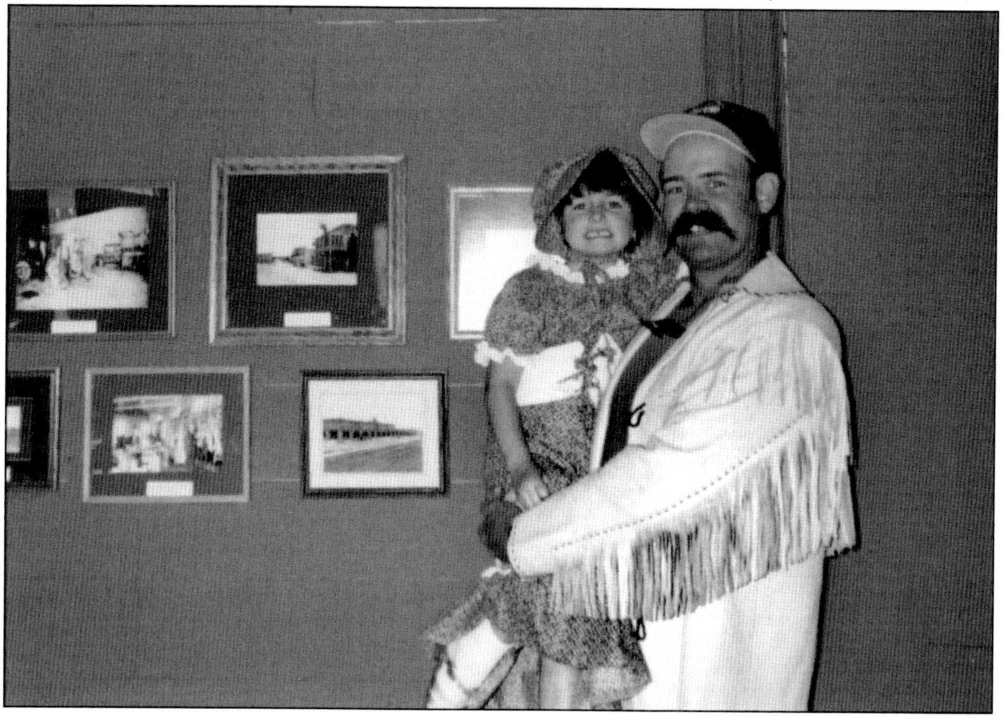

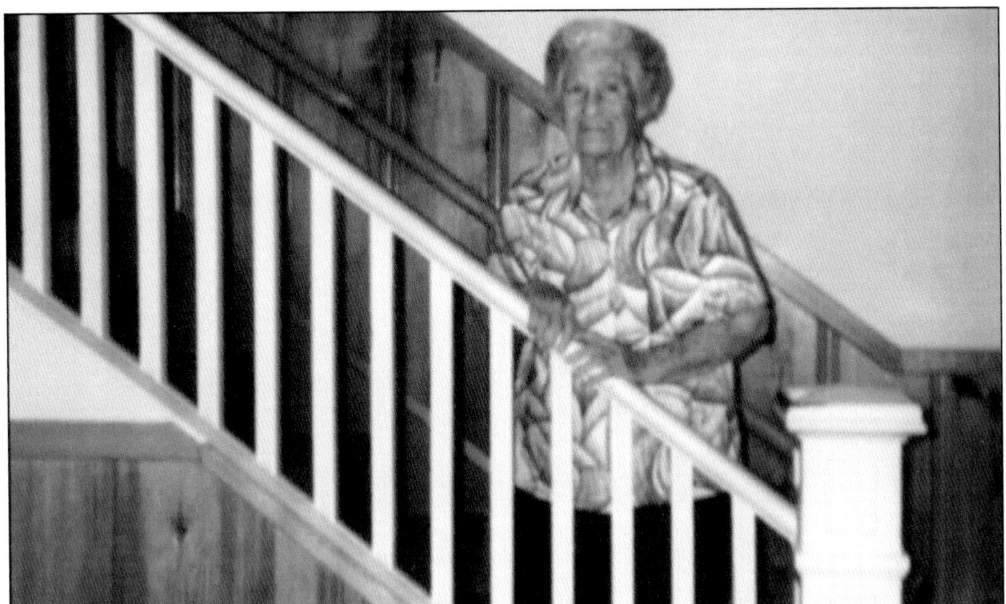

For 65 years, the White House Hotel was home to Alma Pouquette. She stands on the staircase of the hotel built by her father in the early 1900s, which she took over in 1939, cleaning the 20 rooms each day until she could afford to hire an assistant. Alma was born into a famous family of Basque sheep ranchers in Northern Arizona. (Courtesy Hume collection.)

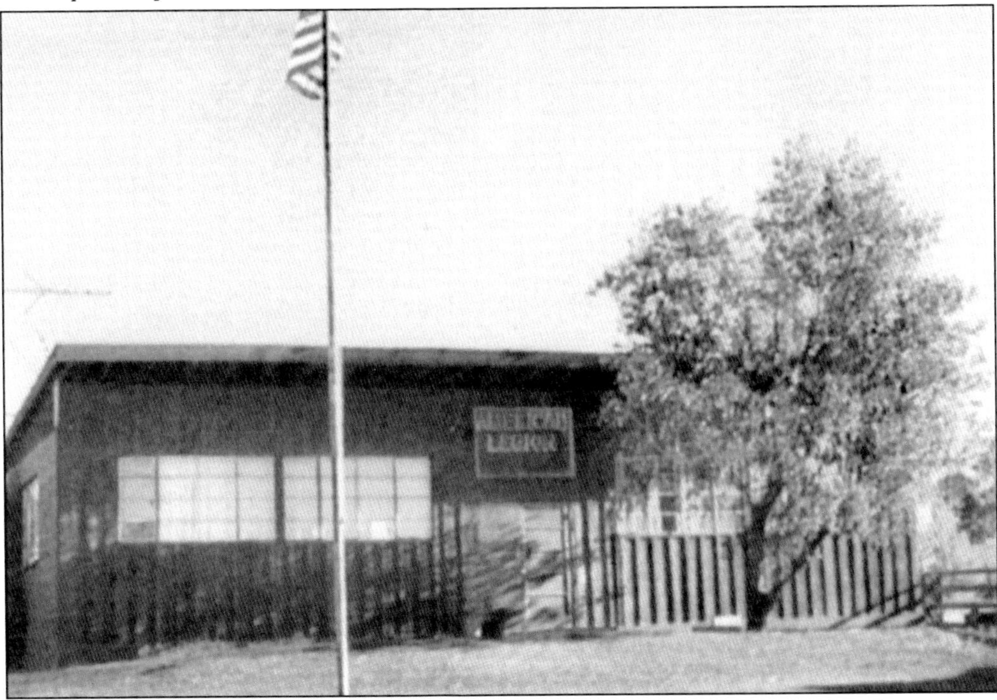

The Robert Fulton American Legion Post No. 57 is not only a social gathering place for veterans, but it's also used by other organizations in the town. The members put up flags along Park and Lewis Avenues on national holidays and act as honor guards at parades and veterans' funeral services. (Courtesy Hume collection.)

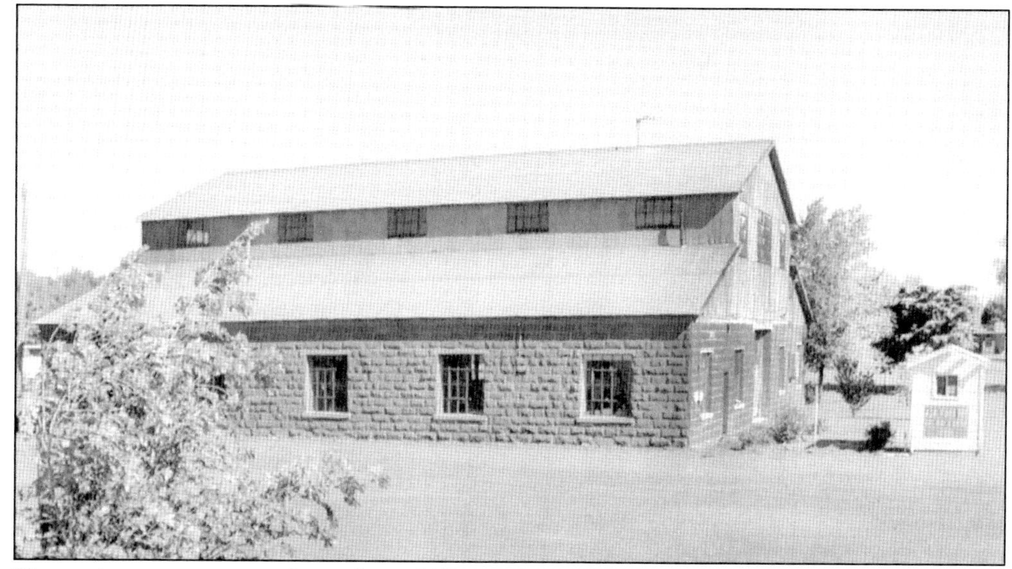

The maintenance camp is located on old Route 66 on the west end of town. When the original railroad depot was demolished in the early 1900s, the stone was used for this building. It remained in operation until 1982, when a new facility was built in Seligman. After receiving a grant for its renovation, the maintenance camp was opened as a historical museum, tourist, and community center in 1998. More than 1,000 visitors toured the museum during the month of July 2007. (Courtesy Hume collection.)

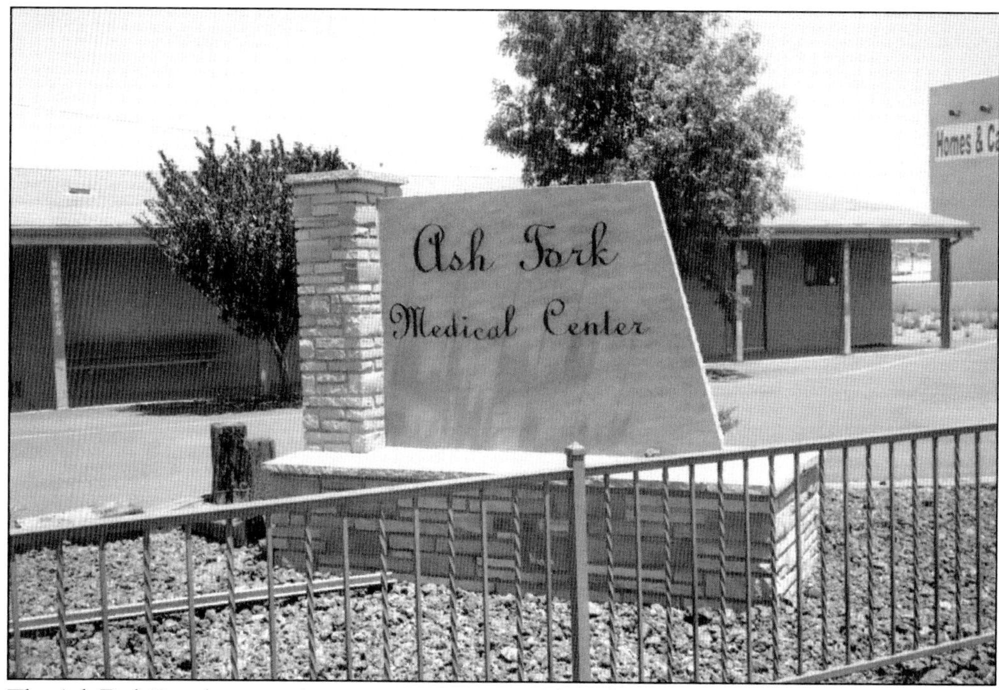

The Ash Fork Development Association was successful in obtaining two grants totaling $250,000 to open a medical and dental health center. The facility opened in October 1999.

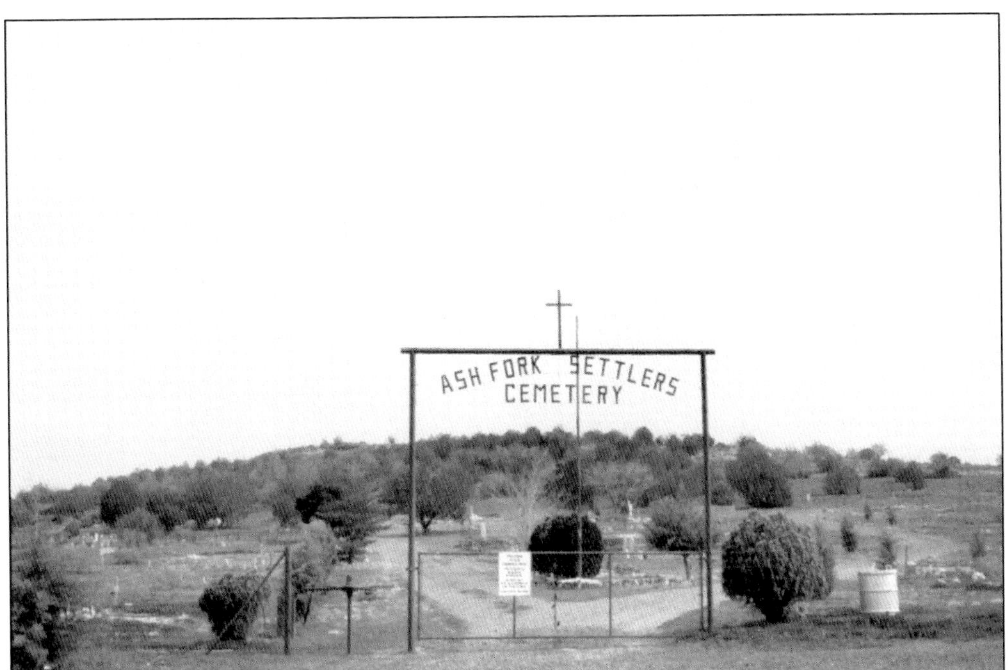

On a hillside north of town is the Settlers Cemetery. The town didn't need a cemetery for the first five years, then, in 1887, a stranger passing through named Tom Kane was "shot by mistake." (Courtesy Hume collection.)

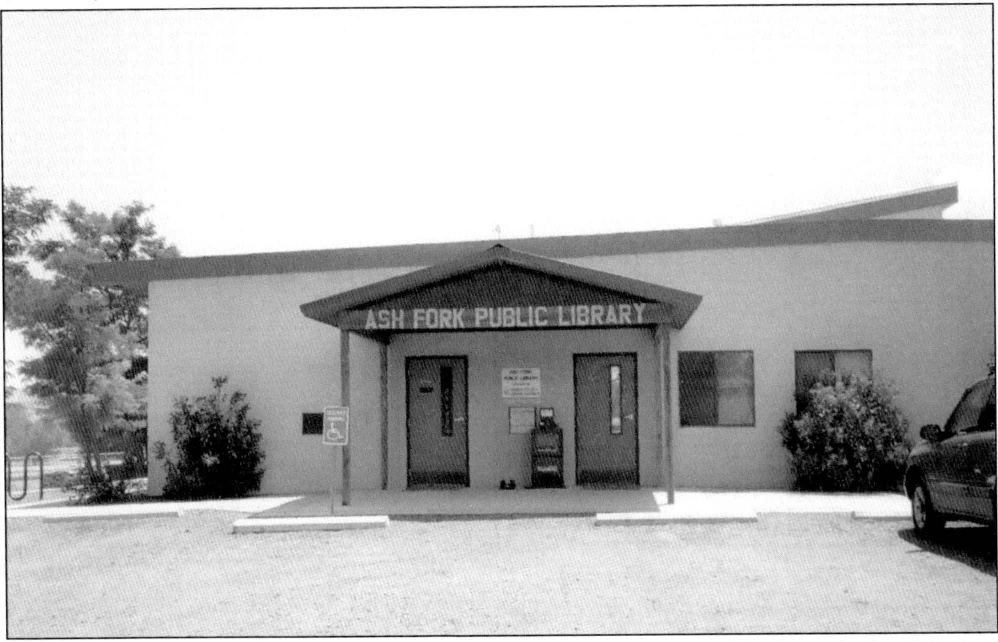

The new Ash Fork Public Library opened in 2005. It was made possible through the Ash Fork Schools, the Ash Fork Development Association, Yavapai County, grants, loans, and lots of volunteer labor under the direction of Lewis Hume, the manager of Ash Fork Water Service. The library also houses Head Start and community college classes. An Escalante Room is planned to commemorate the famous old Harvey House.

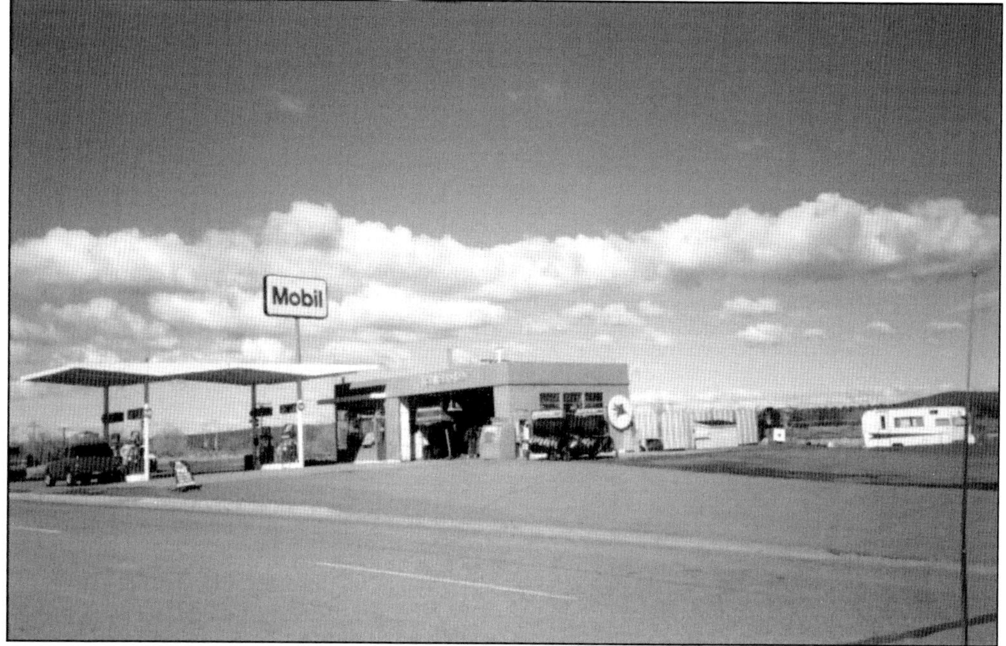

Roy Hume's Mobil station is located on the east end of town. Roy is the eldest of Fayrene and Lewis Hume's three sons and is a fourth-generation native of the town. During the early 1950s, the author worked his way through high school at this station, enabling him to experience firsthand the magic of Route 66 in its heyday. (Courtesy Hume collection.)

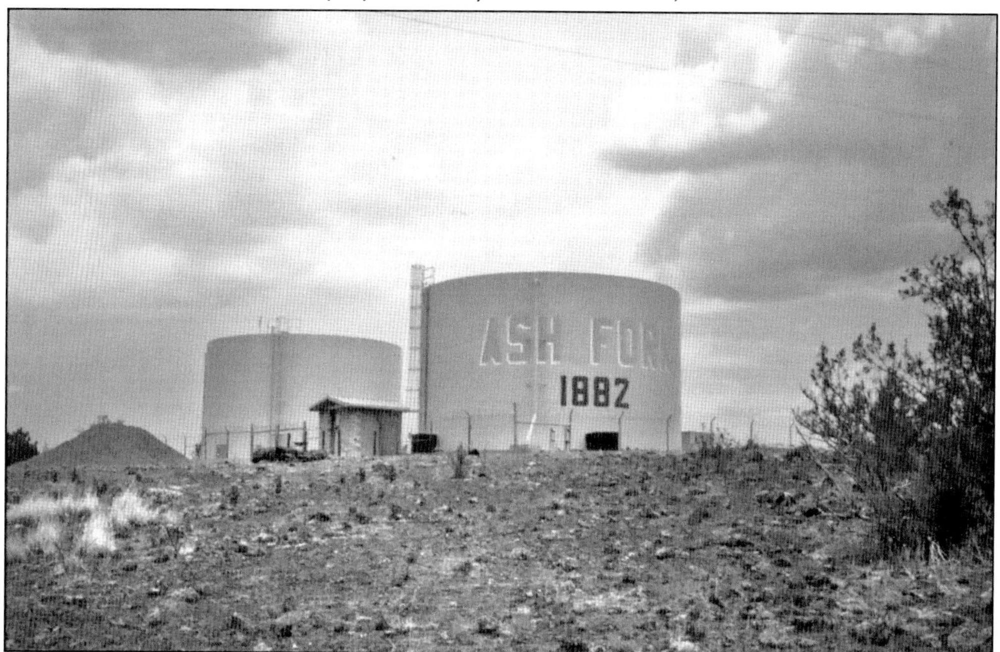

On a hill overlooking the town are two large water storage tanks that provide water for the town. In 1976, a well tapped into a deep aquifer that supplied enough water to sustain the town. A few years later, a second well was drilled. Today the town's water supply is stored in huge tanks south of town. The old Santa Fe water tank now stands empty.

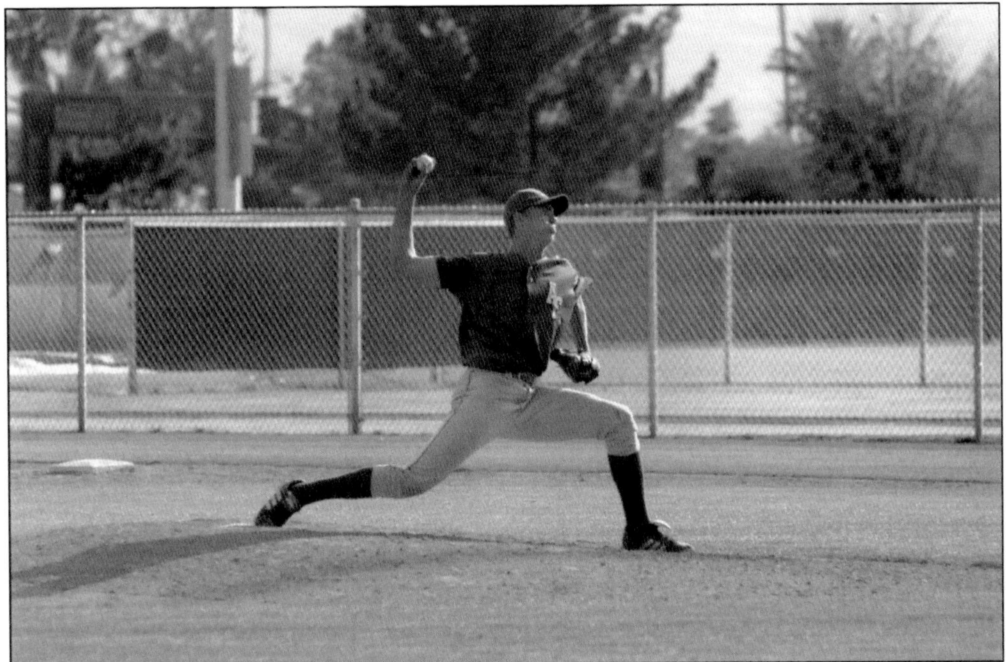

Michael Murphy's blazing 89-mile-per-hour fastball carried the Spartans to the 1-A State Baseball Tournament in 2007, earning him a scholarship to Yavapai Community College in Prescott. During the summer of 2007, he joined a group of collegiate players that went to the national championships at Wichita, Kansas. (Courtesy Eric Hansen.)

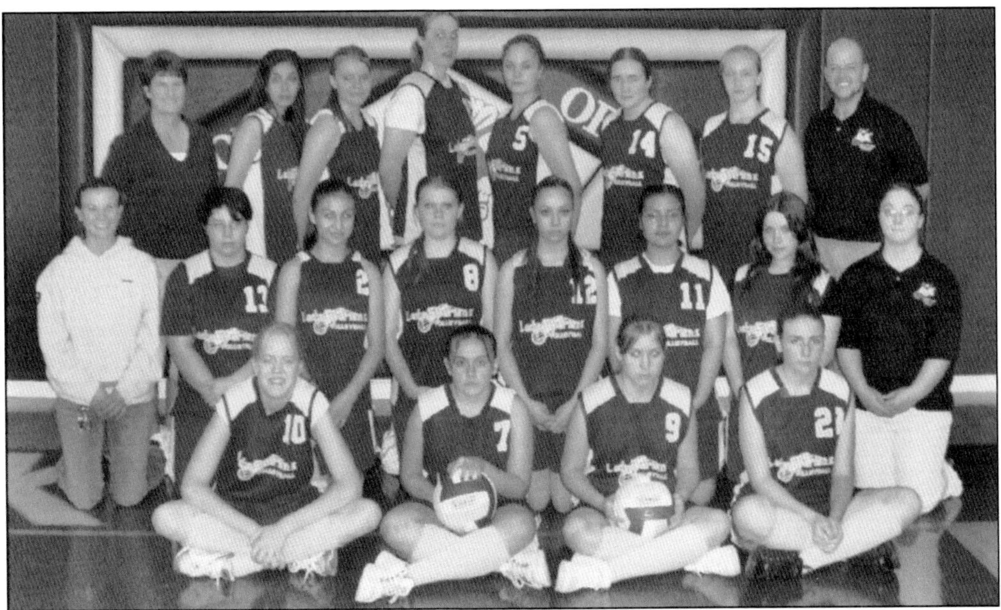

Ash Fork's baseball and girl's volleyball teams enjoyed a banner year in 2007. The Lady Spartans, led by 6-foot-1-inch Jaimie Jackson (top row, fourth from left), were the 1-A Northwest Conference champions, and Jaimie received the Most Valuable Player Award. Jaimie will be attending the University of Arizona on a scholarship. (Courtesy Eric Hansen.)

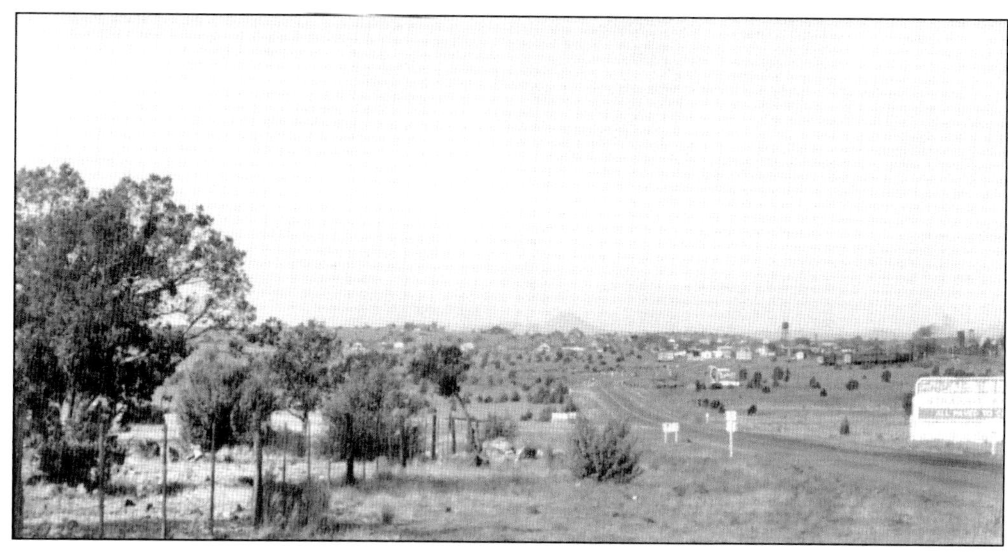

The photograph above was taken in the 1930s. The landmark Santa Fe water tower stands just south of the Harvey House. In the center is the junction of Route 66 and U.S. 89. A sign on the right tells travelers the road is paved all the way to Los Angeles. Another sign closer to town advertises the Fred Harvey Hotel and Restaurant. The cone-shaped mountain in the background is Picacho. The photograph below was taken in 2007 along I-40. The interstate opened in 1979, swinging south and missing the town by a half-mile. On October 13, 1984, I-40 bypassed Williams, 18 miles east of Ash Fork. This was the last section of Route 66 to be closed, marking the end of an era in American history.

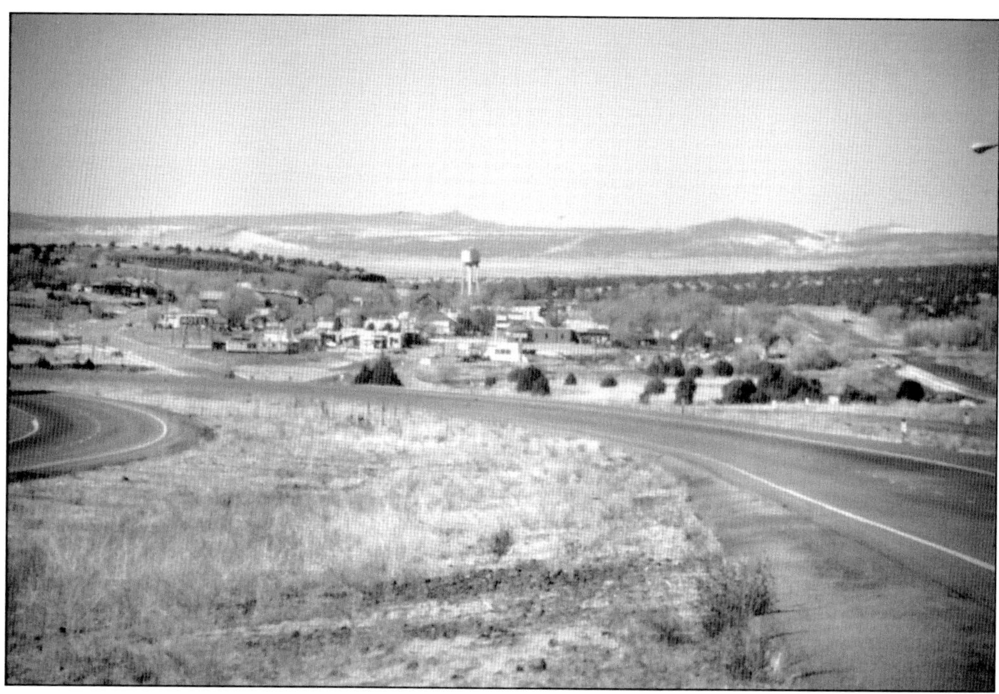

One of Ash Fork's great success stories is Murphy's Chevron. When I-40 bypassed the town in 1979, nearly every business downtown closed. Two years later, Amos Murphy bought a closed Chevron gas station in Holbrook for $1. He dismantled the building and hauled it to Ash Fork, where he resurrected it next to the interstate on the west end of town. Soon the little gas station was doing a land-office business. His son, Rick, and daughter-in-law, Lynn, bought the business in 1991. They designed and opened the new building, seen in these photographs, in 2002. The new Murphy's has a large gift shop, food, towing business, garage, and everything else to meet the needs of tourists and trucks. Rick and Lynn Murphy have that entrepreneurial spirit that every town struggling to survive needs to make it through the hard times.

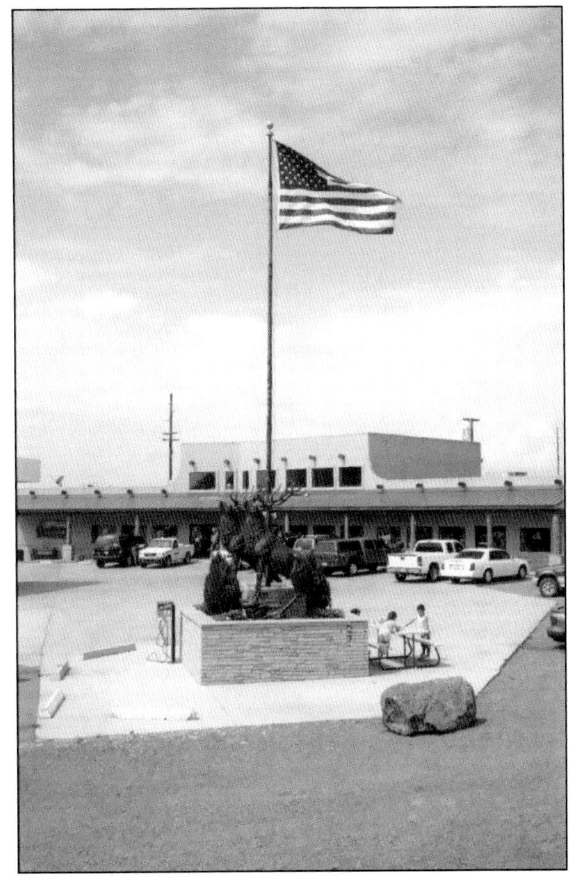

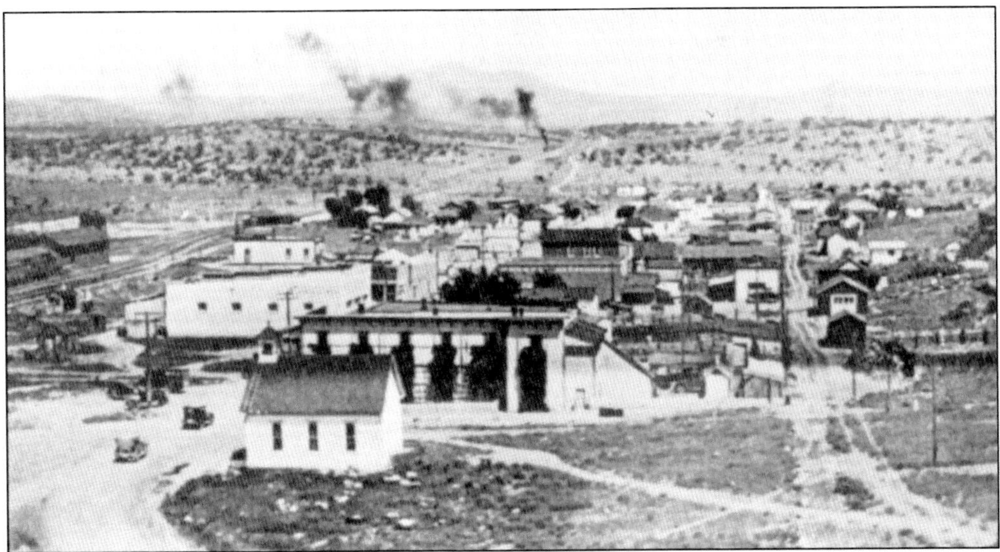

A bird's-eye view of Ash Fork looks east towards Bill Williams Mountain in the 1920s. Route 66 curves around the front of the old Methodist church. In the background, a locomotive is belching black smoke as it begins its climb towards Williams. In 1920, the population was just under 600 residents.

Bibliography

Centennial Committee. *Ash Fork, Arizona: 1882–1982*. Prescott, AZ: Classic Printers, 1982.

Hume, Fayrene, and Carol Popp. *Ash Fork, Arizona: A Pictorial History, 1900–2000*. Prescott, AZ: Classic Printers, 2000.

Kupel, Douglas E. "Ash Fork: Transportation and Town-Building in Northern Arizona." *Journal of Arizona History*. Summer 1998.

Richardson, Cecil C. "Ash Fork." *Arizona Highways Magazine*. September 1956.

Trimble, Marshall. *A Roadside History of Arizona*. 2nd ed. Missoula, MT: Mountain Press Publishing, 2004.

About the Author

Native Arizonan Marshall Trimble, who grew up in Ash Fork, is the state's official historian and the award-winning author of more than 20 books on Arizona and the West. Marshall is heard daily on radio around the state spinning history and folklore. He also hosted an Emmy-winning television show, *Arizona Backroads*. Trimble answers questions about the Old West from readers all over the world in *True West Magazine*'s popular column, "Ask the Marshall."

Trimble taught Arizona history at the college level for more than 35 years and is considered the dean of Arizona historians. The *Arizona Republic* calls him the state's "most recognizable goodwill ambassador." In 2007, the Governor's Council on the Arizona Office of Tourism presented him with its first Lifetime Achievement Award.

INDEX